CAMBRIDGE LIBRARY COLLECTION

Books of enduring scholarly value

Medieval History

This series includes pioneering editions of medieval historical accounts by
eye-witnesses and contemporaries, collections of source materials such as
charters and letters, and works that applied new historiographical methods to
the interpretation of the European middle ages. The nineteenth century saw
an upsurge of interest in medieval manuscripts, texts and artefacts, and the
enthusiastic efforts of scholars and antiquaries made a large body of material
available in print for the first time. Although many of the analyses have been
superseded, they provide fascinating evidence of the academic practices of
their time, while a considerable number of texts have still not been re-edited
and are still widely consulted.

Early Yorkshire Families

First published in 1973, this collection of notes and documents relating to
approximately 100 Yorkshire families who held land of the Crown in Yorkshire
in the middle ages was compiled by the antiquary Sir Charles Travis Clay
(1885–1978). Deeply interested in the history of his home county, he was held
in high esteem for his editing of medieval charters, and the ten volumes of
Early Yorkshire Charters that he edited between 1935 and 1965 (also reissued
in this series as part of the complete thirteen-volume set) were regarded as a
masterpiece. In *Early Yorkshire Families*, Clay's notes on each lineage establish
its provenance, its genealogy, the origin of its land tenure (with further
illustrative documents contained in the latter part of the work), and how land
was held and transmitted. This work is an invaluable source of information for
researchers interested in medieval Yorkshire or the feudal system generally.

T0345414

Cambridge University Press has long been a pioneer in the reissuing of out-of-print titles from its own backlist, producing digital reprints of books that are still sought after by scholars and students but could not be reprinted economically using traditional technology. The Cambridge Library Collection extends this activity to a wider range of books which are still of importance to researchers and professionals, either for the source material they contain, or as landmarks in the history of their academic discipline.

Drawing from the world-renowned collections in the Cambridge University Library and other partner libraries, and guided by the advice of experts in each subject area, Cambridge University Press is using state-of-the-art scanning machines in its own Printing House to capture the content of each book selected for inclusion. The files are processed to give a consistently clear, crisp image, and the books finished to the high quality standard for which the Press is recognised around the world. The latest print-on-demand technology ensures that the books will remain available indefinitely, and that orders for single or multiple copies can quickly be supplied.

The Cambridge Library Collection brings back to life books of enduring scholarly value (including out-of-copyright works originally issued by other publishers) across a wide range of disciplines in the humanities and social sciences and in science and technology.

Early Yorkshire Families

EDITED BY CHARLES TRAVIS CLAY
AND DIANA E. GREENWAY

CAMBRIDGE UNIVERSITY PRESS

Cambridge, New York, Melbourne, Madrid, Cape Town,
Singapore, São Paolo, Delhi, Mexico City

Published in the United States of America by Cambridge University Press, New York

www.cambridge.org
Information on this title: www.cambridge.org/9781108058377

© in this compilation Cambridge University Press 2013

This edition first published 1973
This digitally printed version 2013

ISBN 978-1-108-05837-7 Paperback

The Anniversary Reissue of Volumes from the Record Series of the Yorkshire Archaeological Society

To celebrate the 150th anniversary of the foundation of the leading society for the study of the archaeology and history of England's largest historic county, Cambridge University Press has reissued a selection of the most notable of the publications in the Record Series of the Yorkshire Archaeological Society. Founded in 1863, the Society soon established itself as the major publisher in its field, and has remained so ever since. The *Yorkshire Archaeological Journal* has been published annually since 1869, and in 1885 the Society launched the Record Series, a succession of volumes containing transcriptions of diverse original records relating to the history of Yorkshire, edited by numerous distinguished scholars. In 1932 a special division of the Record Series was created which, up to 1965, published a considerable number of early medieval charters relating to Yorkshire. The vast majority of these publications have never been superseded, remaining an important primary source for historical scholarship.

Current volumes in the Record Series are published for the Society by Boydell and Brewer. The Society also publishes parish register transcripts; since 1897, over 180 volumes have appeared in print. In 1974, the Society established a programme to publish calendars of over 650 court rolls of the manor of Wakefield, the originals of which, dating from 1274 to 1925, have been in the safekeeping of the Society's archives since 1943; by the end of 2012, fifteen volumes had appeared. In 2011, the importance of the Wakefield court rolls was formally acknowledged by the UK committee of UNESCO, which entered them on its National Register of the Memory of the World.

The Society possesses a library and archives which constitute a major resource for the study of the county; they are housed in its headquarters, a Georgian villa in Leeds. These facilities, initially provided solely for members, are now available to all researchers. Lists of the full range of the Society's scholarly resources and publications can be found on its website, www.yas.org.uk.

Early Yorkshire Families
(Record Series volume 135)

This volume contains information about Yorkshire families which descended in the male line, or with not more than one break because of marriage, from the early twelfth to the early fourteenth century. It was originally published with grant aid from the Marc Fitch Fund. The author was Sir Charles T. Clay FBA (1885–1978), who edited the ten-volume continuation of *Early Yorkshire Charters* published in the Extra Series by the Yorkshire Archaeological Society between 1935 and 1965, and five volumes of deeds in the Society's Record Series between 1924 and 1940. Those publications are also now reissued in the Cambridge Library Collection. Professor Diana E. Greenway FBA, who worked with Clay on the present volume, has provided the following prefatory note for this reissue:

> *Early Yorkshire Families* was Charles Clay's final book, published in 1974 when he was in his ninetieth year. It was the culmination of his long and productive study of the records of early feudal Yorkshire. The book is packed with precious information about 'approximately a hundred families' (actually ninety-nine, since he joked that he found the idea of rounding it up to one hundred 'rather vulgar'). It is all expressed in Clay's extremely precise and economical prose, demonstrating for the last time the meticulous treatment of evidence and the masterful handling of complex genealogies which had marked his earlier works for the Yorkshire Archaeological Society, notably his volumes of *Early Yorkshire Charters*, *Yorkshire Deeds* and *York Minster Fasti*. Readers who wish to know about the author are referred to Christopher Brooke's delightful biographical memoir in *Proceedings of the British Academy*, lxiv (1978).

EARLY YORKSHIRE FAMILIES

Printed by
THE WEST YORKSHIRE PRINTING CO. LIMITED
WAKEFIELD

THE YORKSHIRE ARCHAEOLOGICAL SOCIETY

Founded 1863   Incorporated 1893

RECORD SERIES
Vol. CXXXV
FOR THE YEAR 1973

EARLY YORKSHIRE FAMILIES

EDITED BY

SIR CHARLES CLAY

WITH

ILLUSTRATIVE DOCUMENTS

EDITED BY

DIANA E. GREENWAY

PRINTED FOR THE SOCIETY
1973

CONTENTS

PEDIGREES

DOCUMENTS

ABBREVIATIONS and REFERENCES

Anglo-Norman Families	By L. C. Loyd, Harleian Society vol. ciii, 1951
Baildon and the Baildons	By W. Paley Baildon, 3 vols., –1926
Complete Peerage	Revised edition, 14 vols., 1910–59
Danelaw Charters	By Sir Frank Stenton, British Academy, 1920
Dugdale's Visitation, ed. J. W. Clay	3 vols., Exeter, 1899–1917
E.Y.C.	*Early Yorkshire Charters*
Glover's Visitation	Ed. Joseph Foster, 1875
Heads of Religious Houses	Ed. Knowles, Brooke and London, Cambridge, 1972
H.K.F.	William Farrer, *Honors and Knights' Fees*, 3 vols., 1923–25
Lincs. Domesday and *Lindsey Survey*	Lincoln Record Society, vol. 19, 1924
Mowbray Charters	D. E. Greenway, *Charters of the Honour of Mowbray, 1107–91*, British Academy, 1972
Regesta	*Regesta Regum Anglo-Normannorum*, 4 vols., 1913–69
Y.A.J.	Yorkshire Archaeological Journal
York Minster Fasti	Y.A.S. Record Series, vols. 123–4, 1958–59

References to monastic records and serial publications are given in G.R.C. Davis, *Medieval Cartularies of Great Britain*, 1958, and *Texts and Calendars ...*, R. Hist. Soc., 1958.

INTRODUCTION

§1

The notes collected in the present volume relate to approximately a hundred families descending in the male line or with not more than one break due to marriage from an ancestor living before the death of Henry I, and some at least of whose lands passed by inheritance to the reign of Edward I or later.

Among the tenants-in-chief in Yorkshire at the Domesday survey only a few were ancestors of families which are included. There are unbroken male descents from Ralph de Mortemer and Ralph Paynel, and descents with only one break due to marriage from William de Percy and William de Warenne. In the descents from Alan count of Britanny and Ilbert de Lascy there was more than one break, and their families are not included. From Gospatric the king's thegn the families of Allerston, Hebden, Thoresby and Staveley descended. It is probable that the lands of Odo the crossbowman passed by inheritance to the Chauncy family. Although Roger Bigod's Domesday holdings did not extend into Yorkshire the manor of Settrington was acquired by marriage and descended to a younger line.

As a result of forfeitures, royal grants and other causes a large proportion of the Domesday tenancies-in-chief did not pass by inheritance, but became the nucleus of newly constituted honours and fees. Thus the Stuteville fee was originally due to the grant of the main portion of the Domesday holdings of Hugh son of Baldric, and the Trussebut fee was largely based on the holdings of Erneis de Burun. The honour of Mowbray was due to the widespread grants to Nigel d'Aubigny which included the Arches fee and the greater part of the Tison fee, with the grant of the forfeited lands of Stuteville which led to a hundred years of difficulty. The Yorkshire holding of Baliol was due to a grant by William Rufus; the Brus fee to one by Henry I; and the Chamberlain fee to a grant of marriage. The Fossard fee became a tenancy-in-chief on the forfeiture of the overlord the count of Mortain; but as there were two breaks before the inheritance passed to Mauley the family is not included in the present volume.

In addition to the families descending from Gospatric the thegn there are several with an Anglo-Saxon ancestor. The families of Birkin and Thornhill descended from Essulf; Burgh and Longvillers from Swain son of Alric; Constable of Halsham from Ulbert and his wife Erneburga; Eland from Leising; FitzWilliam from Godric son of Ketelbern; Greystoke from Forne son of Sigulf; Grimthorpe from Ulf; Habton from Ansketil son of Gospatric; Horbury from Saxe; Ingoldsby from Colegrim; Manfield from Copsi; Meaux from Gamel son of Ketel son of Norman; Mohaut from Simon son of another Gospatric; Neville of Raby from Dolfin son of Uchtred; and Roall and Vernoil from Gamel son of Baret, the latter also descending from Swain son of Edwin. The details of some of these families show marriages between Anglo-Saxons and Normans. They include the marriage of Meldred, father of Robert son of Meldred, with a lady of the Stuteville family; that of Peter son of Essulf, ancestor of the Birkin family, with Emma de Lascelles; and those of the grand-daughters and coheirs of Swain son of Alric with Normans.

The majority of the families held under-tenancies, usually by knight-service due to a Norman tenant-in-chief. A rough calculation shows that of these about fifty descended in the male line within the prescribed period and about eighteen with only one break due to marriage. There are instances of a son of an heiress taking his mother's name. These include Lascelles, Percy and Warenne; the well-known case of Geoffrey son of Robert son of Meldred, who took his mother's name of Neville; the son of Eustacia de Wyville, who took his mother's name; the son of William de Whatton who took the name of Neufmarché; the adoption of the name of Darel by Geoffrey de Fitling; and the second line of Vescy which descended from Eustace FitzJohn and his first wife. There was some delay before William of York took his grandmother's name of Hebden.

Of the families deriving from Normandy and elsewhere overseas the places of origin of about twenty, largely due to the work of the late Lewis Loyd in his *Anglo-Norman Families*, can be treated with reasonable certainty, and a few more with some degree of possibility. A difficult case is that of Wyville, which requires further investigation.

§2

The Illustrative Documents (pp. 107–117) have been supplied by Dr. D. E. Greenway. They mainly relate to land in Yorkshire held of the lords of the honour of Mowbray, whose charters throughout England have been edited in her book recently published by the British Academy. My thanks are also due to her for her work in looking through the proofs, the preparation of the Index to the Documents, and her help in many other ways.

A special measure of gratitude is due to the Trustees of the Marc Fitch Fund for their grant of a substantial sum towards the expenses of publication. It is not for the first time that the Trustees have shown this welcome interest in the work of our Society.

CHARLES CLAY.

EARLY YORKSHIRE FAMILIES

ALLERSTON

The family descended from Gospatric son of Archil son of Ecgfrid, who in the Domesday survey is recorded as having held a manor of 2 carucates in Cayton and one of 3 carucates in Allerston.[1]

Uctred de Allerston, described as son of Gospatric, gave to Whitby abbey 2 carucates in Cayton, 1087–1109.[2] His successor was Torfin, who is stated to have been his son,[3] and who in 1160 as Torfin de Allerston with Maud de Fribois his wife and Alan his son gave to Rievaulx abbey a carucate in Allerston which he had given in dower to Maud, saving 20s yearly to her.[4] Torfin died c. 1174–76.[5] In 1174 Alan his son confirmed to Whitby abbey the gift of the church of Crosby Ravensworth, Westmorland, made by Torfin his father when Alan was a minor.[6] In 1189 the custody of Helen, Alan's daughter, was given to Alan de Valence;[7] she married Hugh de Hastings, who was dead in 1203, and subsequently was given in marriage to Robert Vipont.[8] Her son Thomas de Hastings succeeded to the inheritance, which descended in the Hastings family.[9] In 1231 Alice widow of Alan de Allerston, who was daughter and heir of Roger Dispenser,[10] quitclaimed to Thomas de Hastings and Thomas his son a third of 2 bovates in Allerston for a render of corn during her life.[11] In 1316 Allerston was held by Nicholas de Hastings.[12]

ARCHES

The family descended from Osbern de Arches, the tenant-in-chief at the Domesday survey of lands in Yorkshire and Lincolnshire.[13] His gifts to St. Mary's abbey, York, of land in Poppleton, Appleton Roebuck and Hessay were confirmed by king William II.[14] The

[1] V.C.H. Yorks., ii, 200–1; and for Gospatric son of Archil pp. 183–4. A chart pedigree is given in the Thoresby section below.
[2] E.Y.C., i, no. 384.
[3] Whitby Chartulary, i, pp. 4, 6.
[4] E.Y.C., i, no. 386; for the original see Yorks. Deeds, vii, no. 11.
[5] Ibid., no. 387n.
[6] Ibid., no. 386n.
[7] V.C.H., N.R., ii, 421, citing Cart. Ant. x, 27, which does not appear in the pd ed. in Pipe Roll Soc., N.S., XIX.
[8] Ibid.
[9] Ibid., p. 422.
[10] Yorks. Fines, 1218–31, p. 157n.
[11] Ibid., p. 141.
[12] Feudal Aids, vi, 178.
[13] D. C. Douglas in Canterbury Domesday Monachorum, p. 44, considers that there is no evidence to support the suggestions (see A. S. Ellis in Y.A.J., iv, 243) that Osbern de Arches was a younger son of Godfrey vicomte of Arques. It can be noticed that Godfrey's father was named Osbern (Complete Peerage, x, app. F, p. 52).
[14] E.Y.C., i, nos. 350, 527 and note.

Lindsey survey shows that by then he had been succeeded by William de Arches,[1] probably his son.[2]

Before 1124 king Henry I gave to Nigel d'Aubigny the fee held by William de Arches,[3] who thus became a tenant of the honour of Mowbray; and in 1166 $8\frac{1}{2}$ knights' fees were held of Roger de Mowbray by Roger de Flamville (*q.v.*), the second husband of Juetta daughter and heir of William de Arches, of which 7 fees constituted the Arches inheritance.[4] Some of these are shown in the charter of William de Arches, 1140–47, enfeoffing Elias de Hou, his kinsman, of 8 carucates in Kirk Hammerton, Kirkby Ouseburn, Hebden and Appletreewick, and of the church of Kirkby Ouseburn,[5] and in another, 1147–53, by which the archbishop of York confirmed his gift with Juetta his wife to their daughter Maud and the nuns of Monkton of 6 carucates, being all his land there, with land in Kirk Hammerton and the churches of Thorp [Arch], Hammerton and Askham [Richard], and the gift of the church of Kirkby Ouseburn made at his request.[6] He had a sister Agnes to whom he gave land in Appleton Roebuck, probably on her first marriage to Herbert de St. Quintin (*q.v.*), by whom she was the mother of Alice, wife of Robert son of Fulk and foundress of Nun Appleton priory.[7]

William de Arches was still living *c.* 1154, as shown by a charter of Roger de Mowbray.[8] Besides his daughter Maud, prioress of Nun Monkton, he had a daughter Juetta who became effectively his sole heir. She married, first, Adam de Brus I, who died in 1143, and secondly Roger de Flamville, who, as noted above, held the 7 Arches fees of the honour of Mowbray in her right in 1166. Her inheritance descended to the Brus family (*q.v.*).[9]

An account of the family of Arches of Shadwell was given by Farrer in his section on the Lascy fee; the probable ancestor was Peter de Arches, living in 1130 and presumably the father of Herbert de Arches I, who held 2 knights' fees of Henry de Lascy in 1166; but no connexion with the family of Osbern de Arches has been established.[10]

[1] *Lincs. Domesday*, p. 162; *Lindsey Survey*, p. 238.
[2] This is left uncertain in the chart pedigree in *E.Y.C.*, i, p. 420; but is so given on p. 415.
[3] D. E. Greenway, *Mowbray Charters*, p. xxv.
[4] *Ibid.*, p. 262.
[5] *E.Y.C.*, i, no. 534.
[6] *Ibid.*, no. 535.
[7] *Ibid.*, pp. 420–1; and see the Kyme section below. Agnes was the foundress and benefactor of the priory at Nunkeeling, where she had dower of her first husband's holding (*ibid.*, iii, nos. 1331–6).
[8] *Mowbray Charters*, no. 359.
[9] Her great-grandson Peter de Brus II held the 7 fees in 1224–30 (*Bk. of Fees*, p. 1460). In 1192 she gave her land of Askham Richard, except one car., to her granddaughter Isabel de Brus (*E.Y.C.*, i, no. 548), whose first husband was Henry de Percy, son of Agnes de Percy and Jocelin of Louvain, who died in 1197–98 (*ibid.*, xi, p. 6). The texts of other charters issued by Juetta have been pd, *e.g. ibid.*, i, nos. 536, 538, 552–3; *Mon. Ang.*, vi, 971. For two more see nos. 1 and 2 below.
[10] *E.Y.C.*, iii, no. 1586n.

ASKE

The family descended from Roger de Aske, who founded Marrick priory, 1154–58, with the assent of Warner son of Wimar and the confirmation of Conan earl of Richmond.[1] Warner son of Wimar held the steward's fee as an immediate tenancy of the honour of Richmond, which included Aske and Marrick.[2] Roger de Aske witnessed a charter of earl Alan, 1136–45.[3] Before 1169 he was succeeded by his son Conan de Aske, who held a knight's fee formerly of the steward's fee, and was succeeded by his son Roger probably by 1208.[4] The latter's lineal descendant Sir Hugh de Aske held a knight's fee in Aske and Marrick in 1280, and in 1284–85 9 carucates in those places and also 3 carucates in Dalton Travers as an immediate tenant of the honour.[5]

From Hugh de Aske the family descended in the male line until the death in 1512 of William Aske, whose coheirs were his granddaughters Anne and Elizabeth; Anne married Sir Ralph Bulmer and Elizabeth married Richard Bowes of South Cowton; and Marrick and Aske were divided between them.[6]

BALIOL

The family derived its name from Bailleul-en-Vimeu, dept. Somme, arr. Abbeville.[7] Guy de Baliol was given by William Rufus the lordship of Bywell, Northumberland, lands in Teesdale from which the lordship of Barnard Castle developed, and lands in Yorkshire which included the manor and soke of Stokesley and manors in Hickleton.[8] In 1112–22 he made several gifts of churches to St. Mary's abbey, York, by a charter mentioning Bernard his nephew.[9] As the latter, his successor in England, was a benefactor of the abbey of Cluny, 1127–44, giving his inherited interest in the altars of several churches including Bailleul,[10] it has been deduced that he was the son and heir of an elder brother of Guy, who may have been Hugh de Baliol, the father of two sons named Eustace and Bernard.[11] In 1123–33 Henry I confirmed to St. Mary's the churches of Stokesley, Stainton and Gainford with the chapel of Barnard Castle, as the charters of Guy de Baliol and Bernard de Baliol testified.[12]

[1] *E.Y.C.*, v, no. 175.
[2] *Ibid.*, p. 18.
[3] *Ibid.*, iv, no. 20.
[4] *Ibid.*, v, pp. 71–2, where there is an account of the early generations.
[5] *Ibid.*, p. 72.
[6] The descent is given in *V.C.H.*, *N.R.*, i, pp. 60–1, 98.
[7] This was shown by Round in *Cal. Docs. France*, preface p. xl, referring to no. 1392; and see *Anglo-Norman Families*, p. 11.
[8] A detailed account of the family is in *Northumberland County History*, vi, 14–71, with chart pedigree pp. 72–3. For the list of Yorkshire lands see *E.Y.C.*, i, p. 438.
[9] *Ibid.*, no. 559; and *cf.* the confirmn charter of Bernard (no. 561).
[10] *Cal. Docs. France*, no. 1392; the date was probably 1138 or shortly before (*N.C.H.*, *ut sup.*, p. 25n).
[11] *Ibid.*, p. 17, citing charters *c.* 1130 and *c.* 1138.
[12] *Regesta*, ii, no. 1890; text p. 385.

Bernard de Baliol I died before 1167 and was succeeded by his son Bernard II, who died before 1193. The descent then proceeded in the male line through Eustace son of Bernard II (died *c.* 1200), Hugh son of Eustace (*d.* 1228), John son of Hugh, who married Devorguil daughter and ultimately sole heir of Alan lord of Galloway, to John their son and eventual heir, who was crowned king of Scotland in 1292, and who after his surrender of the kingdom in 1296 returned to Bailleul-en-Vimeu and died in 1314. His son Edward Baliol, king of Scotland from 1332 to his surrender in 1356, died without issue.[1]

Besides the lands in England mentioned above the family held the manor of Hitchin, co. Hertford, which according to a return of 1212 was of the gift of king Henry I.[2]

BENNIWORTH

The family, whose principal interests lay in Lincolnshire,[3] descended from Walter de Benniworth (*Beningheborda*), who was living at the time of the Lindsey survey as a tenant of Ranulf Meschin,[4] and who witnessed a charter of William de Roumare I, 1123–47.[5] In 1166 Roger de Benniworth held of William de Roumare III 3 knights' fees of the old feoffment and 5½ of the new;[6] and before 1172 William reduced this service, which had been due from Walter, Roger's father, to 6 knights' fees.[7] The family descended in the male line to Geoffrey de Benniworth, who died in 1250–58.[8]

There are two connexions of the family with Yorkshire. Walter de Benniworth gave 22 bovates in Anlaby, par. Kirk Ella, to St. Mary's York, his gift being included in the confirmation charter of king Henry II in 1155.[9] No information is available for the origin of the interest held in Anlaby by Walter, whose gift of the 22 bovates was probably part of the 3½ carucates held there in 1086 by Gilbert Tison.[10]

[1] *N.C.H., ut sup.,* pp. 72–3.

[2] *Bk. of Fees,* p. 123. Guy de Baliol gave land in Hitchin hundred to St. Albans abbey (*N.C.H.,* p. 20).

[3] An account of the family is in *H.K.F.,* ii, 178–82.

[4] *Lindsey Survey,* p. 259. Land in Benniworth was held in 1086 by Odo of Ivo Taillebois (*Lincs. Domesday,* p. 85), and in 1130 Walter son of Odo rendered account of 21*li.* 13*s* 4*d* in Lincs. for right of inheritance *de Comitissa Cestr'* (*Pipe Roll 31 Hen. I,* p. 114), the latter being Lucy countess of Chester, whose first husband, Ivo Taillebois, had probably died in or shortly after 1094 (*Complete Peerage,* vii, 743).

[5] *Reg. Ant.,* Lincoln Rec. Soc., i, 79.

[6] *Red Bk. Exch.,* pp. 377–8.

[7] *Danelaw Charters,* no. 518. Roger married Sibyl sister of Simon son of William de Kyme (*q.v.*) (*H.K.F.,* ii, 179).

[8] *Ibid.,* pp. 136, 180.

[9] *E.Y.C.,* i, no. 354 (p. 276); and for the date *ibid.,* xii, p. x.

[10] *V.C.H. Yorks.,* ii, 272. The 22 bov. were later held by a member of the Anlaby family as a tenancy of St. Mary's (*E.Y.C.,* xii, no. 2; and for an account of that family pp. 24–30).

The second connexion was due to the marriage of Gilbert de Benniworth, son of Roger and grandson of Walter,[1] to Sara, daughter and coheir of Richard de Warwick by Idonea daughter and coheir of Walter the falconer by Maud Tuschet.[2] By this marriage he acquired an interest in Bilbrough and Moor Monkton, together with land in Lincolnshire.[3] These interests descended to Gilbert's grandson Geoffrey de Benniworth, who as noted above died in 1250–58; and then by a family settlement to Geoffrey's two sisters, Lucy wife of Philip de Chauncy (*q.v.*) and Maud wife of Roger de Mortimer.[4]

BIGOD (of Settrington)

The family was a branch of the Bigods, earls of Norfolk, descending from Ralph the staller, who was probably born before 1011 and was created earl of Norfolk and Suffolk, dying in 1068–70.[5] The manor of Settrington passed to that family through the marriage of Roger Bigod to Adeliza sister of Berenger de Todeni and was held by Hugh Bigod, earl of Norfolk, who died in 1176.[6]

The last earl of this line, earl Roger, died in 1306, having surrendered his earldom to the crown.[7] He had a brother John who can be identified with the John le Bigod of Stockton, Norfolk, who with Isabel his wife, with successive remainders to his younger sons John and Roger, was granted the manor and advowson of Settrington by earl Roger in 1302.[8]

John le Bigod of Stockton died in 1305 and was succeeded there by his eldest son Ralph,[9] Settrington in accordance with the final concord passing to his son John, who died without issue. From the latter's brother Roger Settrington then descended in the male line to Sir Francis Bigod, whose heir after the death of his son Ralph in 1569 was the son of his daughter Dorothy, formerly the wife of Roger Radcliffe.[10]

---

[1] Gilbert witnessed a settlement for land in Anlaby in 1205 (*E.Y.C.*, xii, no. 1).
    [2] *Ibid.*, vi, pp. 107–14. The lands were mainly held of the Paynel fee, and for their tenure *ante c.* 1160 by Simon Tuschet, presumably Maud's father, *ibid.*, no. 28 and note.
    [3] *Ibid.*, pp. 109–10.
    [4] *Ibid.*, p. 110; and for the settlement in 1258 *Yorks. Fines*, 1246–72, p. 196. For the issue of Lucy and Maud see *H.K.F.*, ii, 136–7.
    [5] *Complete Peerage*, ix, 568–71; and for the Settrington and other lines the paper by the Rev. C. Moor in *Y.A.J.*, xxxii, 172–213.
    [6] *E.Y.C.*, i, pp. 461, 466–7.
    [7] *Complete Peerage*, ix, 596, with a reference to the decision of the House of Lords in 1906 that the surrender was invalid.
    [8] *Yorks. Fines*, 1300–14, p. 43; and for the identification see Moor, pp. 179, 181.
    [9] Moor, pp. 181–2. The Stockton line descended in the male line to 1416 (*ibid.*, p. 185).
    [10] *Ibid.*, pp. 187–99, with chart pedigree p. 201.

Among the younger branches descending from the Bigods of Settrington was the family settled at Scagglethorpe,[1] a place where Berenger de Todeni held an interest at the Domesday survey.[2]

BIRKIN

The family descended from Peter, the eldest son of Essulf of whom several details, including references to Birkin, will be found in the notes on the family of Thornhill given below. By his wife Emma de Lascelles[3] he was the father of Adam son of Peter, named in 1166 as Adam son of Peter son of Essulf.[4] Adam held a knight's fee of Henry de Lascy in that year.[5] He held land in Birkin,[6] interest there being shown in a record of 1194, when John de Lascelles rendered account of 40s to inquire if a carucate in Birkin of the king's soke was included in the claim whereof a duel was fought between Simon de Lascelles and Adam son of Peter, who recovered against Simon's father 24 carucates in Birkin.[7] Adam married as his second wife Maud daughter and coheir of Robert de Caux, from whom their son John de Birkin inherited her lands including the forestership of Sherwood.[8]

John de Birkin married first Joan daughter of Jordan Lenveise, probably by a sister of master Roger Arundel,[9] and, secondly, Agnes sister and coheir of Hugh de Flamville (q.v.). He was dead in 1227;[10] and, after the death of his son Thomas de Birkin without issue, the heir was the latter's sister Isabel who married Robert de Everingham.[11] They were the ancestors of Adam de Everingham who was summoned to Parliament from 1309 to 1315, and whose son Adam de Everingham died in 1388, leaving as his heirs two granddaughters.[12]

BOIVILLE

Godard de Boiville held the lordship of Millom, Cumberland, for a knight's fee of William Meschin of Copeland, who died in 1130–35; and held the office of steward under Ranulf Meschin his

[1] Moor, pp. 181, 203, with pedigree p. 208.
[2] E.Y.C., i, p. 467.
[3] Ibid., iii, no. 1721. This is an interesting example of a man of Saxon descent marrying a wife of Norman origin.
[4] Pipe Roll 12 Hen. II, p. 46.
[5] Red Bk. Exch., p. 424.
[6] E.Y.C., iii, nos. 1739, 1741–2.
[7] Pipe Roll 5 Ric. I, p. 73. Only one car. in Birkin was recorded at the Domesday survey (V.C.H. Yorks., ii, 245). The 24 car. were a portion of the extensive soke of Snaith (E.Y.C., iii, p. 366); and Farrer suggested that they formed Emma's maritagium (ibid., p. 358).
[8] For Maud de Caux see Reg. Ant., Lincoln Rec. Soc., vol. vii, app. II, giving details of her marriage and family and her father's share of the Alselin inheritance, of which he held 15 k.f. in 1166 (Red Bk. Exch., p. 343).
[9] E.Y.C., x, no. 113n.
[10] Exc. e Rot. Fin., i, 162.
[11] A chart pedigree of the descent from Peter son of Essulf is in E.Y.C., iii, p. 359; an amendment should be made for John de Birkin's first wife.
[12] Complete Peerage, v, 184–92, with a chart pedigree showing the granddaughters' descendants.

son, who died before 1140. He gave to Furness abbey a carucate in Craven, named Bordley (par. Burnsall), which with land in Hetton formed part of the fee of Adam son of Swain held of the honour of Skipton, an inheritance of Alice daughter and an eventual coheir of William Meschin and his wife Cecily de Rumilly. This gift was apparently revoked by Arthur son of Godard de Boiville, who gave Bordley to Fountains abbey. The eventual heir of Godard was his great-great-granddaughter Joan daughter of Adam son of Henry de Millom and wife of John de Huddleston (*q.v.*).[1]

In a charter of Arthur son of Godard he referred to Robert de Boiville, the donor of land in Kirksanton, par. Millom, to Furness abbey not later than 1152, as the son of his uncle.[2] The same Robert de Boiville also gave to Furness a moiety of Newby, par. Clapham, W.R., which he had acquired by marriage with Margaret daughter of Waldeve son of Edmund.[3] Through his son William he was the ancestor of William de Boiville who had an interest in the manor of Kirksanton and also held 3 carucates in Cowling, par. Kildwick, as an immediate tenure of the honour of Skipton in 1287.[4] This is the earliest available reference to the tenure of Cowling by the Boiville family; but it is significant that in 1254 an interest in the manor was held by John de Longvillers,[5] who represented a coheirship of Adam son of Swain;[6] and it is not improbable that the Boiville tenure of Cowling, like that of Kirksanton, dated back to the time of Godard de Boiville and Adam son of Swain.

William de Boiville died in 1305, holding Cowling of the king in chief as of the honour of Skipton for a sixth of a knight's fee, and the manor of Sutton, also par. Kildwick, as an under-tenancy of William le Vavasour (*q.v.*),[7] for a seventh of a knight's fee, together with the manor of Ireby and other holdings in Cumberland, his heir being his son John aged twenty-one or two.[8] The latter was in possession of Cowling in 1302–03 and 1314,[9] and died in 1319, holding Cowling and the under-tenancy in Sutton, together with lands in Cumberland including the manors of Ireby and Kirksanton, his heir being his brother Edmund, aged twenty-six or thirty and more.[10]

---

[1] References, several being taken from *Reg. St. Bees*, are given in *E.Y.C.*, vii, no. 113*n*, where are notes on Godard de Boiville and his descendants, and pp. 4–5 for William Meschin. For notes on the fee of Adam son of Swain see pp. 177–93, and for the close connexion between him and Godard no. 113*n*. A detailed account of the latter and his descendants is in *Cumb. and West. Ant. and Arch. Soc. Transactions*, vol. xli, N.S.; and *cf.* the Huddleston section below.
[2] *Furness Coucher*, ii, 513–4, cited in *E.Y.C.*, vii, pp. 277–8, where are notes on this branch of the family.
[3] *Ibid.*, p. 303, cited *ibid.*
[4] *E.Y.C.*, vii, p. 278.
[5] *Ibid.*, p. 279.
[6] *Ibid.*, iii, p. 318, chart pedigree of Adam son of Swain's descendants.
[7] For the Vavasour holding of the honour of Skipton see *E.Y.C.*, vii, p. 166.
[8] *Cal. Inq. p.m.*, iv, no. 264.
[9] *Feudal Aids*, vi, 108; *Cal. Inq. p.m.*, v, no. 533 (p. 306).
[10] *Cal. Inq. p.m.*, vi, no. 220.

During the latter's tenure the interest in Cowling and Sutton passed to Richard de Denton, who gave it to Adam de Copley, presumably husband of his daughter Margaret. In 1340 Edmund de Boiville released his right to Adam, and in 1362 the 3 carucates in Cowling were held by Margaret de Copley.[1]

BRUS

The family descended from Robert de Brus 1, who witnessed charters in the early years of the twelfth century, including one of king Henry I in 1109, and fought at the battle of the Standard in 1138, dying in 1142; there is evidence that he was given his Yorkshire lands soon after the battle of Tinchebrai in 1106.[2] It is probable that the place of origin of his family was Brix, dept. Manche, arr. and cant. Valognes.[3]

From his elder son Adam de Brus I the family descended in the male line to Peter de Brus III, who died in 1272, leaving sisters as his coheirs.[4]

Robert Bruce, king of Scotland, descended from Robert the younger son of Robert de Brus I.[5]

BULMER (of Wilton)

The main line of Bulmer descended from Ansketil de Bulmer, who died c. 1129, and whose son Bertram de Bulmer, sheriff of Yorkshire, died in 1166, his ultimate heir being his daughter Emma, the mother by Geoffrey de Neville of Burreth of Isabel wife of Robert son of Meldred, ancestor of the Nevilles of Raby (q.v.).[6]

Farrer collected many notes on the descent of the younger lines which, as he said, bristles with difficulties.[7] He showed that the Bulmer family of Wilton descended from a John de Bulmer, whose son and grandson had the same christian name, and suggested that the first of them was a grandson of Stephen de Bulmer, a younger son of Ansketil and younger brother of Bertram.[8] The third John de Bulmer married Tiffany daughter and coheir of Hugh de Morwick and died in 1299.[9] His son Ralph de Bulmer was summoned to Parliament from 1344 to 1348, and the family continued in the male

---

[1] *E.Y.C.*, vii, p. 279.

[2] *Ibid.*, ii, pp. 11–12; and pp. 16–19 for the constitution of the Yorkshire fee.

[3] This was accepted by G. W. Watson in *Complete Peerage*, ii, 358n; but L. C. Loyd in *Anglo-Norman Families*, p. viii, was not satisfied that the evidence was sufficient.

[4] Chart pedigree in *E.Y.C.*, ii, p. 15. Adam de Brus I married Juetta dau. and heir of William de Arches (q.v.), her second husband being Roger de Flamville (q.v.)

[5] *Ibid.*

[6] *Ibid.*, p. 128, a chart pedigree.

[7] *Ibid.*, pp. 126–31.

[8] *Ibid.*, p. 130.

[9] *Ibid.*, p. 131.

line until 1558, when the last member died, leaving seven daughters and coheirs.[1]

BURGH

The family apparently took its name from Burrough Green, co. Cambridge, where the manor (*Burch*) was held by count Alan at the Domesday survey.[2]

In a return of the fees owing castle-guard at Richmond, mainly dating from the time of Henry I, Thomas de Burc owed the service of 4 knights.[3] It is reasonably certain that he was the father of Philip son of Thomas de Burc,[4] who witnessed a charter relating to land in the honour of Richmond shortly before 1148,[5] and who married Ismania daughter of Roald, constable of Richmond, obtaining thereby an additional interest in Great Langton.[6] His son and successor Thomas de Burgh held the office of steward of the honour under duchess Constance, and towards the end of the twelfth century 4 knights' fees, corresponding with the number held by his grandfather, being 2 in Richmondshire, located at Hackforth, Newton le Willows, East and West Appleton and elsewhere, and 2 in Cambridgeshire which included land in Burrough Green and Swaffham.[7] He died in or shortly before 1199, having married as her first husband Sara, a daughter of Amabel, one of the two daughters and heirs of Adam son of Swain, through whom he obtained an interest in Adam's possessions in the West Riding and Cumberland.[8]

The family descended in the male line until 1411, when on the death of Sir Thomas de Burgh the inheritance passed to his three half-sisters, of whom two married members of the families of Ingoldesthorpe and Zouche, and the third William Harpeden, who changed his name to Assenhull.[9]

BUSCEL

The family, which gave its name to Hutton Bushell, wap. Pickering Lythe, descended from Reginald Belet, who was granted by king Henry I in fee farm for 110*s* yearly 11 carucates and a bovate in Hutton and Preston, par. Hutton Bushell, and 13 bovates in

[1] *Complete Peerage*, ii, 414–19.
[2] *V.C.H. Cambs.*, i, 379.
[3] *E.Y.C.*, v, p. 11.
[4] Philip's parentage is discussed in *ibid.*, p. 165*n*.
[5] *Ibid.*, no. 157.
[6] *Ibid.*, p. 165.
[7] *Ibid.*, pp. 164–5.
[8] *Ibid.*, p. 165. A chart pedigree showing the descendants of Adam son of Swain is in *E.Y.C.*, iii, p. 318. The Burgh interest included Cawthorne and Walton nr. Wakefield.
[9] For full details see the paper by J. W. Walker 'The Burghs of Cambridgeshire and Yorkshire' in *Y.A.J.*, xxx, 311–419. Constance, only dau. of Sir William Assenhull and Joan de Burgh, married Richard son of John Waterton (p. 348). The Burgh inheritance of Hackforth, however, had been lost earlier by a compromise with Elizabeth de Burgh, wife of Alexander de Mountford, in whose family it descended for several generations (pp. 329–30).

Ebberston, also in wap. Pickering Lythe; the date, of which the latest limit is 1129, may be in September 1114.[1] As recorded in a charter of his son Alan son of Reginald Buscel he gave the church of Hutton to Whitby abbey.[2] It is stated in a memorial in the Whitby chartulary that Alice niece of William de Percy [I] and prior Serlo, was the mother of Alan Buscel and that she married Hugh de Boythorpe,[3] presumably as her second husband.[4] That Reginald Belet *alias* Buscel married Alice is confirmed by a charter of Alan son of Reginald Buscel to Whitby for the souls of his father Reginald Buscel and his mother Alice de Percy.[5]

Alan Buscel issued other charters to Whitby, including a confirmation of half a carucate in Hutton, a confirmation of the church of Hutton with a carucate, and with Gervase his brother a gift of land by the Derwent called Westcroft [in Hutton],[6] the latter being confirmed by king Stephen.[7] As Alan son of Reginald Buscel he witnessed a confirmation charter of Alan de Percy to Whitby abbey, *c.* 1109–1114.[8] This suggests that Reginald may not have lived long after he was given his land by king Henry I, especially as his wife appears to have had issue by her second husband.

Alan was succeeded by his son Alan, who as Alan Buscel son of Alan Buscel confirmed to Whitby the half-carucate mentioned above.[9] In 1202 and 1208 he was a party to final concords relating to Hutton and the mill of Ebberston.[10] With William his son he had witnessed a charter of Theobald de Wykeham, *c.* 1170–90.[11] He died before Michaelmas 1211, when William Buscel accounted for 40 marks and a palfrey for having seisin of his land.[12] It is possible that there was an intervening generation before the William Buscel who witnessed on 24 February 1246–7 an agreement made by William de Vescy whose court at Brompton in Pickering Lythe is mentioned.[13]

This William Buscel was succeeded by his son Alan, who described as Alan Buscel son of William Buscel of Hutton or as Alan Buscel son and heir of William Buscel or Alan Buscel lord of Hutton or Alan Buscel of Hutton issued four charters of the same period, as is shown by the witnesses, probably in 1250–75, three of which were grants to Wykeham priory, one confirming all the lands

[1] *E.Y.C.*, i, no. 371; *Regesta*, ii, no. 992, where abp T, the addressee, is given as Thomas; but Thurstan, as in Farrer, is probably correct.
[2] *E.Y.C.*, i, no. 375, dated 1135–42.
[3] Pd in *ibid.*, ii, no. 868n.
[4] For Hugh de Boythorpe and his family see *ibid.*, ii, p. 100.
[5] *Ibid.*, i, no. 377.
[6] *Ibid.*, nos. 372–3, 376.
[7] *Ibid.*, no. 374; *Regesta*, iii, no. 943, date assigned 1135–54.
[8] *Ibid.*, ii, no. 859, and xi, no. 4, giving a revised date.
[9] *Ibid.*, i, no. 378; date assigned 1185–1211.
[10] *Yorks. Fines, John*, pp. 47, 135.
[11] *E.Y.C.*, xi, no. 196.
[12] *Pipe Roll 13 John*, p. 29.
[13] *E.Y.C.*, xii, no. 52. A William Buscel occurs as a knight in 1231 (*Yorks. Fines*, 1218–31, p. 149n).

of his fee in Hutton and Preston which the nuns had of the grants of his ancestors,[1] another granting them pasture in Hutton,[2] and the third confirming a half-carucate in Hutton,[3] and the fourth being a grant of pasture in Hutton to William son of John Blundus and his mother.[4]

In 1276 Alan Buscel is said to have had gallows in Hutton for the past sixteen years.[5] He can possibly be identified with Alan Buscel of Wintringham who claimed the advowson of Coxwold against the prior of Newburgh in January 1288-9, as in November 1290 Thomas de Boston and Agnes his wife and Joan her sister, daughters and heirs of Alan Buscel, made a quitclaim of the prior's right.[6] In April 1289 the manor of Wintringham was held by Alan Buscel and Juetta his wife for life.[7] The basis of the claim to the advowson of Coxwold, a church which had been given to Newburgh priory by Roger de Mowbray,[8] is not known; but it may be significant that in 1231 William Buscel had an interest, of which he made a quitclaim, in Oulston, par. Coxwold.[9]

There was a younger line of the family which had an interest in Wykeham and elsewhere in the wapentake of Pickering Lythe.[10] Its later representative may have been the Ralph Buscel whose holding of a messuage and 9 bovates in Hutton Bushell had been forfeited in 1284 as he was outlawed for a felony.[11]

BUTTERWICK

The family descended from Durand de Butterwick, who described as the first Durand gave to Whitby abbey a carucate in Butterwick (par. Foxholes, E.R.) and 2 bovates and a mill in Scampston.[12] His charter recording these gifts, c. 1120-1135, the first being made together with Geoffrey his heir and witnessed by several other sons and by Roger Baarth, the son of his wife,[13] was confirmed by king Stephen, February 1136, stating that the first gift was of the Fossard fee and the second of the fee of Eustace FitzJohn.[14] They were also confirmed by Geoffrey his son, and the latter's son Durand son of Geoffrey de Butterwick.[15] The gift in Butterwick was confirmed by Robert Fossard, c. 1120-1135, referring to Durand

---

[1] *Yorks. Deeds*, ii, no. 231.
[2] *Ibid.*, no. 230.
[3] *Mon. Ang.*, v, 670.
[4] *Yorks. Deeds*, v, no. 90. All four charters were witnessed by Thomas de Ebberston, who occurs in 1268 (*Whitby Chartulary*, i, no. 320).
[5] *V.C.H., N.R.*, ii, 442.
[6] *Yorks. Fines*, 1272-1300, p. 90.
[7] Inq. of John de Vescy in *Yorks. Inq.*, ii, no. 64.
[8] *Mon. Ang.*, vi, 318; *Mowbray Charters*, no. 214.
[9] *Yorks. Fines*, 1218-31, p. 141.
[10] *E.Y.C.*, i, nos. 380-2; the last two being witnessed by Alan Buscel.
[11] *Yorks. Inq.*, ii, no. 18.
[12] *Whitby Chartulary*, i, p. 5.
[13] *E.Y.C.*, ii, no. 1071.
[14] *Ibid.*, no. 868.
[15] *Ibid.*, no. 1074.

as his man, and having offered the gift on the altar with Geoffrey the heir of Durand;[1] and by William Fossard I, 1136–50, stating that the land was of his fee there which Geoffrey son of Durand was holding of him, and that Durand had become a monk at Whitby.[2] The mill and 2 bovates in Scampston were confirmed by William de Vescy, 1157–c. 1170,[3] successor of Eustace FitzJohn.

The elder Durand gave to St. Mary's York half a carucate in Butterwick, the abbot and monks consenting that a priest should celebrate in Butterwick chapel which belonged to the church of Foxholes, 1122–c. 1137.[4] He was succeeded by his eldest son Geoffrey and the latter by his eldest son Durand the younger, whose confirmation to Whitby has been noted above. This Durand must have died before 1166, for in that year 2 knights' fees of the old feoffment were held of William Fossard by Durant son of William.[5] It is therefore difficult to distinguish between him and his predecessor Durand son of Geoffrey or to identify the actual donor, Durand de Butterwick who gave to St. Peter's hospital, York, tofts and pasture in Butterwick, 1160–c. 1175.[6] But it seems clear that it was the Durand of 1166 who gave the advowson of Butterwick to St. Mary's, as recorded in the confirmation of his son Robert, 1184–89.[7]

Farrer has noted that the subsequent descent of the fee is obscure.[8] It is uncertain whether the Robert of 1184–89 is the same man as Robert de Butterwick who quitclaimed to the abbot of Whitby in 1227 land in Hackness in return for the service of Richard de Barevill for a carucate in Butterwick.[9] In the period 1235–49 Robert de Butterwick sold land in Neswick which he had purchased from Sir Richard de Barevill of Butterwick;[10] and in 1255 Ela, widow of Thomas de Butterwick, son and heir of Robert de Butterwick, quitclaimed to the latter a third of land in Sherburn and of the manor of Butterwick, less half a carucate and the advowson, of which Thomas had endowed her at his marriage with Robert's consent, in return for a carucate in Harpsfield, co. Hertford, and a

---

[1] *E.Y.C.*, ii, no. 1072.
[2] *Ibid.*, no. 1047.
[3] *Ibid.*, iii, no. 1891.
[4] *Ibid.*, ii, no. 1073.
[5] *Ibid.*, no. 1003.
[6] *Ibid.*, no. 1075.
[7] *Ibid.*, no. 1076. It is probable that this Durand was the 'Brand' de Butterwick who witnessed a charter of Clement, abbot of St. Mary's, 1161–84 (*ibid.*, i, no. 628n).
[8] *Ibid.*, ii, no. 1071n, with certain details which include a Durand de Butterwick returning to allegiance in 1217. There are many references to the name in the 13th cent., either as jurors or witnesses, but it is not always easy to distinguish between Butterwick in the E. or N. Riding. A Robert de Butterwick gave to his sister Maud in marriage with Thomas de Etton (*q.v.*) half a car. in Butterwick, early 13th cent. (*E.Y.C.*, ix, p. 192n).
[9] *Yorks. Fines*, 1218–31, p. 102; evidently the car. originally given to the abbey by the first Durand.
[10] *Chron. de Melsa*, ii, 54.

rent in St. Albans, being all that Robert held in those places, to hold for life with reversion to Robert and his heirs.[1]

At the death of Peter de Brus in 1272, who had married Hilary de Mauley, Robert de Butterwick held of him a knight's fee in Butterwick and elsewhere;[2] but at the death of Peter de Mauley II in 1279 Ralph son of William held a knight's fee in Butterwick;[3] and in 1284–85 the latter held 12 carucates there for a knight's fee.[4] It seems, therefore, that unless there was a further process of subinfeudation the interest of the main line of the Butterwick family had ended.

CHAMBERLAIN (of Acklam and Wickenby)

The family descended from Herbert the chamberlain of Scotland, who held office under kings David I and Malcolm IV from c. 1136 to c. 1160, and whose gift of the church of Kinneil to Holyrood abbey, made with the consent of his sons Stephen and William, saving the tenure of William the clerk, Herbert's nephew, was confirmed by king Malcolm, 1161–62.[5] King Henry I gave him in marriage Milicent niece of William Turniant, with the land of the said William and Richard his brother and of Osbert the sheriff, their father, and also the land of Marston, co. Lincoln, to hold in chief.[6]

Herbert the chamberlain of Scotland must not be confused with Herbert the chamberlain of Henry I, who died in or shortly before 1130,[7] and who was the father of Herbert the younger and William archbishop of York.[8]

The inheritance of Milicent granddaughter of Osbert the sheriff,[9] being the daughter of Maud his daughter,[10] included land in Scoreby, wap. Ouse and Derwent, and in Wickenby and Westlaby and elsewhere in co. Lincoln, all held of the Percy fee;[11] land in Hayton, wap. Harthill, held of the honour of Mowbray;[12] and the

---

[1] *Yorks. Fines,* 1246–72, p. 194. No reference to a Butterwick holding in Harpsfield is given in *V.C.H., Herts.,* ii, 414. A Butterwick Farm, of which the earliest occurrence is c. 1250, and a Harpsfield Hall are in par. St. Peter's, co. Hertford (*Place-Name Soc., Herts.,* p. 94).

[2] *Yorks. Inq.,* i, no. 114, where Butterwick, N.R., is wrongly given as probable.

[3] *Ibid.,* no. 112 (p. 197). Farrer identified Ralph as Ralph son of William de Grimthorpe (*q.v.*) (*E.Y.C.,* ii, no. 1071*n*).

[4] *Feudal Aids,* vi, 28.

[5] G. W. S. Barrow, *Acts of Malcolm IV,* p. 30 and no. 196; the lands of Kinneil had been granted to Herbert his chamberlain by kg David I (*ibid.,* no. 88).

[6] *E.Y.C.,* xi, p. 214, from a case of 1199–1201 relating to Marston, examined by Farrer in *H.K.F.,* ii, 122; and for the kg's grant, enrolled in the proceedings, *Regesta,* ii, no. 1930, where the note is subject to considerable amendment.

[7] *Pipe Roll 31 Henry I,* p. 37.

[8] *E.Y.C.,* xi, pp. 215–6.

[9] Sheriff of Lincs. from c. 1096, and of Yorks. in the early years of Henry I, probably dying in 1114–16 (*ibid.,* p. 214, citing Farrer's paper in *E.H.R.,* xxx, 277–85). He had a brother Ralph the canon (*Lindsey Survey,* p. 241).

[10] The descent is given in a case of 1223 (*E.Y.C.,* xi, p. 214).

[11] *Ibid.,* p. 213.

[12] *Ibid.,* p. 214.

land of Marston mentioned above. In 1212 it was recorded that
William de Percy [I] had held in chief 3 carucates in Wickenby and
Westlaby and had given them to Osbert the sheriff for the service of
one knight and his heirs were then holding them.[1] It also appears
that the Bardolf family claimed a portion of the inheritance by
descent from Osbert the sheriff including land in Oxfordshire, which
was settled by a final concord, 27 January 1221–2.[2]

Herbert the chamberlain was succeeded by his son Stephen,
who inherited holdings of his mother before 1160, but not those of
his father in Scotland, which may have passed to his brother
William.[3] In 1166 as Stephen the chamberlain he held 2 knights' fees
of the old feoffment of William de Percy II.[4] At the same date he
held rather more than a knight's fee in chief, also of the old feoffment,
which consisted of land in Acklam, Leavening and Wharram Percy,
William de Scures (q.v.) being his principal tenant.[5] On 31 January
1159–60, as Stephen son of Herbert the chamberlain of the king of
Scotland, he confirmed to Kirkstead abbey lands and pastures in
Swinethorpe and Snelland, co. Lincoln,[6] and in 1187, as Stephen the
chamberlain of Wickenby, he issued another confirmation to the
same house.[7] As Stephen de Wickenby the chamberlain or Stephen
the chamberlain of Wickenby he gave and confirmed to Kirkstead,
c. 1175–1184, land in Westlaby and Wickenby held of the Percy fee;[8]
and, as Stephen de Wickenby son of Herbert the chamberlain, he
confirmed the church of Snelland to Barlings abbey.[9] His interest in
Acklam is shown by his confirmation of the gift made by William de
Scures of the church there to Thornton abbey.[10]

In the late twelfth century Robert son of Stephen the chamberlain confirmed to Kirkstead abbey all that it had of his fee in Swinethorpe.[11] In 1207 Robert was holding his land in Wickenby;[12] and he
was a party to the final concord of 1222 and the plaintiff in the case
of 1223 mentioned above. He died before 11 November 1225, when
the king took the homage of Henry the chamberlain, Robert's son,
for a knight's fee in Lincolnshire.[13] From Henry the inheritance

[1] *Bk. of Fees*, p. 172.

[2] *E.Y.C.*, xi, p. 217.

[3] On this point see *ibid.*, p. 216, noting that in 1161–64 William son of
Herbert the chamberlain witnessed a charter of kg Malcolm (Barrow, *op. cit.*,
no. 213).

[4] *E.Y.C.*, xi, no. 88 and p. 213, giving the location in Scoreby and places in
Lincs. in Wickenby and elsewhere.

[5] *Ibid.*, ii, no. 825 and note, giving the location and the suggestion that
Osbert the sheriff had been enfeoffed of these Yorkshire lands.

[6] *Danelaw Charters*, no. 219.

[7] *Ibid.*, no. 231.

[8] *E.Y.C.*, xi, nos. 176–8.

[9] *Ibid.*, no. 180n.

[10] *Ibid.*, i, no. 32, where he is described as Stephen son of Herbert the
chamberlain of the king of Scotland – *Scotie* and not *Stephani*, which was
proposed by Farrer as an amendment.

[11] *Danelaw Charters*, no. 232.

[12] *E.Y.C.*, xi, p. 218.

[13] *Ibid.*

descended in the male line through a younger son until the fourteenth century, eventually passing to a daughter of John son of Robert the chamberlain.[1] In 1284–85 the vill of Scoreby was sub-infeudated, the knight's fee being held immediately of the heirs of Henry de Percy by the heirs of 'le Chaumberlayn'.[2] Although in 1242–43 the tenure in chief in Acklam, Leavening and Wharram Percy, for the service of $1\frac{1}{4}$ knights, was held by Henry the chamberlain,[3] it later became a member of the Ros fee.[4]

CHAUNCY

The lands both in Yorkshire and Lincolnshire, which constituted the Chauncy fees, were held almost entirely at the Domesday survey by Odo the crossbowman,[5] who gave to St. Mary's abbey, York, $4\frac{1}{2}$ carucates in Hanging Grimston, par. Kirby Underdale, which were confirmed by king William II, 1088–93;[6] and with tithes of Skirpenbeck and Bugthorpe were included in the general confirmation of king Henry II.[7]

At the Lindsey survey Amfrey de Chauncy (*Anfrid de Canci* or *Canceio*) held land in Willoughton and Swinhope, and Alfred (*Alfreit*) de Chauncy in Dunham and Bleasby, in all of which Odo had held a tenancy-in-chief in 1086.[8] Amfrey de Chauncy also held a knight's fee of the lord of Richmond, owing the service of castle-guard,[9] and so can be identified with the Anfrid de Canci, a tenant of the count of Britanny in Swinhope at the Lindsey survey.[10] He was the donor to St. Mary's abbey of 4 carucates in Thixendale, par. Wharram Percy,[11] another of the places where Odo held land in 1086. Farrer has suggested as not unreasonable that Amfrey and Alfred were the sons of a sister of Odo;[12] but no proof is available.

Amfrey de Chauncy I presumably died before 1130, when Walter de Chauncy rendered account of 15*li.* in Yorkshire for marrying at his own will, and of 20*s* for the pleas of Blyth.[13] With the consent of Alfred his son and heir Walter de Chauncy gave to Whitby

---

[1] *E.Y.C.*, xi, pp. 218–9. The descent is traced by W. H. B. Bird in his papers on the ancestry and family of Stephen the chamberlain in *Genealogist*, vol. xxxii (1916). It was due to him that the correct parentage of Stephen was proved.

[2] *Feudal Aids*, vi, 33.

[3] *Bk. of Fees*, p. 1100.

[4] *E.Y.C.*, ii, p. 168. In 1316 Acklam was held by William de Ros (*Feudal Aids*, vi, 171).

[5] *V.C.H. Yorks.*, ii, 282; *E.Y.C.*, ii, p. 175; *Lincs. Domesday*, pp. 169–71.

[6] *E.Y.C.*, i, no. 350.

[7] *Ibid.*, no. 354 (p. 271).

[8] *Lindsey Survey*, pp. 240–1, 247, 257; *Lincs. Domesday, ut sup.*

[9] *E.Y.C.*, v, p. 12; date Henry I and later.

[10] *Lindsey Survey*, p. 247. There was thus a division in Swinhope between the Chauncy tenancy-in-chief and the honour of Richmond.

[11] Confirmed by kg Henry II in 1155 (*E.Y.C.*, i, no. 354, p. 273).

[12] *Ibid.*, ii, no. 833*n*, where many details are given of the family, with chart pedigree p. 174. It cannot be supposed that Amfrey and Alfred were the same person as indexed in *Lindsey Survey*.

[13] *Pipe Roll 31 Hen. I*, p. 26.

abbey the advowson of Skirpenbeck and land there, *c.* 1150–1160.[1] Walter also gave to the abbey common of pasture in Skirpenbeck, mentioning his lord king Henry.[2] In 1161 Alfred (*Aluredus*) de Chauncy paid 12 marks in respect of pleas;[3] but by 1165 the succession in Yorkshire had passed to Amfrey de Chauncy II,[4] who in 1166 held 5 knights' fees of the old feoffment in chief.[5]

It is clear that the original tenancy-in-chief consisted of 10 knights' fees, the remaining 5 being in Lincolnshire held by Simon de Chauncy in 1166.[6] To explain this Farrer suggested that the inheritance was divided into two equal parts between Amfrey and Simon, being younger brothers and heirs of Alfred.[7]

Amfrey de Chauncy II confirmed to Whitby abbey the church of Skirpenbeck and land there which his father had given;[8] he also gave land there to Byland abbey, St. Peter's York and St. Peter's hospital.[9] He died before 1190, leaving Walter his son and heir, then a minor, to whom Hugh Murdac, his guardian, gave Maud Murdac in marriage; Walter died in 1228 without issue, being succeeded by Roger his brother, who died in 1238, leaving Robert his son and heir.[10] In 1242–43 Robert de Chauncy held 5 knights' fees in chief in Skirpenbeck, Bugthorpe, Fridaythorpe, Youlthorpe (par. Bishop Wilton) and Swaythorpe (par. Kilham).[11] He died in 1246, dower being held by his mother and by Maud Murdac (widow of his uncle Walter), leaving Thomas his son and heir, nearly two years old.[12] Thomas proved his age, then twenty-three, in 1268, the manor of Skirpenbeck being held of the king by barony;[13] and he died in 1309, described as baron of Skirpenbeck, leaving William his son and heir aged thirty.[14] William died in 1342–43, holding the manor of Skirpenbeck and also the manor of Hutton Wandesley of Robert de Wilstrop for life with remainder to John Chauncy his [younger] son; William's heir being his son Thomas aged thirty and more.[15] The

---

[1] *E.Y.C.*, ii, no. 828.
[2] *Ibid.*, no. 829.
[3] *Pipe Roll 7 Hen. II*, p. 36.
[4] *Ibid. 11 Hen. II*, p. 50.
[5] *Red Bk. Exch.*, p. 426; *E.Y.C.*, ii, no. 833.
[6] See below.
[7] *E.Y.C.*, ii, no. 833*n* (p. 176).
[8] *Ibid.*, no. 831. This charter presents a difficulty. The wording shows that he consented to the gift in his father's charter, but the latter's charter (no. 828) was made with the consent of Alfred his son and heir. Actually there is no proof that Alfred survived his father; and it is possible that after Alfred's death Walter issued another charter in which his eldest surviving son, Amfrey, took part.
[9] *Ibid.*, nos. 838–41, 846; in two of these he is described as Amfrey son of Walter de Chauncy.
[10] References are given in *ibid.*, no. 833*n;* and *Yorks. Inq.*, i, p. 6*n*, where there are several references to the tenure from 1228 to 1268.
[11] *Bk. of Fees*, p. 1102.
[12] *Yorks. Inq.*, i, nos. 7, 8; *Cal. Inq. p.m.*, i, no. 80.
[13] *Yorks. Inq.*, i, no. 60.
[14] *Cal. Inq. p.m.*, v, no. 93.
[15] *Ibid.*, viii, no. 456.

latter held Skirpenbeck in 1346,[1] and Walter Chauncy, baron of Skirpenbeck, in 1382.[2] In 1392 William Chauncy, baron of Skirpenbeck, made an agreement about services in Bugthorpe.[3]

The Lincolnshire line descended from Simon de Chauncy I, mentioned above. In 1166 he held 5 knights' fees of the old feoffment in chief.[4] A record of 1212 shows that he had held lands in Swinhope and elsewhere in Lincolnshire, in places where land was held by Odo the crossbowman at the Domesday survey, and that they were then held by his son Simon, who also held land in Swinhope of the honour of Richmond for a knight's fee[5] – land which had been held by Amfrey de Chauncy at the Lindsey survey.

Simon de Chauncy was living in 1223;[6] and before 1235–36 he had been succeeded by Philip de Chauncy I,[7] who was then holding 5 knights' fees in Lindsey.[8] By his marriage with Lucy sister and coheir of Geoffrey de Benniworth (*q.v.*) he ultimately acquired an interest in Moor Monkton, a member of the Paynel fee in Yorkshire.[9] He died in 1263, being succeeded by his son William, aged twenty-five, from whom the line descended to Gerard de Chauncy, who died in 1322, leaving a daughter Isabel, a year old.[10]

William son of Philip de Chauncy, who died in 1281, held Monkton of John Paynel;[11] but in 1299 his son Philip de Chauncy II sold the manor and advowson to Robert Ughtred.[12]

CHEVERCOURT

The family derived its name from Quièvrecourt, dept. Seine–Maritime, arr. and cant. Neufchâtel, 4 kilometres from Bully, the home of Roger de Busli, the Domesday tenant-in-chief of the lands later known as the honour of Tickhill.[13]

At the Domesday survey Turold was a tenant of Roger de Busli in Carlton in Lindrick, co. Nottingham;[14] and, as Turold de Cheverchort, witnessed Roger's foundation of Blyth priory in 1088.[15]

---

[1] *Feudal Aids*, vi, pp. 215, 237.
[2] *Cal. Inq. p.m.*, xv, no. 598.
[3] *Cal. Close Rolls*, 1392–96, p. 92.
[4] *Red Bk. Exch.*, p. 378. In 1165 he had rendered account of 5 marks (*Pipe Roll 11 Hen. II*, p. 50).
[5] *Bk. of Fees*, pp. 159–60.
[6] In 1220 to 1223 he and his wife Alice were engaged in a plea of land in Walesby, co. Lincoln (*Curia Regis Rolls*, ix, 252; xi, no. 1127). There Amfrey de Chauncy had held 2 car. (*Lindsey Survey*, p. 246).
[7] In Farrer's chart pedigree (*E.Y.C.*, ii, p. 174) he is given as a nephew of Simon, being son of an elder Philip, Simon's brother.
[8] *Bk. of Fees*, p. 548.
[9] *E.Y.C.*, vi, p. 110.
[10] *Cal. Inq. p.m.*, i, no. 561; ii, no. 405; iv, no. 430; v, no. 275; vi, no. 333. Swinhope is mentioned as a tenancy-in-chief in all of them, and the tenure there of the honour of Richmond in two.
[11] *Ibid.*, ii, no. 405.
[12] *Yorks. Fines*, 1272–1300, p. 133.
[13] *Anglo-Norman Families*, pp. 21, 28.
[14] *V.C.H. Notts.*, i, 262.
[15] Hunter, *South Yorkshire*, i, 223; John Raine, *Parish of Blyth*, p. 30.

There were two branches of the family, one descending from Ralph de Chevercourt, the founder of Wallingwells priory, and the other from Walter de Chevercourt whose descendants in the male line held Wyfordby, co. Leicester, most of which was held of the honour of Tickhill, until the middle of the fourteenth century.[1] Nichols, in his account of the family at Wyfordby with a chart pedigree, supposed that Ralph and Walter were the eldest and youngest sons of Alfrid, living temp. Henry I, son of Turold. His evidence for Alfrid is the text of a charter of Henry I confirming to Walter de Chevercourt the land of Alfrid his father which his brother G. had given him.[2] The witnesses to this charter are impossible; but the mention of Alfrid need not be the result of invention. On the other hand, although there is no proof that Turold had a son of that name, it seems reasonably certain that Turold was the ancestor of both branches of the family.

Ralph de Chevercourt's charter founding Wallingwells priory, at a date probably not later than c. 1144, was witnessed by Herbert prior of Pontefract and others including Simon de Chevercourt and Jordan and Richard his brothers,[3] the latter three being presumably the grantor's sons. The connexion of this line with Yorkshire is shown by a charter of Ralph de Chevercourt (*Caprecuria*), evidently the same man, and Beatrice his sister, with the consent of Jordan and Richard his sons, giving to Pontefract priory the vill of Barnsley, held of the Lascy fee, 1144–59.[4] The grantor also held a tenancy of the Caux fee in Yorkshire; and he confirmed to Kirkstall abbey 2 carucates of the land called Bessacar in the soke of Branton (par. Cantley) held of that fee, which had been given by his tenants.[5]

Ralph was succeeded by his son Jordan de Chevercourt before Michaelmas 1165, when the latter owed relief for a knight's fee held of the honour of Tickhill in Carlton.[6] In 1166 Jordan held a knight's fee of the old feoffment of Robert de Caux in his return from Nottinghamshire;[7] and in 1174–77 he confirmed the gift of his father and aunt to Pontefract priory.[8]

Jordan de Chevercourt had a son Ralph who died without issue, and his coheirs were his four daughters, who and their descendants,

---

[1] Nichols, *Leicestershire*, ii (i), pp. 395–7. At Wyfordby 4¼ car. were held of the honour of Blyth (Tickhill) and 1¼ car. by Roger de Mowbray, c. 1130, mainly representing the Domesday holdings (C. F. Slade, *Leicestershire Survey*, pp. 21, 53).

[2] Nichols, *loc. cit*, from MS. Chetwynd. No reference to such a charter is given in *Regesta*, vol. ii.

[3] *Danelaw Charters*, no. 452, from the original, with date assigned c. 1150; but in view of the witness prior Herbert a date not later than c. 1144 can be suggested (see *Y.A.J.*, xxxviii, 458).

[4] *E.Y.C.*, iii, no. 1771, probably not later than 1153 (note thereto).

[5] *Ibid.*, ii, no. 812.

[6] *Pipe Roll 11 Hen. II*, p. 55.

[7] *Red Bk. Exch.*, p. 343.

[8] *E.Y.C.*, iii, no. 1774.

which included the families of Furneaux and Neufmarché, inherited his interests in Carlton.[1]

CLEASBY

The family descended from Harsculf Rufus, who witnessed an Easby charter, *c.* 1152–1162.[2] It has been suggested[3] that he can be identified as the Hasculf son of Ridiou who was one of the principal tenants of count Stephen, lord of Richmond, in 1130;[4] but of this there is no proof.[5]

Harsculf Rufus was given a carucate in Skeeby, par. Easby, a member of the constable's fee held of the honour of Richmond, by Richard de Rollos II; the latter gave it to Harald his nephew to hold of Robert son of Harsculf, 1162–*c.* 1165.[6] Robert de Cleasby, so described, confirmed land in Scotton and Brompton-on-Swale which Harsculf his father had given to Ralph the sheriff (of Ainderby) in marriage with Oriota, his (Harsculf's) sister, *c.* 1175–1201.[7] He gave land in or near Skeeby with his body for burial to Easby abbey late in the twelfth century; and at a later date Harsculf son of Robert de Cleasby confirmed a gift in Skeeby made by his grandfather Robert son of Harsculf.[8] The four generations Harsculf, Robert, Robert and Harsculf can thus be determined.

The younger Harsculf quitclaimed land in Melmerby to Fountains abbey in 1260,[9] and in 1280 Robert son of Harsculf de Cleasby was a party with the abbot of Easby in a final concord for messuages and land in Stapleton.[10] In 1284–85 Robert de Cleasby held 8 carucates in Cleasby with Clowbeck of Roald de Richmond (*q.v.*) (the descendant of Roald the constable), who held of the earl.[11] By his wife Amabel he had an only daughter Emma, who married first before 24 April 1300 Sir Robert Hastang, who died before 15 April 1336,[12] and secondly Henry FitzHugh of Ravensworth (*q.v.*). In 1337–38 a final concord was levied by which the Cleasby inheri-

---

[1] Thoroton, *Nottinghamshire*, ed. Throsby, iii, 408–12, with chart pedigree, in which he made Ralph the elder a son of Turold, thus conflicting with Nichols; on chronological grounds it is likely that there was an intervening generation.

[2] *E.Y.C.*, v, no. 179.

[3] By Farrer (*ibid.*, p. 86); it is given as a possibility in *V.C.H.*, *N.R.*, i, 158.

[4] *E.Y.C.*, v, p. 10.

[5] No tenancy held of the honour temp. Henry I and later gives any clue to Hasculf son of Ridiou's tenancy, as is the case with all the others in the 1130 list.

[6] *Ibid.*, no. 264.

[7] *Ibid.*, no. 204. The date is that of the confirmn of the land given in marriage with a dau. of Ralph and Oriota (no. 203).

[8] *Ibid.*, no. 266 and note.

[9] *Fountains Chartulary*, ii, 512.

[10] *Yorks. Fines*, 1272–1300, p. 31.

[11] *Feudal Aids*, vi, 101.

[12] *Complete Peerage*, vi, 340. Amabel was not, as supposed (*ibid.*), the heiress of Barforth. It was Robert's mother Emma, wife of Harsculf de Cleasby, who was dau. and heir of Richard lord of Barforth (*Pudsay Deeds*, pp. 74–5 and no. 337; and *cf. V.C.H.*, *N.R.*, i, 67).

tance was settled on Emma and her husband with remainder to the latter's right heirs,[1] and the greater part devolved on the latter's descendants by his first wife in default of Emma's death without issue.[2]

A younger line, the Cleasby family of Marske, was closely connected; but the precise nature of the connexion has not been established. It is supposed that the Harsculf de Cleasby from whom the line descended, a nephew of Robert son of Robert de Marske and of Roald lord of Constable Burton,[3] was a younger brother of Robert de Cleasby lord of Cleasby in 1284–85[4] (see above); but as he was apparently described as Harsculf son of William holding a carucate in Cleasby of Robert de Cleasby in that return,[5] and as a Harsculf son of William de Cleasby was a party to a final concord of land in Downholme in 1282,[6] this cannot be accepted. There is no evidence available to identify William, Harsculf's father, who must not be confused with Harsculf's son of the same name;[7] but it is possible that he was a brother of Harsculf de Cleasby, Robert's father, his son Harsculf being thus a first cousin of Robert.

From Harsculf de Cleasby, lord of Marske, the family descended in the male line for several generations to Robert de Cleasby living in the fifteenth century, whose only daughter and heir Elizabeth married William Conyers.[8]

CLERE

The English family of Clere was closely related to the family in Normandy which took its name from Clères, about 11 miles north of Rouen, and held an under-tenancy of the family of Tosny.[9] Roger de Clères was living c. 1040, when he assassinated Robert de Beaumont, evidently in revenge for the killing of Roger de Tosny by Roger de Beaumont, Robert's brother.[10] He was a benefactor of the abbey of Conches, a Tosny foundation,[11] and of the abbey of St. Ouen at Rouen.[12]

---

[1] *Yorks. Fines*, 1327–47, p. 122.

[2] *Pudsay Deeds*, pp. 80–1, giving reference to James de Cleasby who claimed to be Emma's brother.

[3] 'Marske in Swaledale' by Canon Raine in *Y.A.J.*, vi, 218–9.

[4] So given in the pedigree of Barforth and Cleasby in *Pudsay Deeds*, pp. 74–6.

[5] *Feudal Aids*, vi, 101.

[6] *Yorks. Fines*, 1272–1300, p. 65; and *cf.* the final concord of 1289 (*ibid.*, p. 88). Downholme descended in the Cleasby family of Marske (*V.C.H.*, *N.R.*, i, 228).

[7] Raine, *op. cit.*, p. 220.

[8] *Ibid.*, pp. 221–3. The paper must be read with caution, especially as it includes the fictitious charter of earl Conan (p. 213; *cf. E.Y.C.*, iv, p. 73). References to other members of the Cleasby family of later date are given in *V.C.H.*, *N.R.*, i, 159.

[9] *Anglo-Norman Families*, p. 29.

[10] *Orderic*, ed. Le Prévost, iii, 426–7, where the editor confuses this family with that of Clare; D. C. Douglas, *The Rise of Normandy*, Brit. Academy, p. 20.

[11] Delisle-et-Berger, *Rec. des Actes de Henri II*, i, no. 423 (p. 553).

[12] Le Prévost, *Mém . . . de l'Eure*, iii, 467.

The family in England held lands in Yorkshire and Lincoln-shire, of which the tenants-in-chief at the Domesday survey were Robert de Todeni and Berenger his son, who presumably represented a younger line of Tosny of Conches,[1] and also land in Sussex of the honour of Warenne, both Tosny and Warenne holding interests in Bellencombre in Normandy,[2] about 10 miles from Clères.

Roger de Clere I, the first recorded member of the family in England, enfeoffed Eustace FitzJohn, not later than 1129–33, of land in Brompton, wap. Pickering Lythe,[3] where Berenger de Todeni held a manor at the Domesday survey. His son and successor Roger de Clere II gave to Lewes priory land at Atlingworth, par. Portslade, Sussex, which was confirmed by Hamelin earl de Warenne after 1164;[4] and in 1166 he held 2 knights' fees of Hugh Bigod as of the fee of Aubreye de Lisle,[5] which can be located in Sinnington and Wilton, par. Thornton Dale.[6] Not later than 1185 Roger de Clere II was succeeded by Ralph who, described as his brother and heir, confirmed his gift of Atlingworth to Lewes priory, making an agreement therefor in that year;[7] and who gave the church of Sinnington and 4 bovates to Yeddingham priory.[8] From him the succession passed to his son Ralph de Clere II, who was dead by 1239, and to his grandson Roger de Clere III, whose daughter and heir Agatha married William le Rus; their daughter Alice married Richard de Brewse as her second husband.[9] In 1309 their son Giles de Brewse sold the manor of Sinnington to William le Latimer.[10]

CONSTABLE (of Flamborough)

The family descended from Robert Constable of Flamborough, who was very probably the illegitimate son of William son of William son of Nigel, all constables of Chester, from whom his name of Constable was derived.[11] He married one of the four daughters and

[1] *Anglo-Norman Families*, p. 104. That Clères held of Tosny in Normandy and Clere of the Todeni fee in England increases the probability.

[2] *Ibid.*, p. 112; Stapleton, *Rot. Scacc. Norm.*, ii, 431.

[3] *Regesta*, ii, no. 1722 and p. 375; see also no. 1730. This descended to the Vescy family as heirs of Eustace, and in 1284–85 John de Vescy held a k.f. there of Roger Bigod (*Feudal Aids*, vi, 82).

[4] *Lewes Chartulary*, Sussex Rec. Soc., i, 45; ii, 52.

[5] *Red Bk. Exch.*, p. 397. Aubreye was the widow of Berenger de Todeni and Roger Bigod, Hugh's father, married Adeliza, Berenger's sister; see the chart pedigree in *E.Y.C.*, i, p. 461.

[6] Roger de Clere's interest in these places is shown in *Pipe Roll 9 Hen. II*, p. 60; *13 Hen. II*, pp. 97, 99; *15 Hen. II*, p. 41; and in *E.Y.C.*, i, nos. 594, 610.

[7] *Lewes Chartulary, ut sup.*, ii, 51–2.

[8] *E.Y.C.*, i, no. 595.

[9] Documentary evidence is given in an unpublished paper on the family of Clere by the present writer, giving details of lands in other counties including Surrey, Hampshire and Norfolk.

[10] *Yorks. Fines*, 1300–14, p. 73. Giles's father Richard was a younger son of John de Brewse, lord of Bramber, and his descendants continued in the male line to 1489, still holding some of the Clere inheritance (*Complete Peerage*, ii, 304–7).

[11] *E.Y.C.*, xii, pp. 142–5, where the parentage of Robert is discussed; he was living in the period 1147–85.

coheirs of William Tison (*q.v.*), obtaining an interest in Holme upon Spalding Moor and other places of the Tison fee.[1]

From him the family descended in the male line to William Constable, who was created a baronet in 1611 and sold the manors of Flamborough and Holme upon Spalding Moor, dying without surviving issue in 1655.[2]

The Constables of Everingham descended from a younger son in the sixteenth century.[3]

CONSTABLE (of Halsham and Burton Constable)

The family descended from Ulbert who held the office of constable under William le Gros, count of Aumale and lord of the honour of Holderness. By his marriage with Erneburga de Burton he obtained interests in Fraisthorpe and probably in Burton [Constable] and Halsham. The date of birth of their son Robert the Constable I can be placed as *c.* 1130–35. The latter was succeeded by his nephew Robert the Constable II, from whom the family descended in the male line until the death without issue of William Constable, 4th Viscount Dunbar, in 1718.[4]

CONYERS

The family descended from Roger de Conyers who witnessed the charter of king Henry I, probably issued in 1101, giving the manor of Howden to Ranulf bishop of Durham.[5] He was given by bishop Ranulf not later than 1128 lands in Durham including Sockburn and in Yorkshire several lands including the places known subsequently as Hutton Conyers and Norton Conyers;[6] and in 1129–33 he had a confirmation from the king of his ward in respect of the knights doing castle-guard at Durham.[7]

As a result of a division in 1195–96 and consequent disputes between members of the family the interest in Hutton and Norton Conyers had a different descent from that in Sockburn.[8] The family holding Sockburn ended in the male line in 1635, when William Conyers died leaving three daughters,[9] and the elder branch holding Hutton and Norton Conyers ended in the male line in the fourteenth century, when Robert Conyers died leaving an only daughter Joan who married Sir Christopher Mallory.[10]

[1] *E.Y.C.*, xii, pp. 8, 145.
[2] *Ibid.*, pp. 145–51, with chart pedigree facing p. 145; and for the later generations *Dugdale's Visitation*, ed. J. W. Clay, ii, 288–91.
[3] *Ibid.*, pp. 291–4.
[4] 'Early Generations of Constable of Halsham' in *Y.A.J.*, xl, 197–202; and for the later generations *Dugdale's Visitation, ut sup.*, ii, 302–7.
[5] *Regesta*, ii, no. 546.
[6] *E.Y.C.*, ii, no. 944 and note.
[7] *Regesta*, ii, no. 1825; text p. 381.
[8] *V.C.H., N.R.*, i, pp. 393, 403, 451; *Y.A.J.*, xi, 179–80 and note.
[9] Surtees, *Durham*, iii, 247–8, with chart pedigree.
[10] *V.C.H., N.R.*, i, pp. 393, 403.

DAIVILLE

A family of Daiville held land both in Normandy and England of the counts of Eu, and derived its name from Déville, dept. Seine-Maritime, arr. Neufchâtel, cant. Londinières, comm. Grandcourt;[1] and as Nigel d'Aubigny was a tenant of the count of Eu in Normandy[2] it can be deduced that this was the place of origin of the Daiville family in England which held knights' fees of the honour of Mowbray.[3]

In a charter, 1109–14, Nigel d'Aubigny stated that he had given to Richard de Dauiduile land in Freeby and Welby, co. Leicester.[4] Richard witnessed two of Nigel's charters;[5] and in 1130 he rendered account of 10 marks for freedom of pleading for his land of Weston, co. Nottingham.[6] Before his death in 1129 Nigel d'Aubigny gave to Robert Davil or de Ayvile, described as his special friend, the vill of Egmanton, co. Nottingham.[7] A Robert de Davidvilla was described as lord of Kilburn in 1147, when he had disputes with the monks of Byland.[8] Robert de Daiville, also perhaps of a younger generation than the Robert living *ante* 1129, was an important tenant of the honour of Mowbray, holding 5 knights' fees in 1166.[9] As Robert de Daiville he witnessed a large number of charters issued by Roger de Mowbray and his son Nigel,[10] some being as early as *c.* 1147 and others as late as *c.* 1170–1186.[11] He was constable of Axholme;[12] and a benefactor of Byland and Rievaulx abbeys and St. Peter's hospital, York.[13] He married first a sister of Robert de Stuteville III (*q.v.*), and secondly, not later than 1170, Juliana daughter of Thurstan de Montfort.[14] Juliana was living in 1202, when she and her son John de Daiville received a quitclaim of land in Kilburn.[15]

[1] *Anglo-Norman Families*, p. 37.
[2] *Mowbray Charters*, no. 19.
[3] It is significant that in 1242–43 Robert Daiville (see below) held ¾ k.f. of the countess of Eu as of the honour of the castle of Tickhill in Greetwell, co. Lincoln (*Bk. of Fees*, p. 1065).
[4] *Mowbray Charters*, no. 3. These places later formed part of the Daiville fee held of the honour of Mowbray (*Bk. of Fees*, p. 1467).
[5] *Mowbray Charters*, nos. 5, 13.
[6] *Pipe Roll 31 Hen. I*, p. 11.
[7] *Mon. Ang.*, v. 346; vi, 320. As Egmanton formed part of the Daiville fee (see below) it can be assumed that the family descended from him, as well as from Richard (as above); but the relationship between Richard and Robert has not been established.
[8] *Ibid.*, v, 351–2.
[9] *Mowbray Charters*, no. 401; and for their location p. 264. The returns of 1284–85 show that John de Daiville was then holding Mowbray lands in Yorkshire in Kilburn, Nawton, Butterwick, Thornton on the Hill and Baxby (*Feudal Aids*, vi, pp. 52, 58, 65–6).
[10] *Mowbray Charters*, passim.
[11] *e.g.*, nos. 45, 313.
[12] *Ibid.*, no. 221.
[13] *E.Y.C.*, ix, nos. 140–1 for Rievaulx; no. 168 for Byland; and for the hospital charter no. 5 below; also no. 4 for another Byland charter, and no. 3 for one to Geoffrey de Rouen.
[14] *Ibid.*, no. 17.
[15] *Yorks. Fines, John*, p. 36.

In 1186–90 Nigel de Mowbray restored to John son of Robert de Daiville the land which Robert had held of his father (Roger de Mowbray) and himself.[1] John de Daiville, who held a knight's fee in Egmanton in 1235–36,[2] married Maud daughter of Jocelin of Louvain and his wife Agnes de Percy.[3] He died befoie 1242–43, when his son Robert was holding 2½ knights' fees of the honour of Mowbray in Yorkshire.[4] Robert was the father of Sir John de Daiville of Egmanton, Adlingfleet, Kilburn and Thornton [on the Hill], Chief Justice and keeper of the forests north of Trent, 1257–61, dying before October 1291. From his son Sii John the family descended in the male line to Robert Daiville of Adlingfleet, clerk, who succeeded his brother in 1351 and whose coheirs were three sisters. The manor of Kilburn had been sold in 1319.[5]

DAREL (of Sessay)

The family descended from Marmaduke Darel, who like Thomas Darel of Wheldrake (q.v.) was probably a son of Geoffrey de Arel, a witness to a charter of Fulk son of Reinfrid to Whitby abbey, c. 1100–1118.[6] Marmaduke was succeeded by his son William, living in the reign of John, from whom the family descended in the male line to George Darel of Sessay who died in 1466, being succeeded by his three sons, each dying without issue, the heir being their sister Joan wife of Guy Dawnay of Cowick.[7]

DAREL (of Wheldrake)

The family descended from Thomas Darel, probably the elder son of Geoffrey de Arel (as above). He was living c. 1147–1154 and died 1175–80; and his eldest son Geoffrey died 1183–85, leaving two daughters, Geoffrey de Fitling the younger, the son of the elder, taking the name of Darel.[8] From him the second line of Darel of Wheldrake descended; William son of Thomas Darel being the representative in 1368.[9]

ELAND

The family descended from Leising or Lesing, whose son Henry, described as Henry son of Lesing de Eland or Henry de Eland, gave land in Crigglestone to St. Peter's hospital, York, and to Nostell

[1] E.Y.C., ix, no. 137; *Mowbray Charters*, no. 361.
[2] Bk. of Fees, p. 534.
[3] E.Y.C., xi, p. 6 and no. 84, showing that he had land in Catton in marriage.
[4] Bk. of Fees, p. 1097.
[5] Complete Peerage, iv, 130–4, giving a full account of Sir John, C.J., and his descendants.
[6] E.Y.C., i, nos. 529–30; xi, pp. 189, 336.
[7] Ibid., xi, p. 337; and V.C.H., N.R., i, 447.
[8] E.Y.C., xi, pp. 186–91, with chart pedigree p. 188.
[9] Fountains Chartulary, ii, 836–7.

priory, *c.* 1188–1202.[1] He witnessed charters of Hamelin earl de Warenne, 1164–*c.* 1185 and 1164–96.[2]

Rochdale in Lancashire, held of the Lascy fee, was held as to one moiety by Henry de Eland, each of whose daughters inherited a sixth;[3] and as to the other by the descendants of Hugh de Eland who also held Elland and Southowram.[4] The evidence strongly suggests that Leising had made over a moiety of Rochdale to his son Henry, and that Hugh was his elder son.[5]

From Hugh the family descended through Richard his son to Sir John de Eland, sheriff of Yorkshire in 1340–41, who was murdered in 1350 and who and whose son John are well known in connexion with the 'Eland Feud';[6] the heiress Isabel, probably a granddaughter and not daughter of Sir John, married Sir John Savile, in whose family the inheritance descended.[7]

ETTON (of Skerne and Gilling)

The families of Etton descended from Odard de Mawnsell, a French knight, to whom, according to the Meaux Chronicle, king Henry I gave the tenement of which he had deprived Hugelin, lord of Skerne and of lands in Hutton Cranswick, the husband of Aubreye, one of the three daughters of Robert de Octon.[8] The lands appear to have consisted of about 10 carucates in Etton, 8 carucates in Skerne and 2 carucates in Hutton Cranswick, held of the Stuteville fee.[9]

Odard was the father of Geoffrey de Etton, who was succeeded by his son Thomas.[10] In 1154–*c.* 1160 Thomas gave land in Etton to Watton priory,[11] and in *c.* 1175–95, with the consent of Thomas his son and heir, land in Skerne to his daughter Maud in marriage.[12]

In a case of 1194 Thomas de Etton, who on chronological grounds was probably Thomas the younger, was one of the three successful claimants for land in Kilnwick Percy against William de

[1] *E.Y.C.*, viii, nos. 135–6.
[2] *Ibid.*, nos. 67, 69.
[3] Details are given in 'The Family of Eland' in *Y.A.J.*, xxvii, 228; and *cf. E.Y.C.*, viii, p. 192.
[4] *Y.A.J.*, *loc. cit.*, and chart pedigree p. 248.
[5] *Ibid.*, p. 231; *E.Y.C.*, viii, p. 192. It is suggested that Hugh was born *c.* 1110 and Henry *c.* 1115, and that Hugh was succeeded by his son Richard before 1166. Farrer has noted that 'as both Rochdale, Elland and South Owram were held T.R.E. by Gamel there is a strong presumption that the Ellands were his lineal descendants' (*E.Y.C.*, iii, p. 212). No connexion, however, between Gamel and Leising is known.
[6] *Y.A.J.*, xxvii, 241–5 for details.
[7] *Ibid.*, p. 245.
[8] *Chron. de Melsa*, i, 316–8, where is an account of the early history of Skerne and the benefactions to the abbey. On this was based the detailed account of the two families of Etton in his paper on Gilling Castle by John Bilson in *Y.A.J.*, xix, 105–92.
[9] *E.Y.C.*, ix, pp. 191–2, giving details of the early generations.
[10] *Chron. de Melsa*, i, 317.
[11] *E.Y.C.*, ix, no. 105.
[12] *Ibid.*, no. 106.

Percy of Kildale as son of one of the latter's three aunts,[1] and from this it can be deduced that it was Thomas the elder who married a sister of Ernald and Robert de Percy of Kildale (*q.v.*).

Thomas de Etton the younger died in 1223–26, and was succeeded by his son Robert.[2] The latter was presumably the father of Henry de Etton, who held half a knight's fee in Etton in 1282;[3] but no proof of this is available.[4] The family descended in the male line to the father of Amanda, who married Patrick de Langdale and was living in 1336.[5] Etton thus passed to the Langdale family.[6]

The Ettons of Gilling, evidently a branch of the same family, descended from William de Etton, who occurs in documents of 1252 and 1267; from him the descent through Sir Ivo his son continued in the male line to the fifteenth century; and eventually Gilling passed to the Fairfax family by virtue of a settlement made in 1349.[7] No proof has been found of the parentage of William de Etton; but it has been supposed as probable that his father was Ivo de Etton,[8] constable of Tickhill, who may have been the son of Geoffrey de Etton, living early in the thirteenth century.[9] Geoffrey can be identified with Geoffrey second son of Thomas de Etton the elder, mentioned above; and it is known that Geoffrey held an interest in Gilling.[10]

FAUCONBERG

The earliest known ancestor of the family[11] was Franco the man of Drogo de Bevrere the Fleming of whom he held tenancies in Catfoss and Rise in Holderness at the Domesday survey.[12] He is named in the Meaux Chronicle as Franco de Fawconberge of Rise.[13] It is reasonably certain that he was the father of Robert de Fauconberg who by Agnes, sister of William de Arches and widow of

[1] *E.Y.C.*, ii, no. 749*n*.
[2] *Ibid.*, ix, p. 192.
[3] *Yorks. Inq.*, i, no. 131 (p. 241).
[4] Henry does not appear in the eldest line in the pedigree in *Y.A.J.*, xix, 108, where Robert's son is given as Laurence de Etton; but the reference given (*ibid.*, xi, 372) suggests a confusion with Laurence de Etton, Amanda's father, and not great-grandfather.
[5] *Ibid.*, xix, 110; *Yorks. Fines*, 1327–47, p. 104.
[6] The Langdale evidences are pd in *Y.A.J.*, xi, 272 *et seq.*
[7] *Ibid.*, xix, 111–23.
[8] In 1224–30 Ivo de Etton held a k.f. in Gilling and elsewhere of Nigel de Mowbray (*Bk. of Fees*, p. 1460). William de Etton's son Sir Ivo may well have been named after his grandfather.
[9] *Y.A.J.*, xix, 110–11.
[10] *Ibid.*, p. 110; *Yorks. Fines*, 1218–31, p. 5. A charter of Geoffrey son of Thomas de Etton, early 13th cent., to Meaux abbey, confirming land in Skerne and rights given by Thomas his father and Thomas his brother, and also mentioning Odard his brother, is pd in *E.Y.C.*, ix, no. 107.
[11] *Complete Peerage*, v, 268*n*, with details of the descent from Robert de Fauconberg. Franco is given as apparently of the family of the Châtelains de St. Omer, Seigneurs de Fauquembergue.
[12] *V.C.H. Yorks.*, ii, 267–8.
[13] *Chron. de Melsa*, i, 78.

Herbert de St. Quintin, was the father of Peter de Fauconberg.[1] From the latter's son Walter the family descended to Sir Walter de Fauconberg, who was summoned to Parliament from 1295 to 1302, and so in the male line to Sir Thomas Fauconberg who died in 1407, leaving a daughter.[2]

In 1284–85 among the holdings of Sir Walter were Rise, Withornwick and Catfoss.[3] He had obtained Skelton castle in Cleveland in marriage with Agnes sister and coheir of Peter de Brus.[4]

FITZALAN (of Bedale)

The family descended from Scolland,[5] who witnessed a charter of count Stephen, lord of the honour of Richmond, before 1100 and others in the period 1125–c. 1135, occurring as one of the men of count Stephen in 1130; he was steward under earl Alan and was living as late as 1146.[6] He held land in Bedale and Melsonby and other places which had formed part of the fee held at the Domesday survey by Bodin, a half-brother of count Alan I.[7] There is no clue to his origin; but his name is preserved in the eleventh-century building in Richmond castle known as Scolland's hall; and it is known that he was buried at the priory of Castle Acre, to which he gave the church of Melsonby and tithe in Bedale and elsewhere.[8]

He was succeeded by his son Brian, who held 5 knights' fees of the honour; and the inheritance passed before 1171 to Alan son of Brian, who died in 1187–88,[9] and so in the male line to Brian son of Alan [FitzAlan], who was summoned to Parliament in 1295 and died in 1306,[10] leaving two daughters and coheirs. The Bedale fee was then divided between them and passed to their descendants by their respective husbands, Sir Gilbert de Stapleton, a younger son of Sir Miles de Stapleton of Carlton, and Sir John de Grey of Rotherfield.[11]

---

[1] See the Arches and St. Quintin sections. Farrer gives the birth of Peter as before 1130 (*E.Y.C.*, i, no. 540*n*). Agnes was known as Agnes de Catfoss (*ibid.*, iii, no. 1334).

[2] *Complete Peerage*, v, 267 *et seq.*

[3] *Feudal Aids*, vi, 40.

[4] Chart pedigree in *E.Y.C.*, ii, p. 15; and *Complete Peerage*, v, 268.

[5] The traditional descent from Brian brother of Conan earl of Richmond, followed in *Complete Peerage*, v, 393*n*, has now been abandoned, the amended descent being accepted in *ibid.*, x, 781*n;* the evidence is given in *Y.A.J.*, xxx, 281–90 and *E.Y.C.*, v, pp. 200 *et seq.*

[6] *Ibid.*, p. 201.

[7] *Ibid.*, pp. 196 *et seq.*, giving an account of the descent of the lands held by Bodin.

[8] *Ibid.*, p. 202 and no. 311.

[9] *Ibid.*, pp. 201–4, giving details of the early generations.

[10] *Complete Peerage*, v, 393; he held no lands in chief.

[11] *Ibid.*, pp. 395–8; and chart pedigree for the Stapleton coheirship p. 397. The descent of Grey of Rotherfield is given in *ibid.*, vi, 146–50; and for the interest of the two families in Bedale *V.C.H.*, *N.R.*, i, 294.

FITZHUGH (of Ravensworth)

The family descended from Bardulf, another of the illegitimate sons of count Eudo of Penthièvre and so a half-brother of count Alan I. Bardulf acquired a large portion of the Domesday holdings of his brother Bodin, which included Ravensworth and several other places in Richmondshire. He was succeeded by his son Acaris, a principal tenant of count Stephen in 1130, who gave to St. Martin's priory, Richmond, tithe from his demesne lands of Ravensworth and elsewhere. He held 3⅛ knights' fees, rendering castle-guard at Richmond, the same service being rendered by his grandson Henry son of Hervey; and he took a prominent part in founding the house which became known as Jervaulx abbey.[1]

Hervey son of Acaris gave land in Ravensworth to Marrick priory and was given the forestership of the New Forest and Arkengarthdale by earl Conan; he was succeeded by his son Henry before 1184.[2] From Henry's son Ranulf and the latter's grandson Hugh son of Henry[3] the family descended to Henry son of Hugh of Ravensworth, who was summoned to Parliament from 1321 to 1351 under the name Henry son of Hugh [FitzHugh], and so in the male line to George lord FitzHugh, who died in 1513, leaving as his coheirs his aunt, who married Sir John Fenys or Fynes son of Richard lord Dacre, and his first cousin Sir Thomas Parr of Kendal.[4]

FITZWILLIAM (of Emley and Sprotborough)

The family descended from Godric son of Ketelbern. This is proved by a case of 1211 when William son of William son of Godric claimed against Alexander de Crevequer a carucate in Hopton, of which Ketelbern his ancestor was seised in 1135, the right having descended to Godric, then to William and then to William his son, the claimant.[5] In 1191–c. 1200 William son of William confirmed to Byland abbey facilities in Emley by a charter showing that Emley had been in his father's possession;[6] and there is evidence that these facilities had been granted by Godric son of Ketelbern.[7] William son of Godric was living in the period 1169–80 and was dead in 1194; by his marriage as the third husband of Aubreye de Lisours, daughter of Robert de Lisours by his wife Aubreye de Lascy, he obtained Sprotborough.[8] Their son William son of William married Ela daughter of Hamelin earl de Warenne.[9]

---

[1] Evidence is given in the account of the Ravensworth fee in *E.Y.C.*, v, pp. 316–20.
[2] *Ibid.*, p. 318.
[3] In 1280–82 he held the same 3⅛ k.f. (p. 320).
[4] *Complete Peerage*, v, 416–33.
[5] *Curia Regis Rolls*, vi, 138. The case was in progress in 1212–14 (*ibid.*, p. 362; vii, pp. 11, 124, 189), and was settled by a final concord between the plaintiff and Alexander de Neville in 1219 (*Yorks. Fines, 1218–31*, p. 22).
[6] *Hatton Bk. of Seals*, no. 464. Hopton and Emley are both in wap. Agbrigg.
[7] *E.Y.C.*, iii, no. 1690*n*.
[8] For accounts of the family see *Baildon and the Baildons*, i, 343 *et seq.*; *Complete Peerage*, v, 518–20; *E.Y.C., ut sup.*; Hunter, *South Yorkshire*, i, 332–9.
[9] *E.Y.C.*, viii, p. 20.

The main branch of the family descended in the male line to the death of William FitzWilliam early in the sixteenth century, and the inheritance was divided between the families of Savile and Copley, representing the heirs general.[1]

FLAMVILLE

Hugh de Flamville was enfeoffed of the vill of Dalby, wap. Bulmer, for 15s yearly rent by Geoffrey abbot of St. Mary's York, and his claim to land between Dalby and Skewsby was to be tried by a jury, 1122–c. 1130.[2] This was the manor of 3 carucates in Dalby held at the Domesday survey by Berenger de Todeni,[3] whose gift of 3 carucates there was confirmed to St. Mary's by king William II.[4]

The importance of the Flamville or Flammaville family in Yorkshire in the twelfth century is due to Roger de Flamville, presumably Hugh's son, who married as her second husband Juetta daughter and heir of William de Arches (q.v.), her first husband having been Adam de Brus of Skelton who died in 1143.[5] In virtue of this marriage Roger held 7 out of his 8½ knights' fees of the old feoffment in the *carta* of Roger de Mowbray in 1166,[6] the remaining 1½ being held in his own right.

In 1130 Roger de Flamville rendered account of 20 marks of the pleas of Blyth, paying 10 marks.[7] He was a constant witness to charters of Roger de Mowbray,[8] who confirmed to Malton priory the church of Norton, wap. Buckrose, given by Roger de Flamville and his wife Juetta, c. 1150–1169,[9] and in the same period to the hospital of Norton the church of Marton, wap. Claro, 12 bovates in Welham (in Norton) and 8 bovates in Norton, given by Roger de Flamville and his son Hugh.[10] The fact that Hugh was a joint donor in the latter charter shows that part of the gift formed a portion of the 1½ fees constituting the Flamville fee, for he could not have

---

[1] For authorities see note above; and for other confirmations to Byland of lands in Emley, Bentley and Denby belonging to the FitzWilliam fee, *Yorks. Deeds*, v, pp. 37–8 and notes.
[2] *E.Y.C.*, i, no. 637; the limits of date for Geoffrey's abbacy were c. 1119–c. 1137 (*Heads of Religious Houses*, p. 84); but, if, as is probable, Hugh succeeded by Roger 1130 would be the latest date. There was also a Thomas de Flamma[villa] who witnessed another charter of abbot Geoffrey (*E.Y.C.*, i, no. 105).
[3] *V.C.H. Yorks.*, ii, 242, the abbot of St. Mary's holding it of Berenger.
[4] *E.Y.C.*, i, no. 350.
[5] See the chart pedigree of Arches in *ibid.*, p. 420. The date of death of William de Arches can be put forward to after c. 1154 (*Mowbray Charters*, no. 359).
[6] *Red Bk. Exch.*, p. 419; *Mowbray Charters*, p. 262. In 1224–30 these 7 fees were held by Peter de Brus II (*Bk. of Fees*, p. 1460), who was great-grandson of Adam de Brus and Juetta de Arches, and so the latter's heir; the Flamville interest had ended on Roger's death.
[7] *Pipe Roll 31 Hen. I*, p. 27.
[8] *Mowbray Charters, passim.*
[9] *Ibid.*, no. 183. Roger's charter is pd at no. 6 below.
[10] *Ibid.*, no. 184.

inherited any interest in the Arches fee. Moreover Hugh issued a charter of his own, confirming the church of Marton to the hospital (see below).[1]

Roger de Flamville, dying not later than Easter 1169,[2] was succeeded by his son Hugh, who witnessed several charters of Roger de Mowbray and his son Nigel[3] and a charter relating to Rainton, c. 1180–1189.[4] In 1188 as Hugh de Flammavilla of Fryton he was the first witness, Hugh de Flammavilla son of Alan (see below) being the second, to an acknowledgement by Henry de Hastings of a loan of 5 marks from Henry de Cornhill.[5] He confirmed to the hospital of Norton the church of Marton which his father had given (see above), an earlier confirmation having been made before he had given Maud his sister in marriage to Robert de Hastings.[6] He also gave to Rievaulx abbey the mill of Fryton, par. Hovingham;[7] and in 1197–1201 to St. Peter's York 4 carucates in Marton.[8] He was living in 1203,[9] and died before Trinity term 1212, when Maud de Conyers claimed against Peter de Brus dower of a third of land in several places, most or all of which were members of the Arches fee, saying that Hugh de Flamville, formerly her husband, had endowed her on marriage with a third of all that could fall to him in inheritance and that the lands had afterwards descended to him, but Peter replied that Hugh was never seised, either at his marriage or afterwards; and the case was postponed.[10]

As Hugh de Flamville died without issue his heirs were his sisters Maud, who married Robert de Hastings, and Agnes who married first William de Percy of Kildale (q.v.), who died in 1202–03, and secondly John de Birkin (q.v.).[11] In 1205 Maud de Flamville successfully claimed against Geoffrey de Marton services for 4 bovates

---

[1] This rules out the possibility that Hugh's interest in Marton was due to his father's marriage to Juetta, suggested in *York Minster Fasti*, i, 72 (no. 25n), for his father only held a life interest in her inheritance. Details given below show that Fryton, par. Hovingham, was another member of the 1½ fees.

[2] *Pipe Roll 16 Hen. II*, p. 49, showing that he had been dead for three half-years. He may be the Roger de Flamville living in 1167 (*ibid. 13 Hen. II*, p. 1); but this may be Roger of Northumberland (see below).

[3] *Mowbray Charters, passim.*

[4] *E.Y.C.*, xi, no. 148.

[5] *Ancient Charters*, P.R.Soc., vol. x, no. 54. There was evidently a connexion between Henry de Hastings and Robert de Hastings who married Maud sister of Hugh de Flamville.

[6] *Mon. Ang.*, vi (2), 972; the text is pd below at no. 7.

[7] *Rievaulx Chartulary*, no. 311, from MS. Dodsworth vii, f. 116v, mentioning his wife Maud. Another Fryton charter is pd at no. 8 below, and one to Robert de Hutton at no. 9.

[8] *York Minster Fasti*, ii, 120 (no. 78)

[9] *Curia Regis Rolls*, iii, 56, a case relating to Dalby (see above).

[10] *Ibid.*, vi, 345. The defendant was Peter de Brus I, grandson and heir of Juetta de Arches. Hugh may have made some claim to Arches land before his death in 1209 Peter owed 3 palfreys for agreeing with him, and on to 1212 when the debt was 2 palfreys (*Pipe Roll 11 John*, p. 123; *14 John*, p. 32).

[11] Chart pedigree, *E.Y.C.*, i, p. 420; and *ibid.*, x, no. 113n. A charter of Agnes is pd at no 10 below.

in Marton,[1] and in 1224–30 she and Walter de Percy each held half a fee of the honour of Mowbray in Fryton and elsewhere.[2] In 1233–40, in her widowhood, she gave to St. Peter's York and the prebend of Dunnington the homage and service of Sir Godfrey de Louvain for land in Marton.[3]

In 1202 Juetta de Arches recognised 29 bovates in (Kirk) Hammerton as the right and inheritance of William de Percy of Kildale and Agnes (de Flamville) his wife, saving 4 bovates which she had given to Nun Monkton priory and the advowson which the nuns had of the gift of William de Arches, her father.[4] The heir of Agnes was her son Walter de Percy, who in 1224 after a controversy confirmed to Rievaulx abbey the mill of Fryton which Hugh de Flamville his uncle had given (see above).[5] In 1240 William son of Walter de Percy recognised the right of the prioress of Nun Monkton in 27 bovates in Kirk Hammerton as of the gift of Agnes de Flamville his grandmother.[6] The family of Percy of Kildale (q.v.) descended in the male line to the sixteenth century.

Another line of the family in which the names Alan and Elias occur was closely connected. Alan de Flamville witnessed two charters of Roger de Mowbray, 1146–56 and 1154;[7] and two more, also witnessed by Roger de Flamville in a senior position.[8] In 1169 and on to 1172 he was seeking the right of his land in Yorkshire against Roger de Millieres.[9] He had a son Hugh who occurs as a witness in 1188 (see above).

Elias de Flamville made a final concord with Hugh de Flamville (evidently son of Roger) for 8 acres in Marton, and in 1214 Alan his son and heir[10] gave a mark for a writ in respect of this, Hugh's heirs being given as Maud de Flamville and Agnes her sister.[11] In 1226 Alan had a quitclaim of a carucate in Skewsby,[12] and witnessed a Hovingham charter on 11 May 1231.[13] He married Imeria daughter

[1] *Yorks. Fines, John,* p. 94. Maud was evidently sister of Hugh de Flamville and had probably acquired her interest on marriage.

[2] *Bk. of Fees,* p. 1460.

[3] *York Minster Fasti,* i, 71 (no. 25). In 1251 Elias de Flamville (see below), described as of Norton, brought a writ of novel disseisin against Matthew de Louvain for his free tenement in Norton, but did not proceed (*Yorks. Assize Rolls,* p. 58).

[4] *Yorks. Fines, John,* p. 34. Agnes occurs as the wife of William de Percy, 1171–c. 1195 (*E.Y.C.,* ii, no. 750). The reference suggests that her brother Hugh had acquired an under-tenancy in Kirk Hammerton, a member of the Arches fee.

[5] *Rievaulx Chartulary,* p. 219n.

[6] *Yorks. Fines, 1232–46,* p. 72.

[7] *Mowbray Charters,* nos. 253, 237.

[8] *Ibid.,* nos. 236, 240.

[9] *Pipe Roll 15 Hen. II,* p. 35 to *18 Hen. II,* p. 58.

[10] This suggests that Elias was the son of the elder Alan; and that he gave to his son the name of his own father.

[11] *Rot. de Obl. et Fin.,* p. 537. The reference to this in *Pipe Roll 16 John,* p. 94 gives the defendants as Hugh de Flamville and Maud and Agnes his sisters, but this cannot prove that Hugh was still alive (see above).

[12] *Yorks. Fines, 1218–31,* p. 65.

[13] *R. R. Hastings MSS,* Hist. MSS Comm., i, 188.

of Roger de Aske (*q.v.*),[1] and died before 10 July 1232, when the abbot of St. Mary's made a presentation for the church of Dalby by reason of the minority of the heir of Alan de Flamville, dame Maud de Flamville opposing the presentation.[2] This suggests that both Alan de Flamville and Maud derived their interest by a common descent from Hugh de Flamville the elder, who as noted above was granted a tenancy in Dalby by the abbot of St. Mary's early in the twelfth century. If so, it can be deduced that Roger de Flamville and Alan I, who were certainly contemporaries, were brothers and sons of Hugh.

In 1242–43 Elias de Flamville, presumably son of Alan II and the minor in 1232, held 8 carucates of the fee of Peter de Brus in 'Stokesby',[3] evidently Skewsby, par. Dalby.[4] He gave woodland in Scackleton, par. Hovingham, to the abbot of Byland before August 1240;[5] and in 1260–66, as a knight, quitclaimed to the abbot of St. Mary's all his land in Dalby with the dower of his mother and the advowson, Ymanya widow of Alan de Flamville also quitclaiming her right of dower in the wood there.[6] In 1279 he, or another Elias, together with Roger de Mowbray made claims when land in Norton and Sutton by Malton was the subject of a final concord.[7] In 1302–03 the heir of Elias de Flamville held 4 bovates out of 2 carucates in North Cave of the fee of Percy of Kildale.[8]

There were two other families, apparently unconnected, bearing the same name and holding land in England. Roger de Flamenvilla, who must not be confused with Roger de Flamville the Mowbray tenant, was given land in Whittingham, Northumberland by king Henry II in 1160–73.[9] He was succeeded by his son William who died without issue, leaving four sisters as his heirs.[10]

The second family held lands in Leicestershire, which included Aston, hund. Sparkenhoe, later known as Aston Flamville. The descent was from Robert de Flamville, to whom the bishop of Coventry gave these lands for the service of 2 knights' fees, *c.* 1100; Robert's heir was Erneburga daughter of his brother Hugh, whom king Henry I gave in marriage to Hugh de Hastings; and the lands descended in the Hastings family, a younger line of Flamville holding an under-tenancy.[11]

[1] *E.Y.C.*, i, no. 637*n*.
[2] *Reg. Gray*, p. 55.
[3] *Bk. of Fees*, p. 1098; not identified in the index.
[4] So identified by Farrer in *E.Y.C.*, i, no. 637*n;* and actually 8 car. was its Domesday assessment (*V.C.H., Yorks.*, ii, 222).
[5] *Yorks. Fines*, 1232–46, p. 91.
[6] F. Drake, *Eboracum*, pp. 611–2; both witnessed by John de Oketon, sheriff of Yorks.
[7] *Yorks. Fines*, 1272–1300, p. 20.
[8] *Feudal Aids*, vi, 153. In 1202 the earlier Elias de Flamville with two others were parties to a final concord for a carucate in Cave (*Yorks. Fines, John*, p. 73); and in 1226 Alan de Flamville quitclaimed a bovate there (*ibid.*, 1218–31, p. 93).
[9] *Northumberland County Hist.*, xiv, 508.
[10] *Ibid.*, p. 509.
[11] Nichols, *Leicestershire*, iv, pt. ii, 455–7.

In Normandy a family took its name from Flamanville–
L'Esneval in the pays de Caux near Yvetot. In 1059 Hugh de
Flamenvilla witnessed a charter of Rodulf de Warenne to the abbey
of Holy Trinity, Rouen, selling four churches of which Flamenvilla
was one; and in 1074, with Rainald and William his sons, a charter
of Rodulf to the same house, to which the sale by Hugh de Flamen-
ville of tithe and interests in Flamanville and elsewhere, held of
Rodulf de Warenne, was confirmed by the latter *c.* 1060, the witnesses
including Hugh de Flamenvilla with Robert and Gilbert his sons.[1]
In 1210–20 William de Flanmenvilla held half a knight's fee at
Criquetot and Flamenvilla.[2]

There is, however, no evidence to identify this place or others
of the same name in Normandy as that from which any of the English
families noticed above derived its origin.

FLEMING

The family[3] descended from Reiner, known as Reiner the
dapifer, who witnessed a charter of William Meschin founding the
priory of St. Bees, *c.* 1125, and two charters of Cecily de Rumilly to
Embsay priory, 1136–40. In 1166 his grandson Reiner son of William
le Fleming held 1½ knights' fees of the new feoffment of the honour of
Skipton, including land in Wath-upon-Dearne and elsewhere, and
also land in Rathmell, par. Giggleswick, of William de Percy.[4]

The family descended in the male line to the death in 1471 of
William Fleming who left two daughters. Reiner son of John le
Fleming, living in the middle of the thirteenth century, married
Eglantine or Rosamund, daughter and in her issue coheir of Sir
Ralph de Horbury (*q.v.*)

FOLIOT

The family descended from William Foliot, a leading baron
of the honour of Pontefract in the reigns of Henry I and Stephen.
With the archbishop of York and the sheriff he was addressed by
king Henry I in a confirmation to Nostell priory.[5] His gift to Nostell
of two mills in Norton (par. Campsall) and Firsby (*Frisobeia*) was
included in the king's general confirmation, probably 10 January
1121–2;[6] and his gift to Pontefract priory of a carucate in Bag Hill
in Pontefract was confirmed by his son Jordan, 1159–70,[7] who was

---

[1] *E.Y.C.*, viii, no. 1 and note; and see L. C. Loyd in *Y.A.J.*, xxxi, 97–113.
Rodulf was the father of William de Warenne, first earl of Surrey.
[2] *Ibid.*, pp. 104–5.
[3] Details for these statements are given in the account in *E.Y.C.*, vii,
pp. 193–202; and for later generations Hunter, *South Yorkshire*, ii, 65–7, and
W. Keble Martin, *Hist. of Wath-upon-Dearne*.
[4] For Rathmell see *E.Y.C.*, xi, p. 283.
[5] *E.Y.C.*, iii, no. 1434; *Regesta*, ii, no. 1628. In both the date is given as
1120–29; and it has been suggested (W. E. Wightman, *Lacy Family*, p. 244) that
it was not later than April 1116.
[6] *E.Y.C.*, iii, no. 1428 (p. 130); *Regesta*, ii, no. 1312.
[7] *E.Y.C.*, iii, no. 1528.

his son by his first wife. He married secondly not later than 1130, when he was pardoned 43s 2d of the old pleas of Holderness,[1] Agnes daughter of Osbern de Arches, known as Agnes de Catfoss (in Sigglesthorne, Holderness), successively the widow of Herbert de St. Quintin and Robert de Fauconberg.[2] By her he had a son William, who gave land in Bewholme (in Nunkeeling, Holderness) to Nunkeeling priory, of which his mother Agnes de Arches was a benefact01.[3] For the health of the souls of himself, his father William Foliot and Agnes his mother and Henry his brother, he gave 3 bovates in Shafton (par. Felkirk) to Nostell priory, 1165–80;[4] and for the souls of his father and mother and his brothers Jordan, Henry, Pain and Richard, he gave land in the same place to Pontefract priory, 1175–91.[5]

William Foliot the elder was living in 1136–40, when he witnessed a charter of Ilbert de Lascy II.[6] Jordan Foliot I, his eldest son, probably born c. 1120–25, held 3 knights' fees of Guy de Laval's 20 fees as recorded in Henry de Lascy's *carta* of 1166 and 2 fees directly of Henry.[7] He witnessed charters of Henry de Lascy, 1147–54;[8] and gave land in Snapethorpe (in Lupset, par. Wakefield) to St. Peter's hospital, confirmed by pope Adrian IV in 1157.[9] He gave the west mill of Norton to Pontefract priory, with the consent of Beatrice his wife, 1159–70;[10] and land there to the Templars, 1160–70.[11] He was living in 1176;[12] and was succeeded by his son Jordan Foliot II, who described as Jordan Foliot son of Jordan Foliot, confirmed all the gifts of his ancestors to Pontefract priory as testified by his father's charter.[13] In 1206 he was a party to a final concord of land in Fenwick (par. Campsall);[14] and in 1208 to another

---

[1] *Pipe Roll 31 Hen. I*, p. 26; *E.Y.C.*, iii, no. 1535n.

[2] See the Arches chart pedigree in *ibid.*, i, p. 420; and the Arches section above.

[3] *Ibid.*, iii, no. 1336. In no. 1332, a Nunkeeling charter, 1143–54, Agnes is named with her sons William Foliot and Hugh Foliot. Of the sons of William Foliot the elder Farrer gave Jordan and presumably Pain and Richard as sons of his first wife and William, Henry and Hugh sons of his second (*ibid.*, no. 1535n). For Hugh, a tenant of William de Percy in 1166, see *ibid.*, xi, pp. 202–3 and no. 109, mentioning Henry his brother.

[4] *Ibid.*, no. 1535.

[5] *Ibid.*, no. 1539, which shows that a *pro animabus* clause was not necessarily for those who were dead, as it was witnessed by the grantor's brother Jordan Foliot, so described.

[6] *Ibid.*, no. 1493; the date is after the death of William Maltravers and before the resignation of abp Thurstan.

[7] *Ibid.*, no. 1508.

[8] *Ibid.*, i, no. 641; iii, no. 1501.

[9] *Ibid.*, i, no. 186. *Cf.* ii, no. 849, giving further land there in exchange for a payment by William his father and Richard his brother, 1160–70.

[10] *Ibid.*, no. 1528, confirming the carucate in Bag Hill (see above). It was he and not Jordan II who confirmed to Nostell the mill of Norton, given by his father, 1159–70 (*ibid.*, no. 1529, wit. by Henry de Lascy).

[11] *Ibid.*, no. 1531.

[12] *Ibid.*, no. 1534n.

[13] *Pontefract Chartulary*, no. 91.

[14] *Yorks. Fines, John*, p. 101.

of land in Ramesholme.[1] He was presumably the Jordan Foliot who held a knight's fee in Saxby, co. Lincoln, and one in Firsby and Hackthorn in 1212, in all of which Hugh de Laval had held interests at the Lindsey survey.[2]

In later generations the family acquired important additions to the Norton inheritance by marriage. The first was that of Richard Foliot with one of the five sisters and in their issue coheirs of Robert Bardolf and his brother Hugh Bardolf the justice, by which their son Jordan acquired an interest in the Bardolf inheritance in Great Carlton, co. Lincoln, and Hoo, Kent, being a coheir in 1225;[3] and the second was that of this Jordan's son Sir Richard Foliot with Margery, sister and in her issue heir of Sir Robert de Stuteville of Cowesby, N.R., and Gressenhall, Norfolk.[4]

In the account of Sir Jordan Foliot of Norton, Fenwick and Cowesby, in Yorkshire, and of Gressenhall and elsewhere, who was summoned to Parliament in 1295,[5] his descent is given through his father Sir Richard, husband of Margery de Stuteville, and his grandfather Jordan, the Bardolf coheir, son of Richard Foliot, whose descent from the early lords of Norton is stated to be uncertain. The inquisitions after the deaths of Sir Jordan and his father Richard,[6] both occurring in 1299, show that the former was aged fifty and more; this places his birth as not later than 1249 and that of his father, therefore, not later than c. 1225–28. Although no proof has been found for the elder Richard's parentage, it can be suggested as probable that he was son of Jordan Foliot II, whose father Jordan I, as noted above, was probably born c. 1120–25. There would then be the successive generations, alternatively named, of Jordan II (b. c. 1150), Richard (b. c. 1175), Jordan (the Bardolf coheir, b. c. 1200), Sir Richard (b. c. 1225) and Sir Jordan (b. c. 1248). The continuance of the tenure of Norton makes this suggestion plausible.

GRAMARY

At the Domesday survey Rannulfus held of Ilbert de Lascy 4 carucates in Knottingley, par. Pontefract, and 4 carucates in Sturton Grange, par. Aberford, and Shippen, par. Barwick in Elmet;[7] and, as Randulfus Grammaticus, was a benefactor at the foundation of St. Clement's chapel in Pontefract castle, ante c. 1093, in Darrington and apparently in Knottingley.[8] Ralph Grammaticus

---

[1] *Yorks. Fines, John*, p. 139. For Ramesholme see the Vernoil section below.
[2] *Bk. of Fees*, p. 190; *Lindsey Survey*, p. 240. For charters of the Foliot family in Hackthorn see *Danelaw Charters*, pp. 22–4.
[3] *Complete Peerage*, v, 538–9n; and in greater detail in 'Hugh Bardolf the Justice and his Family' in *Lincs. Hist. and Archaeology*, no. 1 (1966).
[4] *Complete Peerage*, v, 539; and *E.Y.C.*, ix, pp. 34–7 for this family.
[5] *Complete Peerage*, v, 538–42, for him and his descendants, ending in the male line in 1325.
[6] *Ibid.*, v, 539n; *Yorks. Inq.*, iii, no. 70.
[7] *V.C.H. Yorks.*, ii, pp. 244, 248.
[8] *E.Y.C.*, iii, no. 1492.

witnessed with Nigel d'Aubigny and others a confirmation of archbishop Thomas II to Selby abbey, 1109-14;[1] and king Henry I confirmed to Nostell priory land given by Robert de Lascy and Ralph Grammaticus,[2] which lay in West Hardwick, par. Wragby.[3]

Although no proof is available it is probable that Rannulfus was the lineal ancestor, possibly through Ralph, of Richard Grammaticus,[4] whose first occurrence is in 1153, when he and his brother Jordan witnessed a charter of Henry de Lascy to Kirkstall abbey.[5] In 1166 he held a knight's fee of Henry de Lascy,[6] which included a third of a fee in Becca Hall in Aberford, where it was held by Andrew de Gramary in 1284-85,[7] and, as references below suggest, land in Middleton, par. Rothwell. He also held a quarter of a knight's fee of Roger de Mowbray in Bickerton, par. Bilton,[8] and half a knight's fee of the barony of William Meschin, which included land in Horsforth, Rawdon and Yeadon.[9] He was living in 1176,[10] and died before 1188, when John Grammaticus had a dispute with William his brother for land in Middleton.[11]

William son of Richard le Gramaire, evidently the elder son,[12] witnessed a charter to Fountains abbey;[13] and, as William Grammary, an agreement in the county court of York in 1198.[14] He was a member of Roger de Lascy's court in 1201,[15] when he was holding a knight's fee of Roger.[16] He had a prolonged dispute for woodland near Middleton, lasting from 1201 to its settlement in 1209.[17] In 1212 he was holding an interest in Becca Hall,[18] and presented Robert le Gramar for institution to the church of Aberford in 1229.[19] Having supported the barons he returned to allegiance in 1217, and served as a justice from 1221 to 1224.[20]

---

[1] *Cal. Papal Letters*, i, 295-6, a confirmn of pope Innocent IV in 1254, where it is cited.

[2] *E.Y.C.*, iii, no. 1434; *Regesta*, ii, no. 1628; and for the date see the note in the Foliot section above.

[3] *E.Y.C.*, iii, no. 1428.

[4] Farrer gives Ranulf as 'the ancestor of a long line' (*V.C.H. Yorks.*, ii, 165), and Ralph as the possible successor of Ranulf (*E.Y.C.*, iii, no. 1434n).

[5] *Mon. Ang.*, v, 532.

[6] *Red Bk. Exch.*, p. 423.

[7] *Feudal Aids*, vi, 19.

[8] *Red Bk. Exch.*, p. 420; *Bk. of Fees*, p. 1460.

[9] *E.Y.C.*, iii, no. 1865 and note.

[10] *Pipe Roll 22 Hen. II*, pp. 110, 117.

[11] *Ibid. 34 Hen. II*, p. 94.

[12] He may be the William who witnessed several Mowbray charters *c.* 1170-86, two being dated 1176 (*Mowbray Charters, e.g.*, nos. 126-7, 208).

[13] *Fountains Chartulary*, i, 355.

[14] *Ibid.*, p. 263.

[15] *E.Y.C.*, iii, no. 1526.

[16] *Curia Regis Rolls*, i, 377.

[17] *Ibid.*, p. 379, and entries to *ibid.*, v, 241; *Yorks. Fines, John*, p. 155.

[18] *Curia Regis Rolls*, vi, pp. 212, 268.

[19] *Reg. Gray*, p. 28, where the spelling is given as *Cramar*.

[20] *E.Y.C.*, iii, no. 1434n. His charter to the hospital of Jerusalem is pd at no. 11 below.

William's successor was his son Richard who with his father witnessed a charter in 1204–09.[1] As Richard son of William le Gramar' he witnessed a Fountains charter,[2] and another as Richard Grammaticus of Bickerton.[3] In 1244 he was granted free warren in the manors of Becca Hall and Bickerton,[4] and in 1251 a market and fair at his manor of Aberford.[5] He died before 1275, when he had been succeeded in those places by Andrew le Grammare, then in debt to the Jews.[6] In 1284–85 Andrew le Gramare or de Gramary held $7\frac{1}{2}$ carucates with others in Bickerton of Roger de Mowbray, and the vill of Becca Hall for a third of a knight's fee of the earl of Lincoln (the Lascy fee).[7] As son of the late Sir Richard de Grammayre he gave a messuage with land and rents in Aberford to Sir Hugh le Despenser.[8] He died before 1301,[9] and in 1302–03 John his son and heir held the interest in Bickerton.[10]

John de Gramayre died before 24 June 1310, when William, his brother and heir, released his right in the manor of Middleton to Sir Simon de Creppinges, whose father Richard had it of the grant of Andrew, William's father;[11] and in 1316 William was the tenant in Bickerton.[12] In 1335 William de Gramary was granted a market and fair at Aberford.[13] In 1348 he released all right in the lands in Aberford to Sir Philip heir of Hugh le Despenser, who had them of the grant of Andrew his father[14] (see above). He died in 1352, holding the manors of Becca Hall and Bickerton by knight-service, his heir being William son of his son John, aged nineteen or twenty,[15] who proved his age in 1356.[16] Inquisitions after the death of William in 1352 also state that he had enfeoffed his son Sir Henry of rents in Snaith and elsewhere, held in chief by the serjeanty of carrying the king's bow in war; but it was found that no such feoffment had been made and that William had died seised. Sir Henry, who was collector of taxes in the West Riding in 1377,[17] can presumably be identified as the father of Agnes, his heir, who married Alexander Anne of Frickley.[18]

---

[1] *Pontefract Chartulary*, i, no. 175; Robert Waleys, [under] sheriff, being the first witness.

[2] *Fountains Chartulary*, i, 363.

[3] *Ibid.*, p. 430.

[4] *Cal. Ch. Rolls*, i, 280.

[5] *Ibid.*, p. 354.

[6] *Yorks. Inq.*, i, no. 86.

[7] *Feudal Aids*, vi, pp. 15, 19.

[8] *Yorks. Deeds*, i, no. 1; with his seal *a cinquefoil with a label of five points*.

[9] *Yorks. Inq.*, iii, no. 107 (p. 165); John then holding the interest in Bickerton.

[10] *Feudal Aids*, vi, 125; the tenancy in Becca Hall being held by Andrew's heirs.

[11] *Yorks. Deeds*, i, no. 316.

[12] *Feudal Aids*, vi, 188.

[13] *Cal. Ch. Rolls*, iv, 345.

[14] *Yorks. Deeds*, i, no. 2; also a release same day by William his son, who must have been a younger son, as the inq. of 1352 says he survived his father.

[15] *Cal. Inq. p.m.*, x, no. 58.

[16] *Ibid.*, no. 272.

[17] *Cal. Fine Rolls*, ix, 56.

[18] *Dugdale's Visitation*, ed. J. W. Clay, ii, 86.

Becca Hall passed before 1388 to Sir Roger Fulthorpe;[1] but the family continued at Bickerton, William Gramery of Bickerton, who may be the William of age in 1356, occurring as a witness in 1411.[2] It is stated that William, the heir in 1352, had a daughter and heir who married Thomas Stokes.[3]

GREYSTOKE

It has been established that the family descended from Forne son of Sigulf.[4] Although nothing is known of the holdings of Sigulf there is much documentary evidence for Forne. He witnessed the foundation charter of Wetheral priory, not later than 1112, by Ranulf Meschin,[5] to whom his tenure of Greystoke, Cumberland, not later than 1120, subsequently confirmed by king Henry I, may have been due.[6] He occurs as an official of the crown, witnessing the king's charters and being addressed by him in 1121–30;[7] and was given by him the land of Thornton-le-Moor, par. North Otterington, N.R., of the fee of Robert Malet, 1115–22.[8] He gave to St. Mary's York land in Millington, par. Great Givendale, E.R., and in Hawold, par. Huggate, with the church of Huggate[9] – places which were *terra regis* at the Domesday survey; and he and Ivo his son gave land in Millington to Hexham priory.[10] Besides Ivo, his son and successor, he had a daughter Edith, who married Robert de Oilli of Hook Norton, co. Oxford, and who, as a mistress of king Henry I, was the mother of Robert FitzEdith.[11]

Forne died before Michaelmas 1130, when Ivo his son rendered account of 100s for his father's land;[12] and by a charter of probable date 30 March in that year the king restored to Ivo the land which Forne had held in chief.[13] Ivo died not later than 1156, and the inheritance descended in the male line to Sir John de Greystoke of Greystoke and Morpeth, who was summoned to Parliament in 1295.[14] On his death in 1306 the inheritance passed to his cousin Ralph son

---

[1] F. S. Colman, *Barwick-in-Elmet* (Thoresby Soc. vol. xvii), p. 294, where, p. 297, is a pedigree wrongly criticising Dodsworth's which is pd in *Yorks. Deeds*, i, 1n. The Fulthorpe interest is shown by the holding by William Fulthorpe in 1401–02 of ½ k.f. in Aberford and Becca Hall, late of John Gramory (*Feudal Aids*, vi, 602).

[2] *Yorks. Deeds*, vi, no. 103.

[3] *Ibid.*, i, 1n, citing Dodsworth.

[4] A detailed account of the family with chart pedigree is given by the Rev. James Wilson in *Ancestor*, no. 6, 121–34; and notes on the early generations with chart pedigree by Farrer, *E.Y.C.*, ii, no. 1236n.

[5] *Wetherhal Reg.*, ed. Prescott, no. 1.

[6] *E.Y.C.*, ii, no. 1236n; and for the king's gift to Forne for a cornage rent of 4li., *Bk. of Fees*, p. 198.

[7] *Regesta*, ii, nos. 1264, 1279, 1326, 1494, 1557.

[8] *Ibid.*, no. 1357; *E.Y.C.*, ii, no. 1236.

[9] *Ibid.*, i, no. 354 (p. 273).

[10] *Hexham Priory*, i, 59; ii, 81.

[11] *Complete Peerage*, xi, app. D, p. 108; *E.Y.C.*, ii, p. 506.

[12] *Pipe Roll 31 Henry I*, p. 25.

[13] *E.Y.C.*, ii, no. 1237; *Regesta*, ii, no. 1639.

[14] Wilson, *loc. cit.; E.Y.C.*, ii, pp. 506–9.

of his aunt Joan de Greystoke and her husband William son of Ralph of Grimthorpe (*q.v.*), and thence to Ralph's grandson Ralph de Greystoke, who was summoned to Parliament in 1321; from him the family descended in the male line to Ralph lord Greystoke, who died in 1487, being succeeded by his granddaughter and heir-general Elizabeth Greystoke who married Thomas second lord Dacre of Gilsland.[1]

GRIMTHORPE

The family which bore the name of Grimthorpe and subsequently that of Greystoke (*q.v.*) on succeeding to the Greystoke fee, descended from William son of Ulf. Ulf can presumably be identified as the Ulf who was a benefactor of St. Peter's York, giving land in several places including 3 carucates in Millington and [Great] Givendale,[2] for land in the latter place was held by the Grimthorpe family. Ulf may be the Ulf son of Thorald, the donor of the well-known ivory horn to St. Peter's.[3]

King Henry I confirmed to William son of Ulf and his heirs his land of Fangfoss, [Grim]thorpe, par. Great Givendale, Meltonby, par. Pocklington, and [Great] Givendale by a charter issued at Nottingham *c.* 1120–1129, to which Forne son of Sigulf, ancestor of the Greystoke family, was a witness.[4] These lands belonged to the socage of the royal manor of Pocklington in 1086.[5] Ten years before the death of Henry I William son of Ulf gave to Hexham priory 4 bovates in [Great] Givendale;[6] and in 1158–72 Henry II ordered his heir to permit the priory to hold them in peace.[7] The gift was confirmed by Ralph son of Ralph and grandson of William.[8]

The younger Ralph, who died before Easter term 1198, was succeeded by his son William, who died in 1218, leaving a son Ralph then under age; and in 1219 a detailed return of his holdings, drawn up by jurors in the wapentake of Harthill, includes land in the four places confirmed to William son of Ulf.[9] William son of Ralph, lord of Grimthorpe, married Joan daughter of Thomas de Greystoke, and their son Ralph succeeded to the Greystoke fee (*q.v.*), dying in 1316.[10]

[1] *Complete Peerage*, vi, 190–201.
[2] *Feudal Aids*, vi, 51.
[3] *Mon. Ang.*, vi (3), 1205, recording the gift.
[4] *E.Y.C.*, i, no. 449; *Regesta*, ii, no. 1326, where the autumn of 1122 is suggested for the date.
[5] *V.C.H.*, ii, 197.
[6] *E.Y.C.*, i, no. 450.
[7] *Ibid.*, no. 451.
[8] *Coll. Top. et Gen.*, vi, 40; *E.Y.C.*, i, no. 449*n* for further details of the family.
[9] *E.Y.C.*, *loc. cit.*; *Bk. of Fees*, p. 246.
[10] Chart pedigree in *Ancestor*, no. 6, 132–3; Thomas, Joan's father, died in 1247. See also *Complete Peerage*, v, 513–16 for a full account of Ralph, who was summoned to Parl. from 1295 to 1315; and for his ancestry, p. 513*n*.

HABTON

The family descended from Gospatric, whose eldest son Walter de Ridale (*Riddale*) was granted a knight's fee in Roxburghshire by king David I, 1139–53.[1] In or before 1156 Walter bequeathed his lands there and at Brawby, par. Salton, N.R., to his brother Ansketil.[2]

Ansketil son of Gospatric, known as de Ridale, Habton or Brawby held a knight's fee of the old feoffment of the Bulmer fee in 1166,[3] which presumably included Habton, par. Kirby Misperton; and also land in Brawby of the prior of Hexham to whom archbishop Thurstan had given it with Salton.[4] By his wife Asceria daughter of William de Stonegrave (*q.v.*), with whom he had land in Birdsall, he had three sons, of whom the two eldest, William and Walter, died without issue and the youngest, Patrick, succeeded to the Roxburgh-shire and Yorkshire lands.[5]

Patrick de Ridale, who held land in Habton and was dead by 1209, had two sons, of whom Walter succeeded to the Roxburghshire lands and was the ancestor of the Riddels of Scotland, and Nicholas was given the Yorkshire lands by his father. From Nicholas de Ridale or Habton the family descended in the male line to Alan de Habton, whose daughter and heir Alice married Sir John Gower of Faceby; and in 1342 their son William Gower held the manor of Great Habton, which subsequently passed to the Middeltons of Stockeld.[6]

HAY (of Aughton)

The family descended from Nigel whose son Roger Hay held land in North Cave of the Fossard fee, *c.* 1135–1148 and 1148–56.[7] In 1166 Roger son of Roger held 2 knights' fees of William Fossard, consisting of land in Huggate, North Cave, Everthorpe (par. N. Cave), Aughton and Laytham (par. Aughton).[8] He was the founder of Thicket priory,[9] and was succeeded by his son Thomas, who confirmed gifts in North Cave made by his father Roger Hay to St. Peter's hospital, *c.* 1175–1188.[10] Thomas married Emma daughter and heir of Roger son of Alvred,[11] and died before Michaelmas 1190, when Thomas son of Thomas son of Roger paid 100*s* for a recog-

---

[1] Sir A. C. Lawrie, *Early Scottish Charters*, no. 222; and a more accurate text in G. W. S. Barrow, *Acts of Malcolm IV*, no. 42.

[2] *E.Y.C.*, ii, no. 778, with notes on the family.

[3] *Ibid.*, no. 777; 6½ car. in Great and Little Habton were held of the Bulmer fee.

[4] *Ibid.*, no. 778*n*.

[5] *Yorks. Deeds*, v, 181–3, where there is a detailed account of the family.

[6] *Ibid.*

[7] *E.Y.C.*, ii, nos. 1123–5.

[8] *Ibid.*, no. 1003 and note.

[9] *Mon. Ang.*, iv, 384; *E.Y.C.*, ii, no. 1131, his gifts including land in West Cottingwith and Goodmanham.

[10] *Ibid.*, nos. 1126–7.

[11] The evidence is given later in the text. Emma's charter to St. Peter's hospital is pd at no. 12 below.

nition of the death of his father respecting land in Aughton and Goodmanham, of which Roger de Hay was deforcing him.[1]

It was recorded in an agreement of 1195–1211 that William son of Anketin, grandfather of William son of Peter,[2] had pledged land in Aughton to Roger son of Alvred, grandfather of Thomas Hay [II] of Aughton, which William son of Peter had redeemed in the time of Emma Hay, Thomas's mother;[3] Thomas restored the land and quitclaimed his right to William, who gave to William son of Adam de Burland, his nephew, 6 bovates in Goodmanham in marriage with Emma, Thomas's daughter, and to Roger, Thomas's eldest son, 5 bovates with the chief messuage there, which Emma Hay had held, in marriage with Christiana daughter of Adam de Burland, his niece; all to hold of the said William.[4]

In 1200 a plea in which Thomas Hay II was engaged for 8 carucates in Everthorpe and North Cave was postponed as he was in the king's service overseas.[5] He was living in 1225, when he granted to Adam de Linton and Agnes his wife with certain exceptions a moiety of the lands that he claimed against them, being 18 bovates in Aughton, 10 bovates in Goodmanham and 4 bovates in Laytham.[6] Before 1228 he was succeeded by his son Roger, then described as lord of Aughton,[7] who in 1242–43 held of the honour of Mauley (formerly Fossard) half a fee in Aughton and another half in Everthorpe and [North] Cave.[8]

In a plea of 1251 between John Hay and the prior of Ellerton for land in Aughton the former stated that Emma his ancestor was seised in the time of king Henry II and from her the right descended to her son Thomas, then to the latter's son Roger, then to William

---

[1] *E. Y.C.*, ii, no. 1130n, citing *Pipe Roll 2 Ric. I*, p. 66. This Roger de Hay has not been identified; he may have been a younger brother of Thomas the elder.

[2] The founder of the Gilbertine priory of Ellerton on Spaldingmore in the reign of John (*E. Y.C.*, ii, no. 1133). He held the advowson of a third of the church of Goodmanham (*ibid.*, no. 1122; *ibid.*, xii, no. 14); and was described as William son of Peter de Goodmanham (*ibid.*, x, no. 113; xii, no. 67). The details given here prove that his ancestry dates back to temp. Henry I. He probably died without issue, one of his heirs being his sister Agnes who married Adam de Linton. The latter confirmed his gifts to Ellerton (*Mon. Ang.*, vi, 976); and Agnes, described as sister of William and widow of Adam de Linton, was also a benefactor (*E. Y.C.*, ii, no. 1122n, citing MS. Dodsworth vii, f. 339). She was living in her widowhood in 1231 (*Yorks. Fines*, 1218–31, p. 136). The details given above also show that William had another sister who married Adam de Burland.

[3] In 1180–1200 William son of Peter had granted to Emma Hay for life the land of Aughton and Goodmanham, which had been the subject of the pledge made for 60 marks, and now redeemed (*E. Y.C.*, ii, no. 1129).

[4] *Ibid.*, no. 1130.

[5] *Ibid.*, note.

[6] *Yorks. Fines*, 1218–31, pp. 60–3.

[7] *E. Y.C.*, ii, no. 1130n. In 1228 Roger's right to the advowson of Aughton was established against the prior of Ellerton, Roger quitclaiming to the latter the advowson of Ellerton, formerly a chapel of Aughton (*Yorks. Fines*, 1218–31, p. 118). In 1227 the prior had claimed the advowson of Aughton; in 1230 Roger's presentee was instituted (*Reg. Gray*, pp. 19, 37).

[8] *Bk. of Fees*, p. 1098.

son of Roger, who died s.p. and then to William's brother John.[1]
At the death of Peter de Mauley II in 1279 German Hay held 1½ fees
in Aughton;[2] and in 1284–85 he was a tenant of the Mauley fee in
Spaldington, Laytham, Aughton, Huggate, Everthorpe and North
Cave.[3]

In 1319 Roger Hay of Aughton was a tenant of Peter de
Mauley IV.[4] In 1330 John Hay and Elizabeth his wife were parties
to a final concord for the manor of Everthorpe,[5] and in an extent of
lands made in 1384 after the death of Peter de Mauley VI 14 carucates
in Everthorpe, Cave, Goodmanham, Laytham and Aughton were
held by the heirs of German del Haye by the service of a knight's
fee.[6]

The property passed to a younger branch of the family of Aske
(*q.v.*), tenants of the honour of Richmond, by whom the arms of Hay
were quartered.[7]

HEBDEN

The family descended in the male line from Dolfin son of
Gospatric son of Archil. Until recently no proof had been found
that Dolfin was a son of Gospatric, as stated in a fifteenth-century
genealogy.[8] But a charter is now available recording that Roger de
Mowbray enfeoffed Uctred son of Dolfin of the land of Uctred's
grandfather Gospatric in Ilton (par. Masham); the date being
1138–?1145.[9]

Uctred occurs as Uctred de Ilton;[10] and was later known as
Uctred de Conistone. He held land in Conistone in Kettlewelldale
in 1166 and an interest in Burnsall as an under-tenancy, both of the
honour of Skipton;[11] and he was granted the manor of Hebden in
Craven by Roger de Mowbray.[12] His son Simon, described as Simon
son of Uctred son of Dolfin, was a benefactor of Fountains abbey of
privileges in Hebden.[13] From him, who was living in 1200–01, the line
descended through his son William de Hebden to his granddaughter

---

[1] *Yorks. Fines*, 1246–72, p. 76*n;* the final concord gives details of the
Linton family whom the prior had called to warrant.
[2] *Yorks. Inq.*, i, 196.
[3] *Feudal Aids*, vi, 45–6. The mention of Spaldington suggests a connexion
with the family of de la Hay of that place; but this has not been traced (*E.Y.C.*,
xii, p. 88). William son of Peter held an interest there (*ibid.*, no. 72).
[4] *Mon. Notes*, ii, 45.
[5] *Yorks. Fines*, 1327–47, p. 31.
[6] *Cal. Inq. p.m.*, xv, no. 816.
[7] *Glover's Visitation*, p. 118.
[8] Farrer in *V.C.H. Yorks.*, ii, 184.
[9] *Mowbray Charters*, no. 392, noting that in 1086 Ilton was held by
Gospatric of count Alan of Richmond. See the chart pedigree in the Thoresby-
Staveley section below.
[10] *Ibid.*, no. 393.
[11] *E.Y.C.*, vii, p. 248.
[12] *Mowbray Charters*, no. 395.
[13] *Fountains Chartulary*, i, 350. His charter to his bro. Walter, giving land
in Ilton, is pd at no. 13 below.

Helen, who married secondly Nicholas of York and had issue a son William of York, who died in 1282; the latter's son, a younger William, took the name of Hebden, and his descendants continued in the male line to the fifteenth century.[1]

HORBURY

The family[2] descended from Saxe, who held land in Middle Shitlington [Middletown], par. Thornhill, of William second earl de Warenne in 1118–30,[3] and who as Saxi de Horbiri witnessed a charter of Swain son of Alric, 1120–30.[4] From his son Matthew, who held land of the Warenne fee in Shitlington, Blacker, Flockton, Horbury and Dewsbury, and who died in 1188–96, the main line descended through his son Sir Thomas de Horbury, steward of the Warenne fee in Yorkshire, c. 1202–10, to the latter's son Sir Ralph de Horbury, similarly steward 1248–51.

Sir Ralph's son Sir John de Horbury married Elizabeth Wake, one of the coheirs of William de Beauchamp of Bedford, their purparty being delivered to them in 1278. He was living in 1302, but died without issue, as did his brother Thomas;[5] and the coheirs were the two daughters of Sir Ralph, being Eglantine or Rosamund, wife of Reiner le Fleming of Wath-upon-Dearne, and her sister, wife of Nicholas de Wortley, or their representatives.

HOUGHTON

Swain son of Edwin the priest gave a bovate in Great Houghton to Nostell priory, which was included in king Henry I's confirmation charter of probable date 10 January 1121–2.[6] This land became a tenure of the Paynels of Hooton Pagnell (q.v.); and in 1147–53 Alexander Paynel and Agnes his wife confirmed to Nostell land in Great Houghton which Swain de Houghton had given for the souls of Agnes his wife, Edwin his father and Richard his son.[7] After c. 1153 William son of Alexander Paynel confirmed to Nostell a gift of his father in Great Houghton, and also gifts of Edwin father of Swain de Houghton, of Swain his son with the consent of Richard, Swain's son, and of Jordan Paynel[8] and Agnes his wife, and also of

---

[1] *E.Y.C.*, vii, pp. 248–51, giving an account of the family. It is significant that William de Hebden had an interest in Ilton in 1226, and gave land there to Fountains (pp. 249–50).
[2] Accounts of the family are in *Y.A.J.*, xxvi, 334–44 with chart pedigree; and *E.Y.C.*, viii, pp. 211–14, where references to statements in this section are given.
[3] *E.Y.C.*, viii, no. 11.
[4] *Ibid.*, iii, no. 1663.
[5] He was living in 1306, when he granted land in Shitlington and Flockton to Nicholas de Wortley, William le Fleming and others being warrantors (*Yorks. Fines*, 1300–14, no. 307). The latter was son of Reiner le Fleming (*E.Y.C.*, vii, p. 201; and see the Fleming section above).
[6] *E.Y.C.*, iii, no. 1428; *Regesta*, ii, no. 1312.
[7] *E.Y.C.*, vi, no. 115.
[8] Almost certainly a younger son of Alexander (*ibid.*, p. 41).

Jordan Paynel with the consent of Henry de Vernoil (*q.v.*), heir of the said Agnes.[1] Land in Great Houghton, given to Nostell by Swain son of Edwin, had been confirmed before 1153 by Henry de Vernoil and Agnes his wife, described as daughter of Swain son of Edwin de Houghton.[2] A confirmation to Nostell of the gift of Swain de Houghton and Agnes his daughter and heir, for the soul of Henry de Vernoil, Swain's son-in-law, was also made by Jordan de Lascy, 1147–66.[3] This is explained by a gift of Alexander Paynel to Jordan de Lascy of his service of Houghton with a small exception, to hold by the service of one knight;[4] the service being evidently due from the land held by Swain de Houghton. Jordan de Lascy's interest, however, expired before 1166, when Jordan Paynel held a knight's fee of the old feoffment directly of William Paynel, together with half a knight's fee of the new.[5]

Richard son of Swain de Houghton died without issue, apparently in his father's lifetime, and Swain's coheirs were his daughters Agnes and Edeline. The details given above show that Agnes married first Henry de Vernoil, by whom she had a son Henry, and secondly Jordan Paynel. Notes on the Vernoil family, tenants of the Lascy fee in Eggborough and Kellington, are given in their section below with a chart pedigree showing the descent from Swain de Houghton, noting that Henry de Vernoil of a younger generation held half a knight's fee in Great Houghton in 1284–85.

Edeline, Swain's other daughter and coheir, married William de Lisle, who with her confirmed to Nostell all the lands at Great Houghton which Swain son of Edwin had given.[6] William had held half a knight's fee of William Paynel in Great Houghton which the latter gave to the Templars, 1185–96.[7] It is clear, therefore, that Swain's tenure descended in equal portions to the families of Vernoil and Lisle; and it can be supposed that the whole knight's fee, returned in the name of Jordan Paynel in 1166, represented the interest not only of Agnes his wife but also of her sister.[8]

From Jordan son of William de Lisle[9] the family descended in the male line to Jordan de Lisle, whose two sisters married Sir William Scot and William de Knottingley; and the latter's son released his right in Great Houghton to Sir John son of Sir William Scot in 1354–55.[10] In 1428 Robert Waterton held half a knight's fee in Great Houghton which William Scot formerly held.[11]

---

[1] *E.Y.C.*, vi, nos. 116–7.
[2] *Ibid.*, no. 119.
[3] *Ibid.*, no. 120.
[4] *Ibid.*, p. 219. For what is known of Jordan de Lascy, presumably a younger member of the main Lascy family, see *ibid.*, p. 220.
[5] *Ibid.*, no. 87.
[6] *Ibid.*, no. 121.
[7] *Ibid.*, no. 118.
[8] *Ibid.*, p. 221.
[9] *Ibid.*, nos. 124, 128.
[10] Hunter, *South Yorkshire*, ii, 128–9, citing Dodsworth. Certain generations in the descent so given appear to be missing.
[11] *Feudal Aids*, vi, 276.

HUDDLESTON

The family descended from Nigel the provost of the archbishop of York. In 1109–12, as Nigel the provost, before becoming a monk at Selby, he gave to the abbey 2½ carucates in Hillam (par. Monk Fryston), which he held of the fee of St. Peter, and a portion of his tithe of Huddleston (par. Sherburn in Elmet).[1] This was confirmed by archbishop Thomas before 24 February 1113–4, describing Nigel as the archbishop's provost, for which the archbishop gave to Nigel's son Gilbert 2 carucates in Wetwang, E.R., in exchange.[2]

Gilbert son of Nigel was the first witness to a notification by archbishop Roger, 1154–61;[3] and he held 2 knights' fees of the old feoffment of the archbishop in 1166.[4] In 1165–74 he surrendered to the church of St. Peter and archbishop Roger whatever he had in Clementhorpe, except his demesne messuage and his garden and meadow[5] which he had given to the nuns of St. Clement, and except a bovate in Cawood of the fee of St. Peter; together with another bovate of the fee of St. Mary which his father had received in exchange for half a carucate of the fee of St. Peter in Poppleton; all of which tenements his ancestors and he had held wrongfully; for this surrender they were absolved; his service to the archbishop not being diminished.[6]

The inheritance passed to Richard de Huddleston, who described Gilbert son of Nigel as his uncle (*patruus*),[7] and in 1175–89 leased his capital dwelling-place in Clementhorpe to a man named Avenel, retaining rights when he made visits to York or when there was war in the land.[8] As a knight he witnessed a charter of the prior of Hexham granting a messuage in Goodramgate, 1191–94;[9] he witnessed an agreement in 1196–97,[10] and several charters c. 1175–1210;[11] and in 1204–09 a confirmation to Pontefract priory with Richard and Robert his sons.[12] It is probable that he was dead by 2 November 1208, when the right to land in Fenton was recognised as that of Richard son of Richard de Huddleston.[13] In 1223 a Richard de Huddleston received a quitclaim of land held in dower in Ganthorpe;[14] and on 19 January 1249–50 Sir Richard de

---

[1] *E.Y.C.*, i, no. 45.
[2] *Ibid.*, no. 46.
[3] *Ibid.*, no. 36.
[4] *Ibid.*, no. 38.
[5] For his gift of meadow to St. Clement's see *ibid.*, no. 359.
[6] *Ibid.*, no. 39.
[7] Charter no. 14 pd below.
[8] *Ibid.*, no. 216.
[9] *Ibid.*, no. 345.
[10] *Pontefract Chartulary*, ii, no. 505.
[11] *E.Y.C.*, ii, no. 1031; iii, nos. 1615, 1641n, 1642.
[12] *Pontefract Chartulary*, ii, no. 316; Robert Walensis [deputy] sheriff witnessing.
[13] *Yorks. Fines, John*, p. 137.
[14] *Ibid.*, 1218–31, p. 51. No Huddleston interest in Ganthorpe, N.R., appears to be known, and the place may be Gowthorpe, associated with Wetwang (see below).

Huddleston was granted by Sewal de Boville, dean of York and then prebendary of Fenton, a licence to hear service in the chapel that he had built in Huddleston, saving the rights of the mother-church of Sherburn.[1] On 14 January 1251-2 a Richard son of Richard de Huddleston purchased from John de Huddleston land in Fenton, subject to a ten-year lease to mag. Robert [Haget], treasurer of York.[2]

A John de Huddleston, representing a younger line, acquired Millom, Cumberland, by his marriage, c. 1230–32, to Joan daughter of Adam de Boiville (q.v.) alias Millum; he died c. 1252;[3] and was the ancestor of the Huddlestons of Millom. With the consent of Joan his wife he confirmed a gift to Holm Cultram abbey.[4] It is stated that his son[5] John de Huddleston of Millom claimed the manor of Huddleston in 1289–90 against John de Meaux (q.v.) and his wife Beatrice,[6] the latter being daughter and eventual heir of Richard de Huddleston.[7] John's plea evidently failed, for in 1302–03 Sir John de Meaux was holding a knight's fee in Huddleston;[8] and in 1316 the heirs of Godfrey de Meaux held an interest there.[9]

In a return of the archbishop's fees apparently dating from 1250–75, in which Richard de Huddleston held a fee of 2 knights in Huddleston, John de Meaux is shown as holding the fee in Wetwang, Gowthorpe and Youlthorpe which had belonged to Richard de Huddleston;[10] and it is likely that this had been given by the latter to his daughter in frank-marriage.

INGOLDSBY

The family descended in the male line from Colegrim, who at the Domesday survey was a tenant of count Alan of Britanny at Fulbeck and elsewhere in Lincolnshire, and of Robert de Stafford at Skinnand, and as a king's thegn the holder of a manor in Ingoldsby.[11] Osbert son of Colegrim was a tenant of count Stephen in 1130, and held 4 knights' fees owing castle-guard at Richmond.[12] Alexander son of Osbert and Nigel his heir gave land in Fulbeck to Sempringham

[1] York Minster Fasti, i, no. 27.

[2] Yorks. Fines, 1246–72, p. 55.

[3] Cumb. and West. Ant. and Arch. Soc., Transactions, vol. xli, N.S., pp. 27–8. There are several charters and notes of this line in Reg. St. Bees.

[4] Holm Cultram Reg., p. 31.

[5] More likely his grandson (ibid., p. 30).

[6] Plantagenet-Harrison, Hist. of Yorkshire, p. 367, where, as was his custom, no documentary reference is given.

[7] John de Huddleston seems to have made his claim as heir male. It is known that John de Meaux of Bewick, living in 1290, married Beatrice dau. and heir of Isabel dau. of Walter de Hedon (Y.A.J., xlii, 103); it can therefore be deduced that Richard de Huddleston, Beatrice's father, married Isabel de Hedon.

[8] Feudal Aids, vi, 121.

[9] Ibid., p. 191.

[10] Reg. Giffard, pp. 14, 17; pd in Kirkby's Inquest, pp. 383, 390. Gowthorpe and Youlthorpe are both in par. Bishop Wilton, E.R.

[11] Lincs. Domesday, pp. 66–7, 72, 188, 198.

[12] E.Y.C., v, pp. 10, 11.

priory.[1] In 1166 Nigel son of Alexander held a knight's fee of Robert de Stafford, evidently in Skinnand; in 1195 he owed 3 marks for a disseisin in Yorkshire; and as Nigel son of Alexander de Ingoldsby was a benefactor of Sempringham.[2] Late in the twelfth century, among the fees of the honour of Richmond, Wensley of the fee of Nigel son of Alexander owed the service of one knight;[3] and the same service was due a little later from Osbern son of Nigel de Wensley.[4]

A case of 1208 relating to Fulbeck shows the descent of Osbert (his correct name) from his father Nigel and his grandfather Alexander.[5] He held 3 knights' fees in Lincolnshire at Fulbeck and elsewhere, and the knight's fee in Wensley makes up the 4 fees of the honour of Richmond held by Osbert his great-grandfather.[6] In 1212 as Osbert son of Nigel and Osbern de Ingoldsby he held land of the Clinton fee in Ingoldsby and elsewhere in Lincolnshire.[7] With the assent of Roger his son and heir he issued a charter relating to land in Wensley.[8]

Roger de Ingoldsby who succeeded his father had issue a younger Roger as his heir;[9] and through the latter, the family, described as of Skinnand and Ingoldsby, and later by marriage as of Lenborough, co. Buckingham, descended in twelve generations in the male line to Sir Henry Ingoldsby who was created a baronet in 1661.[10]

INGRAM

Early in the reign of Henry I William Ingram held 1½ carucates in High Worsall, par. Girsby, wap. Gilling East.[11] In 1130 John Ingelr[am] owed a good horse for the right of his father's land; this is under the Dorset[12] heading, *sed positus est in Euerwicsc'* being added.[13] These two men were probably father and son, for *c.* 1150–60 John Engelram son of William Engelram, with the consent of Adeline his daughter and heir, gave to Guisborough priory a carucate in Ayresome, par. Middlesbrough.[14] Adeline married Robert son of Erneis, a member of the Lincolnshire family of Goushill or Vere,[15] and John Ingram together with them gave land to the church of Middlesbrough,[16] and with his son-in-law land

[1] *E. Y.C.*, v, p. 256, where details of the family and its descent from Colegrim are given.

[2] *Ibid.*, p. 257.   [3] *Ibid.*, p. 13.
[4] *Ibid.*, p. 16.   [5] *Ibid.*, p. 256.
[6] *Ibid.*, p. 257.   [7] *Bk. of Fees*, pp. 180, 183–4.
[8] *E.Y.C.*, v, p. 257; *Yorks. Deeds*, ii, no. 506.
[9] *V.C.H.*, *N.R.*, i, 270, showing that after the younger Roger's death in 1313 the family's interest in Wensley passed to Henry le Scrope of Bolton.
[10] *Genealogist*, N.S., iii, 137–9.
[11] *E.Y.C.*, ii, no. 707n, where there are notes on the family.
[12] Not Wiltshire as in *ibid.*   [13] *Pipe Roll 31 Hen. I*, p. 16.
[14] *E.Y.C.*, ii, no. 707.   [15] *Ibid.*, note.
[16] *Ibid.*, no. 708.

near there to Whitby abbey.[1] John Ingram was still living in 1168.[2]

A younger branch descended from Walter Ingerram, who, mentioning his lord Adam de Brus, for the souls of his parents and that of his uncle (*patruus*) William Ingerram, gave to Guisborough priory the churches of Ingleby Arncliffe, Welbury and West Heslerton with the chapel of East Heslerton, *c.* 1150–1172, John Ingeram being a witness.[3] With the consent of Holdeard his wife he gave land in Welbury and [Ingleby] Arncliffe to Rievaulx abbey, *c.* 1160–1170, which was confirmed by his son William.[4] Farrer notes that there can be little doubt that William, Walter's uncle, was the father of John Ingram of Ayresome.[5] The name of Walter's father is not recorded, but his mother's name was Maud, so named as his grandmother by William son of Walter Ingram in a charter to Rievaulx abbey.[6]

In 1184–88 William son of Walter confirmed to Guisborough priory the three churches and the chapel named above.[7] He was living in 1206 and was succeeded by his son Robert,[8] who in 1242–43 was a tenant of the Brus fee, his holdings including a knight's fee in Heslerton and half a fee in Welbury and Sawcock.[9] The inheritance passed after 1255 to the Colville family, apparently by the marriage of Philip de Colville with Ingelisa, sister of a Robert Ingram.[10] They occur in final concords of 1208.[11] In 1284–85 William de Colville held an interest in West Heslerton; and in 1302–03 Robert de Colville land of the Brus fee in East Heslerton.[12]

JERNEGAN (of Tanfield)

The family descended from Jernegan the father of Hugh son of Jernegan, who witnessed charters of count Stephen, *c.* 1130 and *c.* 1135, and held the office of steward of the honour of Richmond under earl Alan; he was living in 1154. His grandson, another Hugh son of Jernegan, who held the Tanfield fee with the service of $2\frac{1}{2}$ knights, acquired a moiety of Manfield by his marriage to Maud daughter of Torfin son of Robert.

[1] *E.Y.C.*, ii, no. 709.
[2] *Ibid.*, no. 707*n.*
[3] *Ibid.*, no. 711.
[4] *Ibid.*, no. 710 and note.
[5] *Ibid.*, no. 711*n*, giving an account of this line. In the Ingram pedigree by William Brown in 'Ingleby Arncliffe' (*Y.A.J.*, xvi, 154–5) two Williams, father and son, are given as the grandfather and father of John Ingram of Ayresome; but for this no evidence is available.
[6] *E.Y.C.*, ii, no. 716*n.*
[7] *Ibid.*, no. 717.
[8] *Ibid.*, no. 711*n;* iii, no. 1840*n.*
[9] *Bk. of Fees*, p. 1098. In *Y.A.J.*, xvi, 158 it is suggested that there were two Roberts.
[10] *Ibid.*, pp. 158–9; *E.Y.C.*, ii, no. 711*n.*
[11] *Yorks. Fines, John*, pp. 145–6.
[12] *Feudal Aids*, vi, pp. 39, 154. William is given as great-grandson of Philip and Ingelisa in the Colville pedigree in *Y.A.J.*, xvi, 166–7.

The inheritance passed to his son Jernegan son of Hugh, who was dead by Michaelmas 1214 and whose daughter and heir Avice married Robert Marmion, in which family (*q.v.*) it descended.[1]

KILTON

If, as is probable,[2] Ilger son of Roer, who held a knight's fee of the old feoffment of William de Percy in 1166, his tenure including land in Kirkleatham,[3] can be identified with Ilger de Kilton, a tenant of the Brus fee in Kilton,[4] the family of Kilton descended from Roer, who was presumably living in the reign of Henry I.

Ilger was succeeded by his son William de Kilton, who gave the church of Kirkleatham to Guisborough priory, 1195–1206,[5] and William by his niece Maud who married as her second husband Robert de Thweng (*q.v.*), the inheritance descending to their son Marmaduke de Thweng,[6] and so to his descendants in the male line to the death of Thomas de Thweng in 1374.[7]

KYME

Farrer has given a detailed account of the early generations of the Lincolnshire family of Kyme, concluding as the most likely solution that the original ancestor was William the man of Waldin *ingeniator*, the latter being a tenant-in-chief in 1086; and that it was William's great-grandson Simon son of William who founded Bullington priory, 1148–54.[8]

The family's connexion with Yorkshire was primarily due to the marriages of the two brothers Simon and William de Kyme, sons of Philip de Kyme I, son of the founder of Bullington, to Roesia and Margaret, daughters and heirs of Robert son of Robert son of Fulk, the steward of the Percy fee.[9] As Margaret died without issue Roesia became the sole heir, whose inheritance descended in its entirety to her son Philip de Kyme II.[10]

Roesia's father was the lineal descendant of Reinfrid the knight, later prior of Whitby, who died 1086–*c.* 1091.[11] His son Fulk the steward held tenancies of William de Percy in 1086 both in Yorkshire and Lincolnshire, and also of Osbern de Arches (*q.v.*) in Toulston and Newton, afterwards named Newton Kyme, and elsewhere in Yorkshire. Fulk's grandson Robert the steward held $3\frac{1}{2}$ knights' fees

---

[1] For these statements *E.Y.C.*, v, pp. 13, 40–4 and no. 163.
[2] W. Hebditch in 'The Kilton Fee' (*Y.A.J.*, xxxiv, 306*n*).
[3] *E.Y.C.*, xi, p. 225.
[4] *Ibid.*, p. 227.
[5] *Ibid.*, ii, nos. 722, 724.
[6] *Ibid.*, xi, pp. 205, 227.
[7] *Complete Peerage*, xii(i), pp. 737–44.
[8] *H.K.F.*, ii, 118–25; subsequently adopted in the chart pedigree in *Complete Peerage*, vii, 356. Several charters of the family to Bullington are pd in *Danelaw Charters*.
[9] *E.Y.C.*, xi, pp. 89–99.
[10] *Ibid.*, p. 97.
[11] *Ibid.*, p. 92, with chart pedigree.

of the Percy fee in 1166, which lay in Ilkley and elsewhere in York-shire and in Elkington and elsewhere in Lincolnshire. Robert son of Fulk had married Alice daughter of Herbert de St. Quintin by his wife Agnes de Arches; Alice being the founder of the priory at Nun Appleton, a member of the Arches fee, which she had inherited from her mother and which passed by inheritance to her son Robert son of Robert son of Fulk.[1]

Roesia's son Philip de Kyme II was the grandfather of Philip de Kyme III, who was summoned to Parliament in 1295; and after the death of his son William without issue the inheritance passed to his daughter Lucy, wife of Robert de Umfraville, earl of Angus.[2]

LARDINER

The earliest member of the family of whom there is documentary evidence is John the lardiner,[3] to whom and David his son king Stephen in 1136–37 restored the land held in chief with the office of lardiner and his allowance[4] and all his lands of whomsoever held as he had held them at the death of king Henry.[5] John the lardiner gave land in Ousegate to St. Peter's hospital which was confirmed by king Henry, c. 1120–33, possibly in 1122;[6] and a tenement there, being held by John the clerk, his son, to Whitby abbey, his gift of land being confirmed by pope Eugenius III, 1145–48.[7] He witnessed a charter of Bertram de Bulmer, 1130–36.[8]

He was succeeded by his son David the lardiner, for whom king Henry II issued a mandate, 1155–c. 1170, to the foresters of Galtres that he should have his herbage from the waste of Cortburn as his father had it in the time of Henry I, and pasture in the king's

---

[1] For these statements see *ibid.*, pp. 89–95, giving the locality of the holdings. For Toulston and Nun Appleton charters see *ibid.*, i, nos. 529–32 and 541–45; the chart pedigree, p. 420, being subject to the amendment that Roesia and Margaret were daughters and not sisters of Robert son of Robert son of Fulk.

[2] *Complete Peerage*, vii, 352–7, with chart pedigree showing the eventual descent.

[3] The pedigree of the family in F. Drake, *Eboracum*, p. 326, taken from the Widdrington MS, now pd in *Analecta Eboracensia*, ed. Rev. C. Caine (1897), pp. 258–9, gives John the lardiner's father as 'David Lardinarius Regis venit in Angliam cum Conquestore' – a phrase which always invites suspicion. It may have arisen from the Quo Warranto pleas when Philip le lardiner stated that 'proavus proavi sui . . . venit in Angliam cum . . . Conquestore', without naming his first ancestor (*Plac. de Quo Warranto*, pp. 207b–208a). A detailed account of the lardiner serjeanty from the Widdrington MS is in *Analecta, ut sup.*, chapter xvii. The family held the office of kg's lardiner and the custody of the gaol for forest prisoners. A more recent account is in *V.C.H., City of York*, pp. 494–6.

[4] This was 5*d* a day, *i.e.*, 7*li.* 12*s* 1*d* yearly. It was presumably included in the 12*li.* 12*s* 11*d in liberationibus constitutis* in *Pipe Roll 31 Hen. I*, p. 24, and *ibid. 2 Hen. II*, p. 26 and succeeding rolls; in 1165 7*li.* 12*s* 1*d* was the allowance for David the lardiner (*ibid. 11 Hen. II*, p. 46).

[5] *E.Y.C.*, i, no. 343; *Regesta*, iii, no. 433.

[6] *E.Y.C.*, i, no. 168; *Regesta*, ii, no. 1327.

[7] *Whitby Chartulary*, i, no. 1 (p. 6); *E.Y.C.*, ii, no. 872.

[8] *Ibid.*, no. 783.

forest similarly.[1] In 1166 he returned the *carta* of Bertram de Bulmer, of whom he held a fifth of a knight's fee of the old feoffment, which lay in Skelton.[2] With Thomas his son he witnessed a charter of Bernard de Baliol to Rievaulx abbey, 1161–67;[3] and he died in 1180–81, being succeeded by his son Thomas.[4]

At Michaelmas 1214 in the sheriff's account for half the year Thomas son of David the lardiner received 76s $\frac{1}{2}d$, being half the yearly allowance.[5] Before 1219 he was succeeded by his son David II, who as David the lardiner was then holding a serjeanty and the custody of the forest gaol.[6] At Michaelmas 1230, as David son of Thomas the lardiner, he received the allowance of 7*li*. 12s 1*d*;[7] and in 1250 it was recorded that he had alienated lands of his serjeanty in Bustardthorpe (a lost vill in Acomb), where he held 2 carucates of the lardiner service.[8] He died before 9 November 1271, holding lands in chief in Bustardthorpe and Cortburn for keeping the forest gaol and the king's larder, and also lands in Skelton of Sir Robert de Neville;[9] David his son being the heir and of full age.[10]

In December 1271 the king took the latter's homage; and on his death in 1280 his son Philip, the respondent in the Quo Warranto proceedings, succeeded. Seisin of the serjeanty of the forest of Galtres was ordered for him on 16 January 1283–4;[11] and he died before 16 June 1305, leaving two daughters, Margaret aged twenty and Ellen aged eighteen.[12]

LASCELLES (of Kirby Wiske)

At the Domesday survey Picot was a tenant of count Alan in Kirby Wiske, Maunby (par. Kirby Wiske), Scruton, a moiety of Sowber Hill (par. Kirby Wiske), and Thrintoft (par. Ainderby Steeple), all in Richmondshire, and in Aylesby, Fulstow and Swallow, co. Lincoln.[13] He was living at the Lindsey survey, 1115–18, when as Picot de Laceles he held land in Fulstow.[14] He was succeeded by his son Roger de Lascelles, one of the principal tenants of count Stephen in 1130, holding 5 knights' fees, being succeeded by his son

[1] *E. Y. C.*, ii, no. 422.
[2] *Ibid.*, ii, no. 777 and note.
[3] *Ibid.*, i, no. 562.
[4] *Pipe Roll 26 Hen. II*, p. 61; *27 Hen. II*, p. 34.
[5] *Ibid. 16 John*, p. 84.
[6] *Bk. of Fees*, p. 247.
[7] *Pipe Roll 14 Hen. III*, p. 267.
[8] *Bk. of Fees*, pp. 1201–2. A list of liberties claimed for the serjeanty, for which he made a final concord with the mayor of York in 1253, is given in an inq. of Jan. 1251–2 (*Yorks. Fines*, 1246–72, p. 191 and note).
[9] Successor to the Bulmer fee (*q.v.*)
[10] *Yorks. Inq.*, i, no. 69.
[11] *Exc. e Rot. Fin.*, ii, 555; *Cal. Fine Rolls*, 1272–1307, p. 133; *Cal. Close Rolls*, 1279–88, p. 249.
[12] *Yorks. Inq.*, iv, no. 76. For the descendants of Margaret through the families of Leek, Thornton and Thwaites to that of Fairfax see *Analecta, ut sup.*, pp. 259–60, and *V.C.H., City of York*, p. 496.
[13] *E. Y. C.*, v, p. 182.
[14] *Lindsey Survey*, p. 246.

Picot, who married a daughter of Roald the constable of Richmond and died before Michaelmas 1179, when Roger his son was under age.[1] From Roger II the family descended through his son Picot III, who died *c.* 1252, to the latter's nephew Roger III, whose nephew and heir Roger, son of his sister Avice and Thomas de Maunby, took the name of Lascelles, and was summoned to Parliament in 1295. He died *c.* 1300, leaving four daughters and coheirs.[2]

LEATHLEY

The family descended from Ebrard, who at the Domesday survey held land in Haggenby (a lost vill in Tadcaster), Leathley and elsewhere of William de Percy.[3] He witnessed a charter of Alan de Percy to the monks of Whitby, 1100–*c.* 1115.[4] Hugh son of Everard gave the vill of Stainton, par. Gargrave, to Selby abbey, requesting his son William to maintain the gift, *c.* 1140–1150.[5]

In 1166 William son of Hugh, known also as William son of Hugh son of Ebrard and William son of Hugh de Leathley, held a knight's fee of the old feoffment of William de Percy II, which lay in Haggenby, Leathley and Stainton.[6] He was still living in 1201; and from Hugh his son the elder line descended to the latter's grandson Adam de Leathley the younger,[7] who sold to Henry son of William de Percy, his lord, his rights in Leathley, Haggenby and elsewhere.[8]

LONGVILLERS

The family derived its name from Longvillers, dept. Calvados, arr. Caen, cant. Villers-Bocage.[9] It is reasonably certain that the Norman and English branches were of the same stock.[10]

The earliest member of the English line was Robert de Long-villers who accounted for his father's land in 1130, which probably lay in Cleckheaton and Farnley near Leeds, held of the Lascy fee. He was presumably the father of Eudo de Longvillers I and William, each of whom married a daughter of Hervey de Reineville (*q.v.*), the main line descending from Eudo in four generations to Margaret, daughter of John de Longvillers II and wife of Geoffrey de Neville, from whom the Nevilles of Hornby descended.

---

[1] For these and the following statements evidence is given in *E.Y.C.*, v, pp. 183–6, with chart pedigree.

[2] For them and the division of the inheritance see *Complete Peerage*, vii, 444–9.

[3] *E.Y.C.*, xi, pp. 137–8.

[4] *Ibid.*, no. 2; named as *Euerardus*.

[5] *Ibid.*, no. 123.

[6] *Ibid.*, pp. 137–8.

[7] *Ibid.*, p. 139. A detailed account of the family is in *Baildon and the Baildons*, i, 143–56, with chart pedigree p. 156.

[8] *Percy Chartulary*, no. 211. Henry s. of William de Percy died in 1272 (*Complete Peerage*, x, 456).

[9] *Anglo-Norman Families*, p. 55.

[10] 'The family of Longvillers' in *Y.A.J.*, xlii, 41–51, with chart pedigree of the English line, giving details of the lands held by both branches. The statements given here are based on that paper.

The family acquired several interests by marriage. The Reineville marriage brought interests in Badsworth and Gargrave; and several holdings in Penistone and elsewhere of the Lascy fee and in Craven of the honour of Skipton, with a moiety of Appleby, co. Lincoln, were the result of the marriage of Eudo de Longvillers II with a coheir of Adam son of Swain son of Alric.[1] In addition Hutton Longvillers was acquired by a Mowbray feoffment; and the castle and manor of Hornby, co. Lancaster, as a presumed gift to John de Longvillers I by his half-uncle Roger de Montbegon.

A younger line descended from William de Longvillers, apparently a younger brother of John de Longvillers II, who acquired by marriage an interest in Tuxford, co. Nottingham, and whose eventual representative was a great-granddaughter born in the middle of the fourteenth century.

LUVETOT

The family took its name from Louvetot, dept. Seine-Maritime, arr. Yvetot, cant. Caudebec,[2] close to the abbey of St-Wandrille, of which the family in England were benefactors. Their earliest recorded member in England[3] was Roger the man of Roger de Busli, the lord of what was afterwards known as the honour of Tickhill, holding lands of him in about ten places in Nottinghamshire at the Domesday survey.[4] As Roger de Lovetot, so named, with the barons of Blyth, he was addressed by queen Maud notifying her gift of the church of Laughton-en-le-Morthen for a prebend in the church of York, 1101–06;[5] and a precept was addressed to him by the queen relating to the tithes of the same church, with a precept of king Henry to the same effect, issued on the same occasion, 1104–07.[6] As Roger de Luvetot he held 2 knights' fees of the abbey of Peterborough;[7] and in Southoe, co. Huntingdon, the fee of Eustace the sheriff passed to him.[8]

In Farrer's account of the family with a chart pedigree it is stated that Roger was succeeded by his nephew Richard, son of his brother Nigel.[9] The reference is to the Peterborough chronicle;[10] but

---

[1] The coheirs are shown in the chart pedigree in *E.Y.C.*, iii, p. 318.

[2] *Anglo-Norman Families*, p. 56.

[3] Ralph Lunetot (*sic*), who witnessed a gift to the abbey of Jumièges before 1079 may have been a member of the family in Normandy (*Chartes de l'Abbaye de Jumièges*, ed. Vernier, i, 89).

[4] *V.C.H. Notts.*, i, pp. 259, 262–3, 265–8. In several places, e.g. Gringley and Walkeringham, the interest was held later by the Luvetot family; and the churches of six were included in William de Luvetot's gift to Worksop priory (*ibid.*, p. 226; *Mon. Ang.*, vi, 118).

[5] *Regesta*, ii, no. 675.

[6] *Ibid.*, nos. 807–8.

[7] *Chron. Petroburg.*, Camden Soc., p. 173. Hugh Candidus in his *Chron.*, ed. W. T. Mellows, p. 161, gives the location as in Clapton and four other places.

[8] *V.C.H. Hunts.*, ii, 347. He was amerced for a false claim to land in Hunts. (*Regesta*, ii, no. 1860b).

[9] *E.Y.C.*, iii, pp. 3–6.

[10] *Chron. Petroburg.*, pp. 173–4.

this is only an insertion in a later hand above the name of Roger 'Ricardus nepos filius scilicet Nigelli'. Farrer also states that Richard and his son William witnessed a confirmation by Henry I to Belvoir priory;[1] but this is not correct.[2] There is also the reference given by Hunter[3] to Dodsworth's statement, based on the register of archbishop Melton, that Richard de Luvetot gave the church of Ecclesfield to the abbey of St-Wandrille in the reign of Henry I; and Eastwood says that it is distinctly stated in Melton's register under the year 1323 that it was Richard de Lovetoft, lord of Hallamshire who gave the church in the time of Henry I.[4] But the reference in the register, being a confirmation of the appropriation, shows that the gift was made by *Roger*.[5]

It seems, therefore, that there is no convincing evidence for the existence of a Richard de Luvetot as the successor of Roger and predecessor of William.[6]

In the time of archbishop Thurstan William de Luvetot gave to Worksop priory, of which he was the founder, with the concession of Emma his wife and his sons the church of Worksop and several other churches in Nottinghamshire of his lordship held of the honour of Blyth, with tithe both in Normandy and England;[7] his gift of the church of Worksop etc. being confirmed by Henry I, 1123–27, probably 1126.[8] In 1126–35 William de Luvetot was addressed by the king, confirming the possessions of Huntingdon priory;[9] and not later than 1129 he and the lieges of Nottinghamshire were addressed on behalf of the lands of Durham priory in that county.[10] In 1130 he accounted for the farm of Blyth for half the year, and for 226*li*. of the pleas of Geoffrey de Clinton and for the

---

[1] Citing *Cal. Ch. Rolls*, iv, 296.

[2] Actually Richard de Luvetot and William his son witnessed not the kg's charter, but one of Ralph son of William de Walterville mentioned therein; this charter of the kg, which if genuine may be of date 1121, is regarded as 'spurious, at all events in form' (*Regesta*, no. 1277*). Moreover, it is more likely that Richard de Luvetot, also mentioned as witnessing a Belvoir charter, would be the Richard who died in 1171, having married as his second wife Maud de Senlis, widow of William d'Aubigny of Belvoir, as noted in the text below, being succeeded by his son William by his first wife Cecily.

[3] *Hallamshire*, p. 258.

[4] *Hist. of Ecclesfield*, pp. 97, 144; but on p. 511 he gives the name correctly as Roger.

[5] Reg. Melton, f. 159v, from a copy kindly supplied by Mrs. Gurney. The entry includes the statement of the proctor of the abbey of the gift *Rogeri de Louetoft tunc domini de Halumshire et confirmacionibus Henrici primi tunc regis Angl'* . . .

[6] W. T. Mellows in his notes on the family in his edition of *Pytchley's Bk. of Fees*, Northants. Rec. Soc., pp. 93n–96n, regarded William as the successor of Roger and the insertion in Chron. Petriburg as 'difficult to explain.' No suggestion can be made for the precise relationship between them.

[7] *Mon. Ang.*, vi, 118; the canons being mentioned as at Worksop. The traditional date of foundation, 3 Hen. I (*ibid.*, p. 116) is not possible; *c.* 1120 is given in Knowles, *Religious Houses*, p. 90.

[8] *Regesta*, ii, no. 1463 and p. 356.

[9] *Ibid.*, no. 1659.

[10] *Ibid.*, no. 660.

land which Robert de Caux had held with his (apparently William's) mother; he also owed 40s in Yorkshire.[1]

His lands were divided between his two sons, Richard having Hallamshire and about half of the Tickhill fees, with the fees held of the Paynel tenancy-in-chief;[2] and Nigel having the honour of Southoe, the fees held of Peterborough abbey and the remainder of the Tickhill fees.[3]

Richard de Luvetot confirmed the gifts of William his father to Worksop priory, adding gifts of his own and confirming those of Emma his mother.[4] In 1150–60, for the soul of Cecily his wife, with the consent of William his son he gave to Kirkstead abbey the hermitage of St. John in the parish of Ecclesfield, confirming and adding to the land there given by his father.[5] In 1161 at St-Wandrille he made an agreement with the abbey relating to assarts on the roadside leading from Sheffield to Ecclesfield, giving to the abbey tithe of his venison of Hallamshire.[6] In 1166 he held 5 knights' fees of William Paynel, lying in Aston and elsewhere in the wapentake of Strafforth.[7] After the death of William d'Aubigny of Belvoir in 1167 he married the latter's widow Maud de Senlis;[8] and from 1168 to 1171 he accounted for the issues of the honour of Belvoir, dying in the latter year and being succeeded by William his son.[9]

William son of Richard de Luvetot confirmed his father's gifts to Kirkstead and made gifts to Worksop priory.[10] He granted land in Brightside and elsewhere in Sheffield and in Handsworth;[11] and made a feoffment of land in Woodhouse, par. Handsworth, witnessed by Maud his wife.[12] After his death in 1181 Maud his widow, daughter of Walter son of Robert, a member of the Clare family,[13] was in the king's custody and in 1185 was said to be aged twenty-four with a daughter aged seven, holding in dower the vill of Dinsley, co.

---

[1] *Pipe Roll 31 Hen. I*, pp. 10, 11, 30; Hugh de Luvetot also occurs on the Notts. and Derby roll (p. 11); but his relationship is not known. The mother here mentioned is obscure. Farrer made the likely suggestion that she was one of the heirs to the fee of Southoe (see above) held by Eustace the sheriff in 1086 (*E.Y.C.*, iii, p. 5). For Robert de Caux see *Reg. Ant.*, Lincoln Rec. Soc., vii, 209–17, where the problem is discussed.

[2] For these 5 k.f. see *E.Y.C.*, vi, pp. 209–11.

[3] *Ibid.*, iii, p. 5. Returns show the division of the Tickhill fees. In 1208–13 Gerard Furnival (see below in the text) held 5¼ and Nigel de Luvetot 5 fees (*Bk. of Fees*, p. 32); and in 1235–36 Maud de Luvetot, Gerard's widow, held 5 in Worksop and Gringley and Nigel 4 fees (*ibid.*, pp. 533–4). In 1242–43 Maud's 5 fees in Notts. are given in detail (*ibid.*, p. 979).

[4] *Mon. Ang.*, vi, 118.

[5] *E.Y.C.*, iii, nos. 1266–7.

[6] *Ibid.*, no. 1268.

[7] *Ibid.*, vi, no. 87 and p. 209.

[8] *Ibid.*, p. 209n, for a discussion of this, amending Farrer's pedigree which gives Emma as Richard's second wife.

[9] *Ibid.*, iii, pp. 5, 6.

[10] *Ibid.*, nos. 1269, 1272.

[11] *Ibid.*, nos. 1270–1, 1273.

[12] *Hatton Bk. of Seals*, no. 299.

[13] Round, *Feudal England*, pedigree facing p. 472.

Hertford, which had belonged to her husband.[1] She subsequently married Ernulf de Magnaville with whom she quitclaimed dower rights in Whiston in 1196.[2]

Maud de Luvetot her daughter, sole heir of William, issued a comprehensive charter to Worksop priory in her widowhood.[3] She had been married to Gerard son of Gerard Furnival; and with him had delivery of her father's lands in 1203.[4] From them the inheritance descended in the male line of the Furnival family to the death of William lord Furnival in 1383.[5]

Nigel de Luvetot, younger brother of Richard de Luvetot (died in 1171), held the barony of Southoe in 1159 and 1166; and his descendants proceeded in the male line to a later Nigel, who died in 1219, the inheritance being divided between his three sisters.[6]

MANDEVILLE

The family of Mandeville, earls of Essex, of which Ernulf de Mandeville, who held an interest in Huggate, E.R., was a member, took its origin from Manneville, now in the combined commune of Le Thil-Manneville, dept. Seine-Maritime, arr. Dieppe, cant. Bacqueville.[7] The family descended from Geoffrey de Mandeville, a Domesday tenant-in-chief in several counties, father of William de Mandeville, dead in 1130, and grandfather of Geoffrey de Mandeville, first earl of Essex.[8]

Ernulf or Ernald de Mandeville, of Highworth, Wilts., and Kingham, co. Oxford, was the eldest son of earl Geoffrey, though not necessarily by his wife Rohese de Vere, and forfeited his paternal inheritance.[9] By his marriage with Alice, almost certainly daughter of Robert de Oilli of Hook Norton, co. Oxford, by Edith daughter of Forne son of Sigulf, ancestor of the family of Greystoke (q.v.), he acquired an interest in Huggate, a member of the Greystoke fee.[10] In 1166 he held a knight's fee of Ranulf son of Walter de Greystoke.[11]

---

[1] *Rot. de Dominabus*, P.R. Soc., p. 67. It is recorded in *V.C.H. Herts.*, iii, 10, without any reference, that a second manor in Dinsley (the other being Temple Dinsley) 'is stated to have been granted by William Rufus to Richard de Lovecest' (*sic*); but no charter to prove this is known. The manor was later known as Dinsley Furnival.

[2] *E.Y.C.*, vi, no. 114. Whiston was held of the Paynel fee.

[3] *Mon. Ang.*, vi, 119.

[4] *Complete Peerage*, v, 580n.

[5] *Ibid.*, pp. 580–92, showing the eventual descent to the earls of Shrewsbury.

[6] *V.C.H. Hunts.*, ii, 347; and chart pedigree in *E.Y.C.*, iii, p. 4. In 1235–36 the heirs of Nigel de Luvetot held 10 k.f. in cos. Cambridge and Huntingdon (*Bk. of Fees*, p. 571).

[7] *Anglo-Norman Families*, p. 57.

[8] *Complete Peerage*, v, 113–4, and chart pedigree pp. 116–7.

[9] *Ibid.*, p. 116 and note in pedigree. Several references to Ernulf, at one time exiled, are in Round, *Geoffrey de Mandeville*, pp. 227–33, where his mother is given as Rohese, though without proof.

[10] *Complete Peerage*, v, 116n; and for Huggate *E.Y.C.*, ii, p. 509.

[11] *Ibid.*, no. 1244.

With Alice his wife Ernulf de Mandeville confirmed land in Huggate to St. Peter's hospital, given by Edith daughter of Forne and Henry de Oilli her son, 1164–78.[1] This was confirmed by his son Geoffrey, 1178–90,[2] who also confirmed to the canons of Osney, co. Oxford, a mark's worth of land in Huggate, which Alice his mother demised and Ernulf his father assigned, 1178–c. 1193;[3] the latter gift being sold by Osney to Newburgh priory, 1184–c. 1200.[4]

Geoffrey, who had succeeded Ernulf in 1179, was succeeded by his son Geoffrey II c. 1193.[5] The latter gave 10 bovates in Huggate to St. Peter's York in 1201[6] and pasture for 200 sheep there to Watton priory, 1200–16.[7] He also demised land in Highworth to his father Geoffrey to hold for life, 1190–94.[8] He died in 1246, being succeeded by his son Ralph, who died in 1280 leaving issue.[9] The returns of 1284–85 show that 10 carucates in Huggate, constituting a knight's fee of the Greystoke fee, were held by the prior of Watton and his tenants in alms, entry being due to Geoffrey de Mandeville.[10]

MANFIELD

The family descended in the male line from Copsi of Waitby and Warcop, Westmorland, son of Arkill. By his marriage with Godreda daughter and heir of Hermer he acquired the latter's tenure of Manfield and Kelfield, par. Stillingfleet.[11] Robert son of Copsi, living c. 1148, was succeeded by his son Torfin son of Robert, to whom duke Conan in 1159–71 restored the Manfield fee of 2 knights, held of the honour of Richmond by Hermer his great-grandfather (*attavus*) and Godreda (*Gutherith*), Hermer's daughter.[12]

The greater part of Torfin's holdings passed to his two daughters Agnes and Maud, but some of it passed to his son Conan, known as Conan de Manfield, who may have been illegitimate or a son by an earlier wife. Eventually, after the death of Agnes without issue, one moiety, perhaps by some family arrangement, passed to Conan's descendants, the other moiety remaining with those of Maud, whose heir became her granddaughter Avice wife of Robert Marmion[13] (*q.v.*). In 1280 Avice Marmion and Henry son of Conan, great-grandson of Conan de Manfield, held 2 fees in Manfield; and the

[1] *E.Y.C.*, ii, no. 1254.
[2] *Ibid.*, no. 1255.
[3] *Ibid.*, no. 1256.
[4] *Ibid.*, no. 1257.
[5] *Ibid.*, no. 1260; and chart pedigree p. 508.
[6] *Ibid.*, no. 1261; and for the date *Y.A.J.*, xxxvi, 429n.
[7] *Ibid.*, no. 1265, with equestrian seal.
[8] *Ibid.*, no. 1260.
[9] *Ibid.*, note; and p. 508; *Complete Peerage*, v, 116n.
[10] *Feudal Aids*, vi, 49.
[11] *E.Y.C.*, v, pp. 33–5, with chart pedigree p. 54. Hermer was living 1108–14.
[12] *Ibid.*, p. 55; Torfin also inherited the Westmorland lands. Duke Conan's charter is pd in *ibid.*, iv, no. 55.
[13] *Ibid.*, v, pp. 57–8. Maud's husband was Hugh son of Jernegan (*q.v.*) of Tanfield.

returns of 1346 show an equality of division between the Marmion family and Henry son of Henry son of Conan.[1]

The heirs male of Henry son of Conan continued to hold a moiety of Manfield until 1496, when John FitzHenry died leaving two daughters as his coheirs.[2]

MARMION

The family in England descended from Roger Marmion who held land in Lincolnshire, including Winteringham and Scrivelsby, at the Lindsey survey, 1115–18. He was possibly the son of Robert Marmion whose interests lay in Normandy and who died in or before 1106. The earliest occurrence of the name there is that of William Marmion who held land at Fontenay [-le-Marmion], dept. Calvados, arr. Caen, and was living in 1060.

From Roger Marmion the eldest line descended through four Robert Marmions to Philip Marmion of Tamworth and Scrivelsby, who died in 1291; and through the youngest of his four daughters the manor of Scrivelsby descended to the family of Dymoke with the office of king's champion.[3]

The Marmions of Tanfield descended from Robert Marmion, a son by his second wife of the third Robert Marmion mentioned above, who was dead in 1218, and half-uncle of Philip Marmion of Tamworth.[4] By his marriage to Avice daughter of Jernegan son of Hugh (*q.v.*) he obtained Tanfield and several other holdings of the Richmond fee.[5] He died in 1241–42. He was the grandfather through his son William, of Sir John Marmion, summoned to Parliament, 1313–22, whose eventual heirs were his granddaughters Avice, wife of John lord Grey of Rotherfield, and Joan, wife of Sir John Bernack.[6]

MAULEVERER

Not later than 1105 Richard Malus Leporarius gave to Holy Trinity, York, and the monks of Marmoutier the church of Allerton and a carucate there, with tithes in other places; and later, to increase the endowments of the priory at Allerton, he gave 7½ carucates in Grafton, Allerton being made a mother-church by the confirmation of archbishop Thurstan, 1109–14; among the witnesses to another of his charters were his brothers Serlo, Helto, Roger, Fulk and Ralph.[7]

[1] *E.Y.C.*, v, p. 58, citing *Cal. Inq. p.m.*, ii, 215 and *Feudal Aids*, vi, 240.
[2] *V.C.H., N.R.*, i, 187.
[3] The above statements are taken from the article on Marmion in *Complete Peerage*, viii, 505–14.
[4] Chart pedigree in *ibid.*, p. 507.
[5] For the manors composing the Tanfield fee see *E.Y.C.*, v, pp. 40–1.
[6] *Complete Peerage, ut sup.*
[7] *Cal. Docs. France*, no. 1233; *E.Y.C.*, ii, no. 729 and note.

From Richard descended the Mauleverers of Allerton, who continued in the male line to the first quarter of the eighteenth century.[1]

The Mauleverers of Beamsley, who were closely connected with the Allerton line, descended from Helto Mauleverer, who died between 1155 and 1166; it is not impossible chronologically that he was Helto brother of Richard Mauleverer mentioned above, but he may have been of a younger generation.[2] With the consent of his wife and his son William he gave land in Beamsley to Embsay priory, not later than 1131–40, and with the consent of Biljoth his wife 12 bovates in Malham.[3] Beamsley itself was held partly of the honour of Skipton and partly of the Percy fee.[4] In 1166 William Mauleverer held a knight's fee of the old feoffment of Skipton in Hellifield, Malham and elsewhere in Craven.[5] From him the descent was in the male line to Richard Mauleverer of Beamsley, living in 1399, who died without issue, his eventual heirs being his sisters Alice, wife of Sir John Middelton of Stockeld, and Thomasine, wife of William Moore of Otterburn, whose daughter and coheir Elizabeth married Thomas Clapham, ancestor of the Claphams of Beamsley.[6]

MEAUX

The family descended from Gamel son of Ketel son of Norman. In c. 1135–1143 Thurstan provost of Beverley restored to John de Meaux land in Sigglesthorne which had been held by the latter's father Gamel, and land in Walkington which had been held by his grandfather Ketel son of Norman.[7]

John de Meaux exchanged his patrimony of Meaux for the manor of Bewick, par. Aldbrough, so that William count of Aumale could found a Cistercian house at Meaux.[8] In 1166 he held an eighth of a knight's fee of the archbishop of York in Sutton-in-Holderness.[9] His son Robert de Meaux married Maud daughter of Hugh Camin, whereby he acquired land in Little Weighton, North

---

[1] *Glover's Visitation*, pp. 66–8; *G.E.C.*, *Complete Baronetage*, ii, 117–8. Glover's pedigree gives a William Mauleverer as father of Richard the founder of the priory, for whom no evidence is available; and Farrer, in his detailed notes on the families, points out that the descent from Ralph brother of Richard is an error, suggesting that William Mauleverer of Allerton in the middle of the 12th century was son of Ralph probably son of Richard (*E.Y.C.*, ii, no. 729n).

[2] *Ibid.*, vii, p. 116.

[3] *Ibid.*, nos. 5, 6, 57.

[4] *Ibid.*, p. 115.

[5] *Ibid.*, pp. 94, 114.

[6] *Ibid.*, pp. 114–25, giving an account of the fee held of Skipton and the family descent, certain links, however, not being completely proved, with a chart pedigree from Helto.

[7] *R. R. Hastings MSS.* Hist. MSS. Comm., i, 164, cited in the account of the family in *Y.A.J.*, xliii, 99–111. The place of origin was Meaux in Holderness and not Meaux in France, as stated in *Chron. de Melsa*, i, 78.

[8] *Ibid.*, p. 77: and for the agreement between William count of Aumale and John de Meaux, made after the foundation of the abbey in 1150, see *E.Y.C.*, iii, no. 1379.

[9] *Red Bk. Exch.*, p. 415; *E.Y.C.*, i, p. 45n.

Cave, Myton, Leppington and Foggathorpe; and from him the family descended in the male line to John de Meaux IV, who died without issue in or shortly after 1377.[1]

The Meaux family of Owthorne, a younger branch of Meaux of Bewick, descended from Peter de Meaux who held three-quarters of a knight's fee of the new feoffment of William de Percy in 1166, and land in Owthorne of the honour of Holderness.[2] He can probably be identified as Peter brother of John de Meaux I of Bewick, who witnessed with him a charter of William count of Aumale, 1160–c. 1170.[3] From him the family descended in the male line to Peter de Meaux who died in 1349–50, then a minor, his heirs being the three daughters of Philip de Meaux, his grandfather.[4]

MEINILL (of Whorlton)

The first recorded member of the family in England was Robert de Meinill, who occurs c. 1100–09 and was probably the founder of the original castle at Whorlton. From his son and heir Stephen de Meinill I the family descended in the male line to Nicholas de Meinill, who was summoned to Parliament from 1295 to 1299, and from him to his great-grandson John de Meinill, who died as a minor in 1349 and whose heir was his sister Alice. By 1434 her issue had become extinct. Whorlton had been settled on an illegitimate son by Nicholas second lord Meinill, who died in 1322, the elder brother of Alice's grandfather.[5]

MOHAUT

The family (de Mohaut or de Monte Alto) descended from Simon son of Gospatric, who so described witnessed charters of Cecily de Rumilly and William son of Duncan to Embsay priory, 1135–54,[6] and as Simon de Mohaut with Simon his son a charter of Alice de Rumilly to Pontefract priory, 1152–54.[7] Nothing definite is known of Gospatric father of Simon I, but possibly he was Gospatric son of Gospatric the king's thegn, living in the reign of Henry I,[8] the latter having held Bingley before the Conquest;[9] for the family held Riddlesden in that parish.

In 1166 either Simon I or his son Simon II, and probably the former, held 3 carucates of the honour of Skipton in East and West Morton and Riddlesden.[10] It is suggested that Simon I was born c. 1115 and Simon II c. 1140, dying 1226–29, the evidence supporting

---

[1] *Y.A.J.*, *ut sup.*, where there is an appendix on the monuments to John de Meaux IV and his wife in Aldbrough church.
[2] *Ibid.*, pp. 108–9, and *E.Y.C.*, xi, pp. 261–4.
[3] *Y.A.J.*, *ut sup.*, p. 108.
[4] *Ibid.*, p. 109.
[5] *Complete Peerage*, viii, 619–32.
[6] *E.Y.C.*, vii, nos. 9, 12, perhaps 1151–53.
[7] *Ibid.*, no. 16.
[8] *V.C.H. Yorks.*, ii, 184.
[9] *Ibid.*, p. 278.
[10] *E.Y.C.*, vii, pp. 252-4.

the existence of two and not three Simons holding the fee during this period.[1] The family descended to Simon III, grandson of Simon II, who died c. 1279, leaving seven daughters as his coheirs.[2]

A short pedigree of a younger line, as of West Riddlesden, entered at the Visitation of 1585, was signed by Arthur Mawhaut *alias* Mawde,[3] and the name Maude replaced the former.

MONCEAUX

Alan de Monceaux, who held lands in Yorkshire and Lincolnshire of the counts of Aumale, was a member of the family deriving its origin from Monchaux-Soreng, dept. Seine-Maritime, arr. Neufchâtel, lying about fifteen miles north of Aumale.[4] He was given an interest in Boynton by Stephen count of Aumale before 1120–c. 1127;[5] and with the consent of Maud his wife and Robert his son and heir he gave to the hospital of Bridlington 2 bovates in Winkton (a lost vill in par. Barmston in Holderness), his charter being witnessed by Eustace, Ingelram, Gilbert and Alexander de Monceaux and his nephews Walter and Philip, 1127–c. 1135.[6] He was the founder of Nun Coton priory, co. Lincoln;[7] and, after the foundation, with Ingeram his son and heir,[8] he gave the vill of Nun Coton in the presence of Henry archbishop of York, 1147–53.[9] He also gave the church of Barmston to Whitby abbey, his gift being included in a confirmation charter of Henry II.[10] He frequently witnessed charters of William count of Aumale, who for a time held the earldom of York, several being of date 1138–54;[11] and he was apparently living in 1161, when as *dominus et testis* he witnessed a demise to Guisborough priory of land in Ugthorpe.[12]

He was succeeded by his son Ingelram or Ingram, who, as Farrer suggested, held a knight's fee of the honour of Holderness in 1166.[13] He confirmed to Guisborough priory a carucate in Ugthorpe which the monks had held in the times of Alan his father and Gilbert his brother, 1182–1205;[14] and with the consent of Robert

---

[1] *E.Y.C.*, vii, p. 254 and note. A charter of Simon I with the consent of his wife Maud and his sons Simon and Robert has the date assigned 1150–70 (*ibid.*, iii, no. 1866), and one of his son Simon II, 1185–1200 (*ibid.*, no. 1868).

[2] *Ibid.*, vii, pp. 253–6, where there is an account of the family.

[3] *Glover's Visitation*, p. 300.

[4] *Anglo-Norman Families*, p. 66, where details are given of another branch of the family which had a co-heirship in the inheritance of Juliane wife of William FitzAldelin, for whom see *H.K.F.*, iii, 376–8, and Round, *King's Serjeants*, pp. 92–6, dealing with a Marshal serjeanty.

[5] *E.Y.C.*, iii, no. 1326.

[6] *Ibid.*, no. 1328.

[7] *Mon. Ang.*, v, 675.

[8] Robert being presumably dead.

[9] *E.Y.C.*, iii, no. 1329.

[10] *Ibid.*, i, no. 379.

[11] *E.g. ibid.*, iii, nos. 1306, 1313–4.

[12] *Ibid.*, i, no. 619.

[13] *Ibid.*, iii, no. 1305n.

[14] *Ibid.*, ii, no. 1062.

his son a gift of Henry Foliot to St. Peter's York of a bovate in Sunderlandwick, 1161–c. 1175.[1] With Alexander his brother and Alan de Monceaux and Robert the latter's brother he witnessed a Lincolnshire charter, c. 1150–1170;[2] and with Gilbert de Monceaux and Alexander his brother and Agnes de Monceaux and her sons Alan and Robert another relating to Immingham, co. Lincoln, c. 1166–80.[3] Late in the reign of Henry II he gave to Nun Coton priory all his land in Cuxwold, co. Lincoln;[4] and made an exchange with Alice daughter of Philip of half a carucate in Killingholme, co. Lincoln, for a similar amount in Lissett, par. Beeford, Yorks., E.R.[5] He was living in 1199, when he claimed a share of the inheritance of Juliane wife of William FitzAldelin;[6] and was probably dead in 1205.[7] Agnes his widow was living in 1231.[8] He was succeeded by his son Robert, who occurs as a knight in 1207[9] and in 1208 received a recognition of land in Ugthorpe, where the prioress of Grindale had held 15 bovates of him.[10] Robert's successor was Sir Ingram de Monceaux, who in 1284–85 held $29\frac{1}{2}$ carucates in Holderness at Barmston, Lissett, Winkton, Boynton, Caythorpe and Reighton.[11] He died in 1292, leaving John his son as his heir, then aged eighteen.[12] The inheritance passed in the male line from the latter's brother to William Monceaux, who died in 1446 and whose heir was his sister Maud, wife of Sir Brian de la See.[13]

MORTIMER

Ralph de Mortimer, tenant-in-chief at the Domesday survey in twelve counties, was the son of Roger de Mortemer, seigneur of Mortemer-sur-Eaulne, near Neuchâtel-en-Brai, the caput of his honour in England being Wigmore, co. Hereford.[14] In Yorkshire he held several holdings, mainly in wap. Harthill, the most important being manors in Kirk Ella, North Ferriby and Wintringham.[15] These were increased by some of the Domesday lands of Robert

---

[1] E.Y.C., ii, no. 682.
[2] Ibid., i, no. 546. Alan de Monceaux witnessed a charter to Whitby abbey, 1165–75 (ibid., ii, no. 891), and with Robert his brother Fraisthorpe charters (Bridlington Chartulary, pp. 199, 203).
[3] E.Y.C., xi, no. 96.
[4] Danelaw Charters, no. 426.
[5] Ibid., no. 427.
[6] E.Y.C., ii, no. 1062n. This shows his connexion with the other branch (see the note above).
[7] Ibid.
[8] Yorks. Fines, 1218–31, p. 163. Chronology suggests that she was a second wife of more youthful age than her husband, unless there was a younger Ingelram.
[9] E.Y.C., iii, no. 1353n.
[10] Yorks. Fines, John, p. 148.
[11] Feudal Aids, vi, 41.
[12] Yorks. Inq., ii, no. 105, with details of his holdings and tenants.
[13] Poulson, Holderness, i, 187–8, with a chart pedigree p. 186.
[14] Complete Peerage, ix, 266, s.n. Mortimer of Wigmore; the early generations being the work of L. C. Loyd with details from Norman sources.
[15] The list is given in E.Y.C., iii, p. 488.

Malet after the latter's forfeiture in 1106, including manors in South Cave and Drewton, also in wap. Harthill.[1]

In 1304 after the death of Ralph's descendant in the male line. Edmund de Mortimer of Wigmore, the number of knight's fees in Yorkshire was 15; and of the twenty-two places no less than seventeen occur among Ralph's holdings in 1086 and two more lay in his holdings in Kirk Ella and North Ferriby.[2]

There was a close connexion between Vescy and Mortimer. It was recorded in a return for the honour of Eustace de Vescy and Roger de Mortimer in 1186–87, then in the king's hand,[3] that the keeper accounted for 110s scutage for 5½ knights of the fee of Roger de Mortimer, the service of which had been given in marriage to the predecessor of William [de Vescy] and had not attained to the third heir.[4] Eventually, as shown in the inquisition of 1304, of the 15 fees in Yorkshire held by Edmund de Mortimer, 14 were held by the heirs of William de Vescy and one by William de Ros of Helmsley.[5]

MOWBRAY

The family descended from William d'Aubigny, seigneur of Aubigny now St-Martin d'Aubigny, dept. Manche, arr. Coutances. Nigel d'Aubigny, younger son of Roger son of William d'Aubigny and brother of William d'Aubigny the butler, ancestor of the earls of Arundel, was granted many holdings by Henry I, including the English lands of Robert de Stuteville and the forfeited lands in Normandy of Robert de Mowbray, earl of Northumberland, including Montbrai, dept. Manche, arr. St-Lô.[6] His other interests included a knight's fee in Masham held of the honour of Richmond.[7]

In 1166 his son Roger de Mowbray held about a hundred knights' fees in chief, scattered over several counties;[8] and from him the family descended in the male line to John de Mowbray, duke of Norfolk, who died without issue in 1476.[9]

---

[1] The list is given in *ibid.*

[2] *Yorks. Inq.*, iv, no. 46.

[3] William de Vescy, Eustace's father, died in 1183; and Eustace was born 1169–71 (*Complete Peerage*, xii (ii), 275).

[4] *E.Y.C.*, iii, p. 486, from *Red Bk. Exch.*, p. 68. Farrer (p. 487) discussed various possibilities for such a marriage without any satisfactory result. It is significant that the 4 car. in Gilling-in-Ryedale, held by Ralph de Mortimer in 1086, were given by Eustace FitzJohn, William de Vescy's father, to St. Mary's York (*E.Y.C.*, iii, no. 1877), to which Ives de Vescy, Eustace's father-in-law, had given 2 car. there (*ibid.*, i, no. 354); the identity of Ives de Vescy's wife has not been determined (*Complete Peerage*, xii (ii), 274; and *cf. E.Y.C.*, xii, pp. 1, 2).

[5] *Yorks. Inq.*, iv, no. 46.

[6] *Complete Peerage*, ix, 366–9; *Mowbray Charters*, pp. xvii, *et seq.*

[7] *E.Y.C.*, iv, no. 19, being a confirmn to Roger de Mowbray of his father's tenure.

[8] For the location of these see *Mowbray Charters*, pp. 262–6.

[9] *Complete Peerage*, ix, 369–85.

MUMBY

The family descended from Eudo the tenant of Alan count of Britanny at the Domesday survey at Mumby and elsewhere in Lincolnshire, who in 1115–18 held land there of count Stephen and as Eudo de Monbi land in Thorpe St. Peter, co. Lincoln. His son Alan son of Eudo was one of the principal tenants of count Stephen in 1130, holding 5 knights' fees of the honour of Richmond; these consisted of 4 fees in Mumby and the soke and one fee in Wycliffe in Yorkshire.[1]

The inheritance descended in the male line to Alan de Mumby son of Eudo II, who died in or before 1216, his coheirs being three daughters of Ralph de Mumby. Of these Beatrice, then wife of Robert de Turribus, was evidently a widow in 1252, when described as Beatrice de Mumby she enfeoffed Robert de Wycliffe of land in Wycliffe. In 1284–85 Robert de Wycliffe held a knight's fee there of William de Kirkton who held of the earl of Richmond; and in 1300 Roger de Edenham and Joan his wife sold to Harsculf de Cleasby the service of a knight's fee in Wycliffe with the homage of Robert de Wycliffe, to hold of the chief lords, warranty being given by Roger and Joan and Joan's heirs.[2] It can therefore be suggested that Joan was a representative of Beatrice de Mumby, and possibly William de Kirkton, the predecessor of Roger and Joan as the immediate tenant of the honour, had acquired his interest by marriage.

MUSTERS (of Kirklington)

The family descended from Robert, a tenant of count Alan at the Domesday survey at Kirklington and other places in Richmond-shire, at Syerston and Treswell, co. Nottingham, in the latter place being described as Robert de Mosters, and at Lea, wap. Corringham, co. Lincoln. His total holding in Richmondshire was about 60 carucates, and of this about two-thirds were held by his descendant in 1284.[3]

It is probable that he was of the same family as Lisois de Monasteriis who accompanied William I on his northern tour in 1069, a Lisoius son of Robert de Musters, noted below, occurring in 1130. It is also probable that he was connected with Geoffrey de Monasteriis who occurs in Britanny in the middle of the eleventh century and was a benefactor of the abbey of St-Sergius at Angers. There is evidence to suggest that Geoffrey derived his name from Moutiers near La Guerche, about twenty-one kilometres south of Vitré in Britanny, and that his family was Angevin in origin.[4] There

---

[1] *E.Y.C.*, v, pp. 269–71, giving an account of the Mumby fee and the family. Unless otherwise stated the documentary references are given there.

[2] A full abstract of the final concord is now pd in *Yorks. Fines*, 1272–1300, p. 143.

[3] For this and the following details see the account of the Musters fee in *E.Y.C.*, v, pp. 242–55.

[4] *Ibid.*, p. 246 and note.

can be no reasonable doubt that Robert de Musters, the Domesday under-tenant, came from Britanny.

Either he, or possibly a second Robert, died shortly before 1130, when Lisoius de Monast[eriis] owed a sum for his father's land.[1] In 1145–46 count Alan III restored to Robert de Musters (*de Monasteriis*) the land of Robert his grandfather, which had been held by his father Geoffrey and his uncle Liserus.[2] Geoffrey had held 8 knights' fees of the honour of Richmond,[3] of which 3 lay in Richmondshire, 2 in Nottinghamshire and 3 in Lincolnshire,[4] the latter holding being subsequently reduced to one.[5]

Robert son of Geoffrey de Musters died in 1184–89 and was succeeded by his son Lisiard.[6] From him the family descended in the male line to Sir Henry de Musters, whose daughter and heir Elizabeth married first Sir Alexander Mowbray, who died in 1368–69, and secondly *c.* 1370 John de Wandesford.[7]

NEUFMARCHÉ

The earliest member of the family holding land in Yorkshire was Ralph Novi Fori who witnessed the foundation of Blyth priory by Roger de Busli in 1088, and was presumably a tenant of the fee later known as the honour of Tickhill, of which his descendants held 4 knights' fees.[8] Although he probably came from Normandy his place of origin has not been determined; there is no known connexion with Bernard de Neufmarché, lord of Brecknock, who came from Neufmarché, dept. Seine-Maritime, arr. Neufchâtel, cant. Gournay.[9]

Pain de Novo Foro, Ralph's brother, was a benefactor of Blyth priory with the consent of William his nephew;[10] and the latter can be identified as William de Novo Mercato, named as the uncle of the son of William de Whatton (co. Nottingham), who rendered account of 25*li.* in 1130 for his son's succession to the land of William de Novo Mercato.[11] This son was presumably Adam de Neufmarché, taking his mother's name, who as Adam de Novo Foro

---

[1] *Pipe Roll 31 Hen. I*, p. 26.

[2] *E.Y.C.*, iv, no. 26.

[3] *Ibid.*, v, p. 11.

[4] *Ibid.*, p. 242.

[5] In Willingham by Stow; the others, in Lea and Great Burton, passed as an immediate tenure of the honour to the Trehampton family (*ibid.*).

[6] *Ibid.*, p. 243. A charter of Lisiard is pd at no. 15 below.

[7] A full account of the descendants is in H. B. McCall, *Story of the Family of Wandesforde of Kirklington and Castlecomer*. Writing in 1904 he recorded that the manor of Kirklington had descended in an unbroken line through thirty generations.

[8] *Complete Peerage*, ix, 543; *E.Y.C.*, viii, pp. 142, 148, with chart pedigree p. 141.

[9] *Anglo-Norman Families*, p. 72.

[10] *E.Y.C.*, viii, p. 142*n;* it being suggested that Pain was Ralph's younger brother and not his heir.

[11] *Ibid.*, p. 142, from *Pipe Roll 31 Hen. I*, p. 36; and for the identification of Whatton (*Waddona*) *Complete Peerage*, p. 543*n.*

witnessed the foundation charters of Roche abbey, founded in 1147.[1]

Henry de Neufmarché, Adam's son and successor, married Denise daughter of Otes de Tilly; and by this marriage the family holdings were increased by 3 knights' fees of the Lascy fee and 3 knights' fees of the honour of Warenne.[2] From him the family descended in the male line to the fifteenth century, when Robert son of Ralph de Newmarch died without issue male, his daughter and heir Elizabeth wife of John de Neville of Althorpe, co. Lincoln, being the mother of Joan her heir and wife of Sir William Gascoigne of Gawthorpe.[3]

Two younger branches can be noted. First, William a younger brother of Adam de Neufmarché, who had the custody of the lands of the latter's son Henry up to 1172, can probably be identified as William de Neufmarché who married Isabel one of the two daughters of Ranulf son of Wilard, a tenant of the Baliol fee, in whose right he acquired land in Hickleton and elsewhere.[4] Their son was known both as Ranulf de Hickleton and Ranulf de Novo Mercato, and left issue.[5]

The second branch descended from Adam a younger son of Adam de Neufmarché of the main line who died in 1247. He received the property at Whatton, which descended through several generations to Elizabeth daughter of Hugh de Neufmarché, who married her distant cousin Robert son of Ralph de Newmarch, mentioned above, thus bringing back Whatton to the main line.[6]

NEVILLE (of Pickhill)

The connexion with Yorkshire of the family which held a knight's fee in Rigsby, co. Lincoln, and another in Rolleston, co. Nottingham, of the honour of Richmond, was due to a gift to Jollan de Neville by Alan constable of Richmond of his daughter Amfelise in marriage, together with Pickhill, including 6 carucates in demesne, and the service of 4 carucates in Whitwell, par. Catterick, to hold for the service of eleven-twelfths of a knight's fee, c. 1175.[7]

At the Domesday survey Losoard held land in Rigsby and Rolleston of the bishop of Bayeux; and at the Lindsey survey Richard son of Losward held 2 carucates 2 bovates in Rigsby of the lord of the honour of Richmond.[8] Richard was succeeded by his son Rocelin, who as Rocelin son of Richard de Rigsby gave land in Rigsby to Greenfield priory; and the gift of Rocelin de Rigsby and Jollan his son was confirmed by king Henry II.[9] In 1231 a case

---

[1] *E.Y.C.*, viii, p. 142, it being assumed, as in *Complete Peerage*, p. 544, that William de Whatton married a sister of William de Novo Mercato.

[2] *Ibid.*, pp. 140, 143–4.

[3] *Complete Peerage*, pp. 544–8.

[4] *E.Y.C.*, viii, p. 143n.

[5] *Ibid.* and *ibid.*, i, no. 584n.

[6] *Complete Peerage*, pp. 546n, 548n.

[7] *E.Y.C.*, v, no. 262, with note giving details of Jollan's origin.

[8] *Ibid.; Lindsey Survey*, p. 254.

[9] *Danelaw Charters*, nos. 117, 119–20.

shows that Joelin son of Rocelin was the father of Johelin de Neville the plaintiff.[1] The collective evidence, especially the details for Rigsby and Rolleston, suggests that Jollan de Neville, the grantee of Pickhill, was the same man as Joelin son of Rocelin and the descendant in the male line from Losoard, and that he possibly took the name of Neville from his mother.[2] He was dead in 1208, and from his son Jollan the family descended in the male line; in 1559 the manor of Pickhill was sold by Sir Thomas Neville.[3] In 1284–85 Andrew de Neville held of the constable's fee 8 carucates in Pickhill and 4 carucates in Whitwell,[4] which can be compared with the land given by Alan the constable to his grandfather Jollan.

NEVILLE (of Raby)

It has been established[5] that the Nevilles of Raby who held Sheriff Hutton in Yorkshire, descended in the male line from Dolfin son of Uchtred, who was granted Staindrop and Staindropshire by the prior and convent of Durham at a yearly rent of $4li.$ on 20 March 1131–2,[6] and who witnessed a charter of Geoffrey bishop of Durham, 1133–41.[7] Until comparatively recently no proof was available for the parentage of Uchtred;[8] but there is now evidence to identify his father with a reasonable degree of certainty as Meldred, from whom bishop William of St. Calais acquired a portion of Kelton in exchange for Winlaton, both in co. Durham.[9] Meldred son of Dolfin, who on this hypothesis was the elder Meldred's great-grandson,[10] held land at Stella near Winlaton; and Winlaton formed part of the Neville fee in the fourteenth century.[11]

Dolfin son of Uchtred was succeeded by his son, a younger Meldred, who with Patrick his brother witnessed a charter of Hugh bishop of Durham,[12] and who died not later than 1195, being succeeded by his son Robert.

[1] *E.Y.C.*, v, no. 262*n.*
[2] *Ibid.*
[3] *Ibid.*; *V.C.H., N.R.*, i, 379. The family is cited by Sir Anthony Wagner (*English Genealogy*, 2nd ed., pp. 66–7) as an example of a non-baronial male descent from the Conqueror's day, noting that Mr. H. R. Nevile of Thorney, Notts., is probably 25th in descent from Losoard.
[4] *Feudal Aids*, vi, pp. 99, 103.
[5] By Round in 'The Origin of the Nevilles' (*Feudal England*, pp. 488–90).
[6] The charter is pd in *Feod. Prior. Dunelm.*, Surtees Soc., p. 56*n.*
[7] *Ibid.*, p. 140*n.*
[8] Round, *loc. cit.;* Sir A. Wagner, *English Genealogy*, p. 25.
[9] *Durham Episcopal Charters*, Surtees Soc., p. 76; the editor, Professor H. S. Offler, noting that a Uhtred son of Meldred occurs in *Liber Vitae*, p. 146. A Uhtred son of Maldred witnessed a charter of Ranulf bishop of Durham, 1116–?1119 (*Durham Ep. Ch.*, p. 75). The parentage of Uchtred was discussed by G. A. Moriarty in 'The Origin of Nevill of Raby' (*New England Hist. and Gen. Reg.*, xvi (1952), 186–90, where although his father is given as an elder Meldred, the latter's origin as suggested cannot be proved.
[10] The descent would run Meldred (b. *c.* 1050), Uchtred (b. *c.* 1080), Dolfin (b. *c.* 1105), Meldred (b. *c.* 1140), Robert (b. *c.* 1170).
[11] *Durham Ep. Ch.*, p. 76.
[12] *Feod. Prior. Dunelm.*, p. 100*n.*

In 1194–95 Robert rendered account of 600 marks for having his father's land.[1] Evidence has been given[2] that Meldred, his father, married a sister and coheir of Roger de Stuteville of Long Lawford and Newbold-on-Avon, co. Warwick, son of John de Stuteville, a younger son of Robert de Stuteville II (q.v.); and in 1214 Robert son of Meldred (*filius Maudredi*) was plaintiff against Roger Pantulf for a moiety of land in those places as his right by descent as a share of the sisters of Roger de Stuteville.[3] It is not unnatural that Meldred, marrying a member of a Norman family, had four sons with the names of Robert, Gilbert, Richard and William.[4]

Robert son of Meldred, whose saltire on his armorial seal[5] was adopted by his Neville descendants, married Isabel sister and eventual heir of Henry de Neville of Burreth, co. Lincoln,[6] and also heir of their mother's Bulmer inheritance (q.v.).[7] Their son Geoffrey took the name of Neville and his issue in the eldest line descended through the earls of Westmorland to 1601.[8] The representative of a younger branch is the present Marquess of Abergavenny,[9] whose ancestry can thus be traced in a direct male line from Uchtred son of Meldred.

PAYNEL

There is some evidence that Ralph Paynel, tenant-in-chief in several counties at the Domesday survey, was a younger son and eventual heir of William Paynel whose original home was at Les Moutiers-Hubert, dept. Calvados, arr. Lisieux, and who may have acquired Hambye, dept. Manche, arr. Coutances, by marriage. Both these places were held by William Paynel, eldest son of Ralph.[10]

Among the wide-spread lands of Ralph Paynel at the Survey were the manor of Drax in Yorkshire and the manors of West Rasen in Lincolnshire and East Quantoxhead in Somerset.[11] Besides his eldest son William, who succeeded him in 1115–24, he had sons Jordan and Alexander by a second wife (see below). William son of Ralph was the founder of Drax priory and of the abbey of Hambye. By his first wife he had with others two sons Hugh Paynel I and

---

[1] *Pipe Roll 7 Ric. I*, p. 26.

[2] *Antiquaries Journal*, xxxi, 201–4; and cf. *E.Y.C.*, ix, pp. 23–6.

[3] *Curia Regis Rolls*, vii, 283, cited in *Ant. Journal, loc. cit.*, where the identification of Robert is discussed. Roger Pantulf was Roger de Stuteville's nephew (*E.Y.C.*, ix, p. 26).

[4] *Ant. Journal, loc. cit.*

[5] *Ibid.*, ii, 211–7; his charter with the seal is illustrated in *Pudsay Deeds*, plate viii.

[6] *Complete Peerage*, ix, 493–4.

[7] This included Sheriff Hutton, Yorks., and Brancepeth, co. Durham; see Round, 'Neville and Bulmer' (*Family Origins*), pp. 56–9).

[8] *Complete Peerage*, ix, 494–503; xii(ii), 544–59.

[9] *Ibid.*, i, 30–44.

[10] *E.Y.C.*, vi (the Paynel fee), giving accounts of the various Paynel families, with chart pedigree facing p. 1.

[11] *Ibid.*, chapter II, giving a survey of the lands held by Ralph and his descendants in the 12th cent.

Fulk Paynel I, and by his second wife a daughter Alice.[1] By an unusual arrangement his property was divided, Hugh obtaining West Rasen and Les Moutiers-Hubert, and Fulk Drax and Hambye. At a later date, at the loss of Normandy, Hugh Paynel I's grandson, Hugh Paynel II, supported king John, and Fulk Paynel I's son, Fulk Paynel II, supported Philip Augustus. As a result Hugh Paynel II lost Les Moutiers-Hubert, taken into the hand of Philip Augustus, and was given Drax in compensation as an addition to his holding of West Rasen, Drax having been lost by Fulk Paynel II of Hambye.

From Fulk Paynel II descended the Norman family of Paynel, lords of Hambye;[2] and from Hugh Paynel II the English family, holding Drax and West Rasen, descended in the male line to John Paynel who died in 1325, leaving two daughters; and the inheritance eventually passed as an undivided whole to the family of Poucher and subsequently to that of Sothill and so to the Constables of Everingham.[3]

PAYNEL (of Hooton Pagnell)

It is probable that Ralph Paynel, the Domesday tenant-in-chief (*q.v.*) married as his second wife a daughter and coheir of Richard de Surdeval,[4] and certain that some of the latter's land, which included Hooton Pagnell,[5] passed in turn to Ralph's sons Jordan and Alexander. On the death of Jordan without issue the inheritance passed to Alexander, who was succeeded by his son William Paynel.[6] It is reasonably certain that a younger Jordan, who married as her second husband Agnes daughter of Swain son of Edwin de Houghton (*q.v.*) and widow of Henry de Vernoil (*q.v.*) was a younger son of Alexander.

William Paynel of Hooton Pagnell succeeded his father Alexander not later than 1153;[7] and at his death his heirs were two daughters, Frethesant wife of Geoffrey Luterel and Isabel wife of William Bastard, the inheritance passing as a whole to Andrew Luterel son of Frethesant.[8] On the death in 1230 of Maurice de Gant, grandson of Alice daughter of William son of Ralph Paynel (*q.v.*), he obtained possession of certain of Maurice's Paynel inheritance, which included Irnham and East Quantoxhead.[9] From Andrew Luterel the family descended in the male line to Sir

---

[1] For Alice's marriages to Robert de Curcy and Robert de Gant and her acquisition of several of the Paynel possessions see *E.Y.C.*, vi, pp. 31–8. This included Irnham, co. Lincoln, and East Quantoxhead; but these later passed to the Luterel family as heirs of the Paynels of Hooton Pagnell (*q.v.*).

[2] *Ibid.*, pp. 24–30.

[3] *Ibid.*, pp. 9–17.

[4] *Ibid.*, pp. 4, 5.

[5] A list of the Yorks. lands is in *ibid.*, p. 58.

[6] An account of this line is in *ibid.*, pp. 38–46.

[7] *Ibid.*, p. 41.

[8] *Ibid.*, pp. 44–6.

[9] *Ibid.*, pp. 37–8.

Geoffrey Luterel who died without issue in 1419, his heir being a sister;[1] but whereas Hooton Pagnell and Irnham so descended, East Quantoxhead had been given by Andrew to a younger son Alexander, from whom the Luttrells of Dunster are descended,[2] holding it in the twentieth century as an unbroken inheritance from Ralph Paynel in the eleventh.

PEITEVIN

At the Domesday survey Roger held Altofts (*Westrebi*), par. Normanton, and Whitwood, par. Featherstone, of Ilbert de Lascy.[3] As Roger Pictavensis he gave 2 thraves of his tithe in Altofts and [?]Towton to the chapel of St. Clement in Pontefract castle before c. 1093.[4] He, or more probably a younger Roger, gave a mill in Saxton to Nostell priory, included in the benefactions confirmed by Henry I, [?] 10 January 1121–2;[5] he rendered account in 1130 for 20 marks of silver for the pleas of Blyth, being pardoned 10 marks;[6] and witnessed a charter of Ilbert de Lascy II to Pontefract priory, 1135–40.[7]

He was succeeded by his son Robert, who confirmed the gift of Roger his father to Nostell of the mill in Saxton, 1154–75.[8] In 1166 Robert Pictavensis held 3 knights' fees of the old feoffment of Henry de Lascy.[9] He gave to Pontefract priory a bovate in Altofts, mentioned when witnessing a charter of Henry de Lascy to that house, 1147–54;[10] and to St. Peter's hospital, York, the advowson of Saxton, which was confirmed by Roger his son not later than 1177.[11] From this last Roger the family descended in the male line to the fourteenth century.[12]

There was a younger line holding land in Headingley, Leeds. A case of 1280 shows four generations in the male line from Thomas le Peitevin living in the reign of John.[13] The connexion with the elder line of Altofts is shown by charters of Robert le Peitevin (of Altofts), confirming to Kirkstall abbey land in Headingley given by William le Peitevin, whom in another charter he described as his knight, 1153–77.[14] As a William Pictavensis gave 2 thraves of his tithe in

---

[1] *Complete Peerage*, viii, 284–9.
[2] *Ibid.*, p. 285n.
[3] *E.Y.C.*, iii, no. 1556n, giving details of the early generations.
[4] *Ibid.*, no. 1492.
[5] *Ibid.*, no. 1428 (p. 131); *Regesta*, ii, no. 1312.
[6] *Pipe Roll 31 Hen. I*, p. 27.
[7] *E.Y.C.*, iii, no. 1493.
[8] *Ibid.*, no. 1561.
[9] *Ibid.*, no. 1508.
[10] *Ibid.*, no. 1499.
[11] *Ibid.*, nos. 1562–3; the latter being witnessed by Robert master of the schools, who was drowned in that year.
[12] *Baildon and the Baildons*, i, 288–300, with full documentary details and a chart pedigree p. 300.
[13] *Ibid.*, p. 289n.
[14] *E.Y.C.*, iii, nos. 1556–8.

Skellow to St. Clement's chapel, Pontefract, before *c.* 1093,[1] it is possible that the two families were separated by that year, and that this William was a brother of Roger the Domesday tenant in Altofts; but there is no definite proof that he was the ancestor of the Headingley line.

PERCY

William de Percy I, tenant-in-chief in Yorkshire and Lincolnshire at the Domesday survey,[2] took his name from Percy-en-Auge, dept. Calvados, arr. Lisieux, cant. Mézidon.[3] His grandson William de Percy II died leaving two daughters as his coheirs; and in 1175 his barony was divided between the earl of Warwick, husband of Maud, and Jocelin of Louvain, husband of Agnes.[4] Maud died without issue; and William de Percy III, son of Henry son of Agnes, became the heir male of his great-grandfather William de Percy II.[5] His inheritance, however, was subject to the gift of a large portion made by Agnes to her younger son Richard de Percy, who obtained a moiety of the barony; and this led to a protracted dispute between Richard and his nephew until Richard's death in 1244 without legitimate issue, when the barony was again united,[6]

From William de Percy III the family descended in the male line to Jocelin Percy, earl of Northumberland, who died in 1670, leaving an only daughter Elizabeth, who married Charles Seymour, duke of Somerset, as her third husband.[7] Thus the family had descended in the male line with only one break by reason of the marriage of Agnes de Percy and Jocelin of Louvain.[8]

PERCY (of Bolton Percy)

The family descended from Picot, a tenant of William de Percy at the Domesday survey; and in 1166 3 knights' fees of the old feoffment were held of William de Percy II by Robert son of Picot, lying principally in Bolton Percy, Carnaby, Nesfield and Sutton upon Derwent.[9] Robert, who was known as Robert de Percy son of Picot, died before 1175, when the 3 knights' fees were held by William son of Robert de Percy, being assigned to the share of Jocelin of Louvain.[10]

---

[1] *E. Y.C.*, iii, no. 1492. He was the William who held Burghwallis and Skellow of Ilbert de Lascy at the Survey (*V.C.H. Yorks.*, ii, 165).

[2] Lists of his lands are given in *E. Y.C.*, xi, chapter II.

[3] *Anglo-Norman Families*, pp. 69, 77; *Complete Peerage*, x, pp. 435*n*–36*n*. This supersedes Percy, dept. Manche, arr. St-Lô, the traditional place of origin.

[4] *E. Y.C.*, xi, no. 89, giving an approximate total of 43 knights' fees.

[5] *Complete Peerage*, x, 435 *et seq.*, giving an account of the family; *cf.* also *E. Y.C.*, xi, pp. 1–7 for the early generations.

[6] *Ibid.*, p. 7; and for details of the dispute *Complete Peerage*, p. 450*n*.

[7] *Ibid.*, pp. 452–68; from Elizabeth's granddaughter Elizabeth Seymour the present family of Percy descends.

[8] Through this marriage Petworth became a member of the Percy inheritance. Alnwick was acquired in 1308.

[9] *E. Y.C.*, xi, p. 104.

[10] *Ibid.*, p. 107.

From William the family descended in the male line to Robert de Percy III, who died in 1321, his coheir being Eustachia, sole heir after the death of her sister under age, daughter of his son Peter de Percy II, who had died in 1315, and subsequently wife of Walter de Heslerton.[1]

The family had acquired an interest in Wharram, later known as Wharram Percy, which was held as a tenancy-in-chief by serjeanty service.[2]

PERCY (of Dunsley)

The family descended from Richard a younger son of William de Percy I, who was succeeded by his son William de Percy.[3] The latter was the founder of Handale priory, giving thereto land and pasture in Dunsley;[4] and from his son Richard, living in 1200–02, the family descended in the male line to Peter son of Simon de Percy, living in the fourteenth century, whose heir was Margaret de Percy, wife of Robert Man of Sneaton.[5]

PERCY (of Kildale)

The family descended from Ernald de Percy who witnessed the charter of William de Percy I to the monks of Whitby, c. 1091–1096,[6] and who gave the church of Ormesby to Guisborough priory, 1129–c. 1135.[7] This gift was confirmed by his son Ernald de Percy II,[8] whose heir at his death in 1170 was William son of his brother Robert, then under age.[9] Robert had held Kilnwick, later known as Kilnwick Percy, a member of the Brus fee, quitclaiming the church to St. Peter's York, c. 1160–1165.[10]

William son of Robert de Percy, whose wife was Agnes sistei and coheir of Hugh de Flamville (q.v.),[11] confirmed gifts to Guisborough made by Ernald (*Ernulfus*) de Percy his grandfather and Ernald his uncle, 1171–c. 1195.[12] The holding of the Brus fee consisted of 3 knights' fees in Kilnwick, Kildale, Ormesby and elsewhere.[13] From Walter son of William de Percy, the latter having died by 1203,[14] the family descended in the male line to early in the sixteenth century.[15]

[1] *E.Y.C.*, xi, pp. 107–12, with chart pedigree p. 106.
[2] *Ibid.*, pp. 107–8, 111–12.
[3] *Ibid.*, p. 8.
[4] *Ibid.*
[5] *Ibid.*, and *V.C.H.*, *N.R.*, ii, 518.
[6] *E.Y.C.*, xi, no. 1.
[7] *Ibid.*, ii, no. 746.
[8] *Ibid.*, no. 747.
[9] *Ibid.*, no. 746n.
[10] *Ibid.*, no. 749.
[11] *Ibid.*, no. 746n; *ibid.*, xi, p. 9.
[12] *Ibid.*, ii, no. 751.
[13] *Ibid.*, xi, p. 9.
[14] *Curia Regis Rolls*, iii, 15.
[15] Farrer's detailed accounts of the early generations are given in his notes to *E.Y.C.*, ii, nos. 746, 749. A summary is given in *ibid.*, xi, pp. 8–10. The later generations are given in *V.C.H.*, *N.R.*, ii, 250–1.

REINEVILLE

The family derived its origin from Reineville, dept. Calvados, arr. Vire, cant. Condé-sur-Noireau, comm. Lassy, being a hamlet of Lassy.[1]

At the foundation of St. Clement's chapel in Pontefract castle, *ante c.* 1093, Ilbert de Reineville (*Ramisvilla*) gave two sheaves of his demesne in Campsall, and Girald de Reineville (*Rameswilla*) a moiety of his tithe in Smeaton.[2] That the main line descended from Ilbert can be presumed in view of its interest in Campsall, but the actual descent to Adam de Reineville I, known as 'vetus'[3] has not been established.[4] In a confirmation charter of Henry I in 1122 to Nostell priory the gift by Adam de Reineville of a bovate in 'Histoft' is recorded.[5] He was succeeded by his eldest son William, who held land in Bramley and Armley in 1154, and who gave to Kirkstall abbey land there, for the soul of Cecily his wife, confirming the gift of his father, 1154–75.[6] He witnessed charters of Henry de Lascy to Pontefract priory, 1147–54, and one with Adam his son, 1154–58;[7] and in 1166 he held 4 knights' fees of the Lascy honour of Pontefract.[8]

His son Adam de Reineville II witnessed as steward a charter of Henry de Lascy, when starting for Jerusalem in 1177,[9] and, as steward, with Robert de Lascy who died in 1193.[10] He also served as constable under Roger de Lascy.[11] He made grants of land in Pontefract, 1180–1200;[12] and issued a charter to the priory for the soul of Alice his wife, witnessed by Thomas his son, *c.* 1180–1206.[13] He witnessed several charters of Robert de Lascy, some with Thomas his son, and one with Richard his brother;[14] and in a charter relating to Leeds, 1175–95, he was described as of Armley.[15] He occurs as a member of Roger de Lascy's court in 1201 and 1209, Robert Waleys being steward on both occasions.[16] In 1208 he received a quitclaim

---

[1] *Anglo-Norman Families*, p. 84; not Ranville nr. Caen as in *E.Y.C.*, iii, p. 248*n.* Lassy was the original home of Lascy.

[2] *Ibid.*, no. 1492. Farrer suggested that Robert, the D.B. tenant of Ilbert de Lascy in Smeaton, was the father of Ilbert and Girald (*ibid.*, p. 257).

[3] In the account of the family in *Kirkstall Coucher*, p. 144, Adam 'Vetus' had sons William, Adam, Swain (? an error for Hervey) and Jordan.

[4] Farrer notes that the pedigree in *Pontefract Chartulary*, ii, 310 is full of errors (*E.Y.C.*, iii, no. 1574*n*).

[5] *Ibid.*, no. 1428; *Regesta*, ii, no. 1312, giving the date 10 Jan. 1121–2. The place has not been identified.

[6] *E.Y.C.*, iii, no. 1574 and note.

[7] *Ibid.*, nos. 1499, 1501; and others dated 1144–50 and *c.* 1160–1177 (*ibid.*, nos. 1496, 1773).

[8] *Ibid.*, no. 1508.

[9] *Ibid.*, no. 1629, also wit. by Thomas de Reineville.

[10] *Ibid.*, no. 1786, also wit. by Thomas son of Adam de Reineville.

[11] *Pontefract Chartulary*, no. 174.

[12] *E.Y.C.*, iii, nos. 1575–9.

[13] *Ibid.*, no. 1660.

[14] *Ibid.*, nos. 1509, 1514–5, 1517, 1520–1.

[15] *Ibid.*, no. 1746.

[16] *Ibid.*, nos. 1526, 1695*n*.

of the advowson of a moiety of the church of Campsall,[1] for which he had made a presentation of a previous rector.[2] He had a daughter Clarice who married Robert de Stapleton I (q.v.).[3]

Thomas de Reineville, his son, died in his lifetime; and in 1218 Adam made an arrangement with Eva,[4] Thomas's widow, who claimed as dower a third of the vills of Bramley, Campsall and elsewhere, by granting her the vill of Allerton [-Bywater] and the service of a knight's fee in Askerne.[5] Thomas was probably the Thomas de Reineville who was steward of the Luvetot fee in Hallamshire in the period 1200–18.[6]

On the death of Adam II his successor was his grandson Adam III, who as Adam de Reineville son of Eva de Boby confirmed to Pontefract priory a rent of 10s in Lincoln which his mother had given in her widowhood.[7] As Adam son of Thomas de Reineville he granted a villein in Bramley with his sequel to the priory, mentioning a charter of Adam his grandfather.[8] A record of 1229 shows that he had sworn not to alienate any of his lands of the fee of John de Lascy, constable of Chester, nor any advowsons including that of Kirk Bramwith, without the constable's consent: and in the following year sold to him the manor of Allerton [-Bywater] and the advowson of [Kirk] Bramwith.[9] In 1231 Jordan Foliot (q.v.) quitclaimed any right in the advowson to Adam de Reineville and the constable, referring to the final concord of 1230.[10]

There are no details of a Reineville holding in Bramley, Armley or Campsall in the returns of 1284–85; but in 1428 Thomas de St. Paul held half a knight's fee in Campsall, formerly held by Robert son of Thomas de Reineville of Campsall.[11]

Notes on the family of Longvillers (q.v.) show that Badsworth with the advowson, which had been given by Adam de Reineville I to his younger son Hervey,[12] descended by marriage to that family and so to the Nevilles of Hornby.

Jordan de Reineville, another younger son of Adam de Reineville I, was probably the Jordan who held land in Ecclesfield in 1150–60 and 1171–81, as recorded in charters of Richard de Luvetot and his son William.[13] In 1208 Henry de Vernoil (q.v.) and Maud

---

[1] Yorks. Fines, John, p. 139; in exchange quitclaiming his right in the advowson of a moiety of the chapel of Fenwick, par. Campsall.

[2] Fasti Parochiales, i, 54–6.

[3] E.Y.C., iii, no. 1540n.

[4] Eva de Boby, as below.

[5] Yorks. Fines, 1218–31, p. 9.

[6] E.Y.C., iii, nos. 1279 (where the identification is accepted), 1291–2, 1294. There was a Thomas de Reineville of an earlier generation, a canon of York in the periods 1149–53 and c. 1170–1177 (ibid., i, nos. 67, 584).

[7] Pontefract Chartulary, ii, no. 302.

[8] Ibid., i, no. 214.

[9] Yorks. Fines, 1218–31, p. 130 and note.

[10] Ibid., p. 164.

[11] Feudal Aids, vi, 282.

[12] E.Y.C., iii, no. 1574n; Fasti Parochiales, i, 18.

[13] E.Y.C., iii, nos. 1266–7, 1269.

his wife and Jordan de Reineville, Maud's son, were parties to a final concord against Jordan Foliot for land in Ramesholme;[1] and possibly Maud had married the elder Jordan's son as her first husband. The younger Jordan witnessed charters, c. 1205–1218 and 1200–18.[2] This branch held an interest in Cowley in Ecclesfield, which passed to the Mounteney family by marriage with Margaret de Reineville, said to be the daughter of a Jordan de Reineville.[3]

RICHMOND

Roald son of Harscod, his constable, was given 6 carucates in Barningham by count Stephen of Richmond, c. 1130.[4] He held the constableship under earl Alan and founded Easby abbey, c. 1152.[5] It has been suggested that both he and Richard de Rollos I, whose families held equal portions of the bulk of the Domesday holdings of Enisan Musard married a daughter of Enisan.[6] The identity of Harscod, Roald's father, has not been determined; but the most likely theory, in view of the evidence relating to Tansor, co. Northampton, is that he was a son of Hascolf de St. James (sur Beuvron), the holder of that place, possibly by a second wife.[7]

Roald was succeeded by his son Alan, who held 6½ knights' fees, being a moiety of the Constable's fee and died in 1201, and then by his grandson Roald son of Alan, also constable of Richmond.[8] The descent continued in the male line, the family sometimes adopting the names of Burton and Richmond. In 1321 Roald son of Thomas de Richmond sold the manor of Constable Burton to Geoffrey le Scrope of Masham, and the entire fee passed to the Scrope family.[9]

The family of Rollos, which shared the Constable's fee, took its name from Roullours, dept. Calvados, near Vire. From Richard de Rollos I the inheritance descended to his son Richard de Rollos II, who died in 1195, and then to his grandson William, who forfeited his English lands on the loss of Normandy, his share of the Constable's fee passing to Roald son of Alan the constable.[10]

---

[1] Yorks. Fines, John, p. 139; for Ramsholme see the Vernoil section.
[2] E.Y.C., iii, nos. 1288, 1297.
[3] Eastwood, Hist. Ecclesfield, pp. 355–6. In the Mounteney pedigree in Hunter, Hallamshire, p. 227 Sir Robert de Mounteney is given as the husband of Margaret de Reineville, dau. and coh. in 1266 of Jordan de Reineville, lord of the manor of Cowley, son of Adam de Reineville 'Vetus'. This is certainly impossible; nor is it likely that she was the dau. of Jordan living in 1208; and her father was presumably a later Jordan.
[4] E.Y.C., iv, no. 9.
[5] Ibid., v, p. 89.
[6] Ibid., p. 84.
[7] Ibid., pp. 85–8.
[8] Ibid., pp. 90–3.
[9] Ibid., pp. 93–4; V.C.H., N.R., i, 234; and Yorks. Deeds, vii, nos. 137 et seq., from the Westminster Abbey Muniments.
[10] E.Y.C., v, pp. 95–8.

ROALL

Before the Conquest Baret held land in Kellington, Roall and Eggborough (both in par. Kellington); and in 1086 he held a total of 8 carucates in these places of Ilbert de Lascy.[1] He had also held a manor in Burton Hall (par. Brayton) with berewicks in Brayton and Thorpe-Willoughby, making a total of $3\frac{1}{2}$ carucates;[2] and a manor and soke in Hensall (par. Snaith) consisting of 4 carucates;[3] and although he is not mentioned as Ilbert de Lascy's tenant in these places in 1086 references given below show that his interests had not been lost.

In 1110–30 Baret's son Gamel, described as Gamellus Barret, and the latter's son Richard gave 4 bovates in Thorpe-Willoughby and 3 bovates in Burton Hall, apart from 2 bovates previously given, to Selby abbey.[4] In all the places mentioned above interests were held by the families of Roall and Vernoil (q.v.); and it can be deduced that they were acquired by marriages with the coheirs of Gamel son of Baret. Not later than 1160, as Osbert the archdeacon was a witness, and probably much earlier, Alexander de Roall, with the free-will and consent of A. his wife, confirmed to Selby abbey 2 bovates in Thorpe-Willoughby,[5] evidently representing part of the gift made by Gamel. There can be little doubt that A., Alexander's wife, was a coheir of Gamel. Farrer suggested that she was possibly a daughter of Richard son of Gamel;[6] but on chronological grounds it is more likely that she was Richard's sister. As Baret was holding interests both in 1066 and 1086, his birth can scarcely have been later than c. 1030–35; and as Gamel and his son Richard issued a charter in 1110–30, Richard's birth can be placed as c. 1080–85. The chronology of the Vernoil family suggests that the member who married the other coheir was of that generation.[7]

In 1166 Humphrey de Roall held half a knight's fee of Henry de Lascy.[8] That this represented an interest in the tenure of Gamel son of Baret is shown by a charter of Roger son of Humphrey de Roall to St. Peter's hospital giving land in Eggborough and Roall, 1190–1210.[9] As Humphrey his gift of land in Eggborough to the hospital was confirmed by pope Adrian IV in 1157,[10] and by Henry de Lascy, 1155–70.[11] As Humphrey de Roall he gave a bovate in Roall to Watton priory, which Roger his son confirmed.[12] He

---

[1] *V.C.H. Yorks.*, ii, 248.

[2] *Ibid.*, p. 245. A church, being the church of Brayton, is recorded in this entry; see below.

[3] *Ibid.*, p. 288.

[4] *E.Y.C.*, iii, no. 1622.

[5] *Ibid.*, no. 1623.

[6] *Ibid.*, no. 1622n; but his addition that Agnes mother of Henry de Vernoil was her sister cannot be correct; see the Vernoil section below.

[7] See the chart pedigree given with the account of the family.

[8] *Ibid.*, no. 1508.

[9] *Ibid.*, no. 1625.

[10] *Ibid.*, i, no. 186.

[11] *Ibid.*, iii, no. 1502.

[12] Burton, *Mon. Ebor.*, p. 415.

witnessed a charter to St. Peter's hospital, 1160–70;[1] and with Roger and Henry his sons and Alexander de Roall a charter of Henry de Vernoil [III], giving land in Eggborough to the hospital, 1180–90.[2] He had several other sons[3] and a daughter Margery, who married Malger de Steeton, bringing 2 bovates in Thorpe-Willoughby which she gave to Selby abbey and which her sons Adam and Robert de Steeton confirmed.[4] Humphrey was presumably the Humphrey son of Hubert de Roall who gave to St. Peter's hospital the land of Lund in Hemingbrough, the first witness being Malger de Steeton, 1165–75,[5] although no other Roall interest there appears to be known. No clue has been found for the relationship between Humphrey and Alexander, the husband of the coheir of Gamel son of Baret.[6] It seems, however, that more than one member of the family shared the inheritance at the same time. This can be seen in the charter of Henry de Lascy to the Templars in 1177, when Henry de Vernoil and three members of the Roall family, Alexander (a younger Alexander), John and Roger, were named as his tenants;[7] and also by the joint tenure by Ralph and (a later) Alexander de Roall of the half knight's fee assigned to the dower of Margaret de Lascy in 1241.[8]

Roger de Roall (son of Humphrey) gave land in Eggborough to the Templars, witnessed by Alexander de Roall and Henry de Vernoil, 1175–77.[9] With Alexander he witnessed a charter of Henry de Vernoil giving meadow in Kellington to Pontefract priory;[10] and with Alexander de Roall and Alexander his son and other members of the family a gift of land in Hensall, 1180–1200.[11] In 1185 the prior of Pontefract gave half a mark for a licence for an agreement with him;[12] and he quitclaimed to Robert de Lascy and his monks of Pontefract a carucate in Kellingley (par. Kellington), in exchange for half a carucate in Extwistle (Lancs.).[13]

[1] *E.Y.C.*, ii, no. 849.

[2] *Ibid.*, iii, no. 1630; Alexander must be a younger member of that name.

[3] *Ibid.*, no. 1625n; and *cf.* the witnesses to no. 1660. One of the sons was John r. of Kellington and rural dean of Pontefract.

[4] *Ibid.*, no. 1743n; *Selby Coucher*, i, nos. 423–5. The dates are not later than 1227, when John de Birkin (*q.v.*) a witness died.

[5] *E.Y.C.*, ii, no. 991; but Farrer's suggestion there that it was Hubert who married the coheir of Gamel son of Baret cannot be upheld, conflicting with his note in *ibid.*, iii, no. 1622n.

[6] Chronology does not make it impossible that Hubert was Alexander's son, if Humphrey's birth can be placed at *c.* 1130; but of this no kind of proof is available.

[7] *Ibid.*, no. 1629; these three witnessed and confirmed Henry de Vernoil's charter to the Templars, 1175–77 (*ibid.*, no. 1626).

[8] *Close Rolls*, 1237–42, p. 262.

[9] *E.Y.C.*, iii, no. 1627.

[10] *Ibid.*, no. 1632.

[11] *Ibid.*, i, no. 498. Hensall is one of the places held by Baret before the Conquest.

[12] *Pipe Roll 31 Hen. II*, p. 73.

[13] *E.Y.C.*, iii, no. 1624. No further reference to him in Extwistle is available; the principal Lascy tenants there were the families of Malbisse and Preston (*V.C.H. Lancs.*, vi, 47).

There is no evidence for the links in the descent from the earliest Alexander or from Roger son of Humphrey; but the former may have been the ancestor of Alexander living in 1177 and with Alexander his son in 1180–1200, and of the later Alexander living in 1241, as noted above. An Alexander de Roall, with the consent of Lena his wife and Roger his heir, quitclaimed to Selby abbey a rent of 4s for 2 bovates in Thorpe-Willoughby and 2 bovates in Burton Hall not later than 1227, John de Birkin being a witness.[1] An Alexander de Roall and Alice his wife occur later than 1290.[2]

In 1202 Ralph son of John de Roall was a party in a final concord with Simon de Roall for land in Sherwood Hall in Eggborough, Amabel, Ralph's wife being mentioned;[3] and in February 1218–9 was called to warranty for land in Hensall.[4] Not later than 1227 he confirmed to Selby abbey his right of patronage in a third of the church of Brayton.[5] He had a son Ralph who quitclaimed to Selby a rent of 4s 9d for 3 bovates in Thorpe-Willoughby and 3 bovates in Burton Hall.[6] It was probably this younger Ralph who shared with Alexander de Roall the half knight's fee in 1241, mentioned above, and who was the father of John son of Ralph de Roall who sold rents in Hensall[7] in the same preiod as Henry son of Henry de Vernoil (*q.v.*) sold lands there.

There is no information in the returns of 1284–85 to show that any members of the Roall family were then holding interests in the places mentioned in these notes. In 1401–02 and 1428 the interest in Roall was held by the Preston family;[8] and, as noted above, that family were tenants in Extwistle where Roger de Roall had acquired land in exchange.

ROS (of Helmsley)

Peter de Ros, whose parentage is unknown, almost certainly took his name from Roos in Holderness. He was steward of the count of Aumale, lord of Holderness, and married Adeline, sister and coheir of Walter Espec, lord of Helmsley. He died before 1130, when Everard his son and heir rendered account of 2 marks that he might no longer be steward of the count of Aumale. Everard died in or before 1153, being succeeded by Robert his brother, who inherited their uncle's tenure of Helmsley. From Robert the family descended in the male line to 1508, when the inheritance passed to George Manners of Belvoir, nephew of the tenth lord Ros.[9]

[1] *Selby Coucher*, i, no. 459.
[2] *Yorks. Deeds*, vii, no. 320.
[3] *Yorks. Fines, John*, p. 46.
[4] *Rolls of the Justices* . . . Selden Soc., vol. lvi, no. 284.
[5] *Selby Coucher*, i, no. 336. An interest in the church was also held by the Vernoil family (*q.v.*).
[6] *Ibid.*, no. 415. This can be compared with Alexander's quitclaim noted above.
[7] *Yorks. Deeds*, x, no. 284.
[8] *Feudal Aids*, vi, pp. 282, 597.
[9] *Complete Peerage*, xi, pp. 90 *et seq.;* and for some further details of the early generations *E.Y.C.*, x, pp. 144–7.

ST. QUINTIN

The family held a tenancy of the honour of Gloucester. It is stated[1] that the descent was from Richard (if his first name is correctly recorded) de St. Quintin, a knight of Robert FitzHamon at the conquest of Glamorgan c. 1090. His relationship to Herbert de St. Quintin I, from whom the family descended,[2] is uncertain; but they were probably father and son, Herbert's son being named Richard.

Herbert de St. Quintin witnessed a charter to Glastonbury abbey c. 1102.[3] In 1115-18 he held land in Thorganby and Stainton le Vale, co. Lincoln, of Stephen count of Aumale, lord of Holderness.[4] By his first wife he had a son Richard (see below); and he married secondly, as her first husband, Agnes sister of William de Arches (q.v.). Agnes was the foundress of Nunkeeling priory, to which she gave the church of Nunkeeling and 3 carucates there with a croft and woodland for the souls of Herbert de St. Quintin her husband and Walter and Alan her sons.[5] Her gifts were confirmed by Richard de St. Quintin (her step-son) of whom she held the land; and by William count of Aumale, and by William archbishop of York at her request being described as mother of Peter de Fauconberg and at the request of her sons William and Hugh Foliot.[6] By Herbert de St. Quintin she was the mother of Walter and Alan who died without issue and of a daughter Alice who married Robert son of Fulk, steward of William de Percy, and was the foundress of Nun Appleton priory and subsequently the wife of Eustace de Merc.[7]

Herbert de St. Quintin died not later than 1129 when Richard his son witnessed an agreement between the bishop of Llandaff and Robert earl of Gloucester.[8] Richard witnessed the foundation of Neath abbey in 1130;[9] and the agreement between William count of Aumale and John de Meaux c. 1150-51[10] and, with Herbert his brother, a charter of the count to Bridlington priory, c. 1147-1168.[11] In 1166 he held 10 knights' fees of the old feoffment of the earl of Gloucester,[12] and apparently one fee of the honour of Holderness.[13]

[1] *Complete Peerage*, xi, 368n.

[2] A. S. Ellis, 'The De St. Quintins' in E. R. Ant. Soc., *Transactions*, vol. x, 19-24. It is clear that Herbert de St. Quintin was the *first* husband of Agnes de Arches and not, as stated there, a widow when he married her.

[3] *Ibid.*, p. 20.

[4] *Lindsey Survey*, p. 244.

[5] *E.Y.C.*, iii, no. 1331. The priory is said to have been founded in 1152 (*Mon. Ang.*, iv, 185).

[6] *E.Y.C.*, iii, nos. 1332-4; the latest date of the abp's confirmn is 1154.

[7] Chart pedigree of the Arches family in *ibid.*, i, p. 420; and see *ibid.*, xi, pp. 94-5 and the Foliot and Kyme sections above.

[8] Ellis, *op. cit.*, p. 21.

[9] *Ibid.*; *Mon. Ang.*, v, 259.

[10] *E.Y.C.*, iii, no. 1379.

[11] *Ibid.*, no. 1340.

[12] *Red Bk. Exch.*, p. 288.

[13] *E.Y.C.*, iii, no. 1305n. This can be located in Brandesburton, and several other places named in *Feudal Aids*, vi, 40, held by his descendant in 1284-85; the total holding was 45 car. 5 bov., 52 car. making a k.f.

In 1147 or later he disclaimed right in the church of Frome, Dorset, of which the advowson was claimed by his son Herbert in 1205.[1]

Herbert de St. Quintin II, son of Richard, who held the 10 fees of the honour of Gloucester,[2] was a benefactor of Thornton abbey, an Aumale foundation, giving land in Stainton,[3] where as noted above Herbert I had a tenancy in 1115–18. He married Agnes one of the five sisters and coheirs of Anselm de Stuteville of Weston Coleville, co. Cambridge, and Burton Agnes, who was dead in 1199, his interest obtained thereby descending to younger lines.[4] He was eventually succeeded by a younger son William, whose son Herbert was summoned for service from 1282 to 1297, but not to Parliament, and died in 1302, holding Brandesburton in Holderness and tenancies of the earl of Gloucester, his heir being his grandson Herbert, aged eighteen.[5] This last Herbert's heir was his granddaughter Lora, ancestress of the Herbert earls of Pembroke.[6]

SALVAIN

The family, which gave its name to Thorpe Salvin, wap. Strafforth, held a tenancy there of the honour of Tickhill, and one in Swinton, par. Wath upon Dearne, of that portion of the Tison fee (*q.v.*) which became a member of the honour of Mowbray.

The earliest ancestor was Osbert Salvain I, sheriff of Nottinghamshire and Derbyshire in 1130, and the donor of land in Swinton to Nostell priory.[7] The family also held a tenancy of the bishop of Lincoln; Osbert Salvain II, grandson of Osbert I, holding a knight's fee of the bishop in 1166, which lay at Silk Willoughby, where his son Ralph II held a knight's fee in 1210–12.[8] The family descended in the male line to Nicholas Salvain living in 1364, having sold the manor of Thorpe Salvin to William de Sandford, clerk.[9]

There were two other families of the name of Salvain. One of these held land in Thorpe le Street, where Gilbert Tison held a manor at the Survey, and continued in the male line to the fifteenth century.[10] The other descended from Hugh Salvain who held 4 knights' fees of the bishop of Lincoln in 1166, and occurs as Hugh

---

[1] *Complete Peerage*, xi, 368*n*.

[2] *Ibid.*

[3] *Mon. Ang.*, vi, 327.

[4] *E.Y.C.*, ix, pp. 29–34, giving details, the St. Quintins of Harpham descending from Sir Alexander de St. Quintin who made his will there in 1257.

[5] *Complete Peerage*, xi, 358 and note; *Yorks. Inq.*, iv, no. 21. The grandson, who was born at Frome St. Quintin, Dorset, proved his age in 1306 (*ibid.*, no. 103).

[6] *Complete Peerage*, *ut sup.*

[7] *E.Y.C.*, xii, pp. 97–103, giving an account of the family with a chart pedigree. Osbert's charters recording his gift to Nostell and noting the overlordships of Roger de Mowbray and Tison are pd at nos. 74–6, of date 1143–54.

[8] *Ibid.*, p. 100.

[9] *Ibid.*, p. 102; and for the sale of the manor *Yorks. Fines*, 1347–77, p. 95; *Yorks. Deeds*, viii, no. 394. Notes on the Sandford family at Thorpe Salvin in the 15th and 16th cents. are given in Hunter, *South Yorkshire*, i, 309–10.

[10] *E.Y.C.*, xii, pp. 109–12.

Salvain of Dunsby, where in 1086 the bishop's tenant was Ralf.[1] It may be significant that Ralf was also the bishop's tenant at Silk Willoughby, where the Salvains of Thorpe Salvin held an interest; and coupled with the fact that Osbert Salvain I's son and heir was a Ralph Salvain the suggestion can be tentatively made that Ralf, the bishop's tenant, was the ancestor of the Salvains of Thorpe Salvin, Hugh being closely related.[2]

SCROPE

By a charter, which can be dated early in the reign of Henry II, Alice the countess (of Northampton), daughter of Gilbert de Gant, confirmed to Robert Scrop of Barton (upon Humber, co. Lincoln) son of Richard Scrop and of Agnes, the grantor's maternal aunt,[3] land which his ancestors had held of her ancestors in Barton, namely a quarter of the vill, for the service of half a knight's fee.[4] Robert can be identified as Robert Scrop or Scropes who held a knight's fee of earl Simon, Alice's husband, as of the Gant fee in 1166.[5] One half of this fee certainly lay in Barton, and the remaining half probably in Flotmanby, par. Folkton, wap. Dickering, where R. Escrop (presumably Robert or Richard his father) gave land to Bridlington priory, his charter being witnessed by earl Simon.[6] The Scropes of Barton descended in the male line to Joice Scrope who died in 1304.[7]

The two Chief Justices Henry le Scrope of Bolton and his brother Geoffrey le Scrope of Masham were descended in the male line from Simon le Scrope of Flotmanby and Wensley, a younger brother of Philip le Scrope of Flotmanby.[8] In 1205 the daughters of Philip conveyed to Simon land in Flotmanby and elsewhere in wap. Dickering;[9] and Simon and his son Henry each gave land there to Bridlington priory.[10] There can be little doubt, especially in view of

[1] *Ibid.*, p. 103.
[2] *Ibid.*
[3] The mother of countess Alice was Rohaise dau. of Richard FitzGilbert de Clare (*E.Y.C.*, ii, pp. 433–4). Agnes wife of Richard Scrop was therefore a sister of Rohaise.
[4] *Ibid.*, no. 1217; and *Bradford Antiquary*, i, 213 from the original. Of five of the witnesses four witnessed a charter of Gilbert de Gant and four another of his charters, both *ante* 1156 when he died (*Hatton Bk. of Seals*, no. 297; *E.Y.C.*, ii, no. 1219). Farrer's date for no. 1217, 1184–85, was based on the assumption that it was issued after the death of Simon earl of Northampton (no. 1216*n*); but there are several instances of an heiress issuing a charter in her husband's lifetime, *e.g.* one of Maud de Percy in the lifetime of her husband the earl of Warwick (*E.Y.C.*, xi, nos. 53–4). The first of Gilbert de Gant's charters noted here was witnessed by Richard Scrop, evidently Robert's father; and the countess's confirmation to Robert was presumably issued shortly after his father's death, and certainly not before 1156.
[5] *Ibid.*, ii, no. 1139.
[6] *Bridlington Chartulary*, p. 80. Farrer assigned Barton and Flotmanby as the location of the k.f. in 1166 (*E.Y.C.*, ii, p. 430*n*).
[7] *Complete Peerage*, xi, 532; giving a survey of the early generations.
[8] *Ibid.*, pp. 532 *et seq.*
[9] *Yorks. Fines, John*, p. 94.
[10] *Bridlington Chartulary*, pp. 82, 87.

the Flotmanby evidence, that Philip and Simon represented a younger line of the Scropes of Barton; but the actual relationship has not been established.[1]

From Henry le Scrope of Bolton, who died in 1366, his descendants continued in the male line to Emanuel, lord Scrope of Bolton, who died without legitimate issue in 1630; and from Geoffrey le Scrope of Masham, who died in 1340, to Geoffrey lord Scrope of Masham, who died unmarried in 1517.[2]

It has been conjectured that the family was connected with the Gloucestershire family of Scrupes, but it has been shown that for this there is no evidence.[3]

SCURES (of Long Riston)

The family descended from Anschetil de Scures, who as stated in the Meaux Chronicle,[4] was lord of Long Riston in Holderness, and who at the Lindsey survey held 6½ bovates at Hackthorn, co. Lincoln, of Stephen count of Aumale.[5] It has been suggested that his family, unconnected with that which derived its name from Escures, arr. Bayeux, and held a tenancy of Port of Basing, came from Ecuires by Montreuil-sur-Mer which belonged to the counts of Ponthieu, count Enguerrand being the first husband of Adeliz mother of Stephen count of Aumale.[6]

In 1130 Alan de Scures, who can be identified as the son of Anschetil, was pardoned 75s for the old pleas of Holderness, and rendered account of 15li. for the dower of his wife, paying 10 marks on account.[7] He built a church at Long Riston which was found to be harmful to the mother-church of Hornsea.[8] Confirmation charters of William de Scures show that Robert his brother, whom he had succeeded before 1166, gave to Bridlington priory 2 bovates in Acklam in exchange for 4 bovates in [Long] Riston which Anschetil his grandfather had given; and that William gave the demesne toft of Alan de Scures his father in Acklam and added 4 further bovates there.[9] These gifts were confirmed by Stephen son of Herbert the

[1] *Complete Peerage*, xi, 532.
[2] *Ibid.*, pp. 535–72.
[3] 'The Family of Scrupes or Crupes of Whittington, co. Gloucester' in *Trans. Bristol and Glos. Arch. Soc.*, lxv, 129–40, where the account of the Scrope family by Sir Harris Nicolas in *Scrope and Grosvenor Roll*, vol. ii, in which there is confusion between the two families, is examined.
[4] Vol. i, pp. 96–8, giving a detailed account of the family.
[5] *Lindsey Survey*, p. 239.
[6] *Anglo-Norman Families*, p. 97.
[7] *Pipe Roll 31 Hen. I*, p. 26.
[8] *E.Y.C.*, iii, no. 1348.
[9] *Ibid.*, ii, no. 826; *Bridlington Chartulary*, p. 225. The second charter was issued for the souls of William's grandfather and father, Robert his brother and Alan de Monceaux (*q.v.*). The latter was a benefactor of Nun Coton priory, co. Lincoln, his charter being witnessed by Richard de Scures (*Mon. Ang.*, v, 676). Possibly the two families, both tenants of the honour of Holderness, were connected by marriage. The wife of William de Scures was named Milicent (*E.Y.C.*, iii, no. 1348).

chamberlain, 1170–85, of whose fee the land in Acklam was held, and of whom William de Scures held a knight's fee of the old feoffment in 1166.[1] William de Scures gave to Thornton abbey the vill of Humbleton in Holderness and the churches of Humbleton and Acklam.[2] His heir was his sister Maud, who together with her successive husbands Turgis de Bray and William de Funtenay issued charters relating to Long Riston;[3] and on her death without issue the inheritance passed to her first cousin Walter son of Richard de Scures, the latter being described as her uncle.[4] Walter was succeeded by his son Sir Robert de Scures, whose daughter and heir Joan married Robert de Hildyard;[5] and in 1278 Robert de Scures gave them the manor of Long Riston for a yearly rent of 1d.[6] In 1284–85 Robert Hildyard held 48 carucates in Holderness at Long Riston and elsewhere;[7] and by the marriage of his great-granddaughter Long Riston passed to the family of Nuthill.[8]

STAPLETON (of Stapleton)

At the Domesday survey Gislebert held Stapleton, par. Darrington, and Thorpe Stapleton, par. Whitkirk, of Ilbert de Lascy.[9] As Gilbert son of Dama he gave 2 thraves of his tithe in Stapleton to the chapel of St. Clement in Pontefract castle before c. 1093.[10] He was succeeded by his son Hugh, who as Hugh de Stapleton witnessed a charter of Hugh de Laval to Pontefract priory, confirming a gift of Robert de Lascy, c. 1122–1129;[11] and as Hugh son of G[ilbert] a charter of William Maltravers, the sucessor of Hugh de Laval, to the same, 1130–36.[12] Hugh de Stapleton and William his son witnessed a charter of Ilbert de Lascy II to Ralph le Rus, 1135–41;[13] and they both witnessed an ordinance of archbishop Thurstan notifying an agreement with Pontefract priory relating to the church of Darrington and lands of the chapel of Stapleton, 1137–40.[14]

[1] E.Y.C., ii, nos. 825 with note and 827. For Stephen son of Herbert the chamberlain of the kg of Scotland see ibid., xi, pp. 213–9, and the account of the Chamberlain family above.

[2] Ibid., iii, no. 1312.

[3] Ibid., no. 1349 and note; a charter of hers in her full power being dated 1185–1200.

[4] Chron. de Melsa, i, 97. Richard (see the note above) is mentioned in a confirmn of pope Alexander III to Nun Coton as the son and heir of Juet[ta] de Verli (Mon. Ang., v, 676). She must therefore have been a wife of Anschetil de Scures; and as Richard was her son and heir she was presumably a second wife, Richard being a half-brother of Alan, Anschetil's son and heir.

[5] Chron. de Melsa, i, 97–8. In 1275 a quitclaim of right in the manor of Riston was given to Robert de Hildyard and Joan his wife (Poulson, Holderness, i, 342); for Joan's parentage with notes on the family see E.Y.C., iii, no. 1345n.

[6] Yorks. Fines, 1272–1300, p. 13.

[7] Feudal Aids, vi, 40.

[8] Chron. de Melsa, i, 98. The descent is shown in the pedigree in Poulson, Holderness, i, 341–2.

[9] E.Y.C., iii, no. 1633n, giving details of the early generations.

[10] Ibid., no. 1492.

[11] Ibid., no. 1487.

[12] Ibid., no. 1489.

[13] Lancs. Pipe Rolls and Early Charters, p. 387.

[14] E.Y.C., iii, no. 1470.

William was succeeded by his son Robert, who as Robert de Stapleton son of William de Stapleton gave land in Stapleton to Pontefract priory, 1160–70;[1] and as Robert de Stapleton held 2 knights' fees of the old feoffment of Henry de Lascy in 1166.[2] Robert, who married Clarice daughter of Adam de Reineville (q.v.), was succeeded before 1202 by his son William de Stapleton II,[3] who occurs as a knight of the honour of Pontefract in 1213.[4] William was succeeded by his son Robert II, who as Robert son of William son of Robert de Stapleton confirmed to Pontefract priory a gift of Robert his grandfather,[5] and who held 2 knights' fees less a fifth of the Lascy fee in 1242–43.[6] Robert de Stapleton II was living in 1255, when he was granted free warren in Stapleton, Thorpe Stapleton and Cudworth.[7] He died before 1284–85, when his heirs held Thorpe Stapleton;[8] and the inheritance passed to the families of le Botiler and Scargill into which his two daughters and eventual coheirs had married.[9] In 1401–02 Joan widow of Sir John de Scargill held of the duchy of Lancaster 2 knights' fees less a fifth (the precise holding in 1242–43) in Stapleton and elsewhere, which had been held by Sir Warin de Scargill and Roald le Boteler, subject to certain deductions in favour of members of the Scargill family.[10]

The family had no connexion with that of Stapleton which held a tenancy in Stapleton, par. Croft, of the honour of Richmond.[11]

STONEGRAVE

The family held land by knight-service of the Paynels of Drax (q.v.), which included holdings in Stonegrave and Nunnington, wap. Ryedale;[12] and a sixth of a knight's fee of the old feoffment held by William de Stonegrave of Everard de Ros in 1166.[13]

William and Simon de Stonegrave witnessed a charter of William Paynel to Drax priory, c. 1130–1139[14] From William de Stonegrave the family descended in the male line to John de

---

[1] E.Y.C., iii, no. 1633.
[2] Ibid., no. 1508.
[3] Yorks. Fines, John, p. 72.
[4] E.Y.C., iii, p. 293.
[5] Pontefract Chartulary, i, no. 224, where the date assigned, c. 1180, is far too early.
[6] Bk. of Fees, p. 1102.
[7] E.Y.C., iii, no. 1633n.
[8] Feudal Aids, vi, 18.
[9] Pontefract Chartulary, i, p. xlvi. From a memorandum in the Kirkstall Coucher, no. 203, which however is partly inaccurate, it can be supposed that Robert de Stapleton II had a son and heir William, whose two daughters died s.p., when the inheritance passed to William's two sisters and so to the Scargill and le Boteler families.
[10] Feudal Aids, vi, 597.
[11] Notes on that family are given in E.Y.C., v, no. 338An.
[12] An account of the family is given in ibid., vi, pp. 119–22.
[13] Red Bk. Exch., p. 433. This holding lay in the lost vill of Riccal, wap. Ryedale, where in 1284–85 John de Stonegrave held 2 car. of Robert de Ros for ⅛ k.f. (Feudal Aids, vi, 65).
[14] E.Y.C., vi, no. 13.

Stonegrave who died in 1295.[1] He married Ida, one of the three daughters of Baldwin Wake and his wife Ela, one of the three daughters of William de Beauchamp, thus acquiring in her right a ninth part of the barony of Beauchamp of Bedford.[2] His daughter and heir Isabel married Simon de Pateshull,[3] in whose family the inheritance descended.[4]

STUTEVILLE

Several branches of the family, both in Normandy and England, descended from Robert de Stuteville I, who derived his name from Etoutteville-sur-Mer, dept. Seine–Maritime, arr. Yvetot, cant. Yerville. He was granted the main portion of the lands in Yorkshire and elsewhere, of which Hugh son of Baldric had been tenant-in-chief at the Domesday survey. After his imprisonment, due to his support of duke Robert at the battle of Tinchebrai in 1106, a large portion of his English lands was granted to Nigel d'Aubigny, father of Roger de Mowbray. Certain of his lands, which included Cottingham, were restored to his grandson Robert de Stuteville III, who claimed other lands against Roger de Mowbray; and as a compromise he was enfeoffed by the latter of 10 knights' fees including the manor of Kirkby Moorside. In 1166 he held in chief 8 knights' fees of the old feoffment and an eighth of a fee of the new, in addition to his tenure of the honour of Mowbray.[5] The dispute with Mowbray continued during the twelfth century; and eventually, by a settlement made in 1201, William de Mowbray gave to William de Stuteville, son of Robert III, 9 knights' fees as an increase of the original 10.[6]

The main line of the family in England descended to Nicholas de Stuteville II, who died in 1233.[7] His elder daughter Joan and eventually sole heir married Hugh Wake, the ancestor of Joan wife of Edward the Black Prince.[8]

The Stutevilles of Warwickshire descended from John de Stuteville, a younger son of Robert de Stuteville II;[9] and there is evidence that it was his daughter who married Meldred son of Dolfin, lord of Raby.[10] The Stutevilles of Weston Colville, co. Cambridge, and Burton Agnes descended from Osmund de Stuteville, probably

---

[1] Chart pedigree in *E.Y.C.*, vi, p. 122.
[2] *Ibid.*, pp. 120–1.
[3] *Ibid.*, p. 121. An account of John de Stonegrave is in *Complete Peerage*, xii (i), p. 276.
[4] For the descent in Yorks. see *V.C.H.*, *N.R.*, i, 545; and for the family of Pateshull, taking its name from Pattishall, nr. Towcester, co. Northampton, *Complete Peerage*, x, 311–6.
[5] *E.Y.C.*, ix, pp. 1–5; and for his *carta* of 1166 no. 67. For Mowbray's *carta*, giving only 9 fees held by Robert de Stuteville III, see *Mowbray Charters*, no. 401.
[6] *E.Y.C.*, ix, nos. 42–4.
[7] *Ibid.*, pp. 1–23, with chart pedigree facing p. 1.
[8] *Ibid.*, p. 23.
[9] *Ibid.*, pp. 23–7, with chart pedigree p. 24.
[10] See above in the Neville of Raby section.

another son of Robert de Stuteville II; and the male line ended with the death of Anselm de Stuteville not later than 1199, leaving five sisters as his heirs.[1] And the Stutevilles of Cowesby, wap. Birdforth, held of the main line, and of Gressenhall, Norfolk, held of the honour of Warenne, descended from another Osmund, probably a younger son of Robert de Stuteville III, whose descendant Robert de Stuteville died in 1275, leaving as his heir his nephew Jordan Foliot (*q.v.*).[2]

The main line of the family in Normandy, where the caput of the honour was Valmont, dept. Seine–Maritime, arr. Yvetot, cant. Valmont, descended from Nicholas d'Estouteville, the founder of the abbey of Valmont in 1169, to which he gave not only lands and churches in Normandy, but also the church of Stratfield in Hampshire.[3] His interest in the latter place, where Hugh son of Baldric had held a tenancy-in-chief in 1086, shows that he was of the same family as Robert de Stuteville I; and it is probable that he was the eldest son of Robert de Stuteville II. He died in 1177.[4] By marriage with Leonia daughter of Edward of Salisbury and Adeliz de Rames his son Robert d'Estouteville acquired in her right the manor of Rames in Normandy and considerable interests in England, which included 15 knights' fees mainly in Nottinghamshire and Derbyshire.[5] Leonia's interests in England were inherited by her descendants, the d'Estoutevilles of Normandy, who forfeited them from time to time when war with France was in progress; eventually they passed to a younger line early in the fourteenth century, and finally to the king's hand with the lands of aliens in view of the approaching war with France.[6]

The main line in Normandy descended from father to son until the sixteenth century when Adrienne daughter and heir of Jean d'Estouteville married François de Bourbon; and in 1534 the duchy d'Estouteville was created in their favour.[7]

TATTERSHALL

The family descended from Eudo son of Spirewic who held a tenancy-in-chief at the Domesday survey in Lincolnshire, Norfolk and Suffolk, and his son Hugh who held an interest in Tattershall and several other places in Lincolnshire at the Lindsey survey.[8] Hugh's son Robert, the founder of Kirkstead abbey in 1139, held 25 knights' fees in chief in 1166, one of his tenants being William

---

[1] *E.Y.C.*, ix, pp. 27–34.
[2] *Ibid.*, pp. 34–7; and for two other branches of the Stuteville family pp. 37–40.
[3] *Ibid.*, pp. 41–65, giving a detailed account of the Norman line with a chart pedigree; notes are given of several younger lines.
[4] *Ibid.*, p. 41.
[5] *Ibid.*, pp. 48–54.
[6] *Ibid.*, pp. 63–5.
[7] *Ibid.*, p. 63.
[8] A full account of the family is in *Complete Peerage*, xii(i), pp. 645–53. Documentary references not given here are in that article.

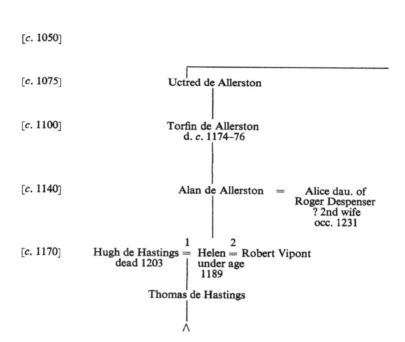

Suggested lines of descent.

[Born *c.* 1020]

[*c.* 1050]

[*c.* 1075]   Uctred de Allerston

[*c.* 1100]   Torfin de Allerston
               d. *c.* 1174–76

[*c.* 1140]   Alan de Allerston   =   Alice dau. of
                                         Roger Despenser
                                         ? 2nd wife
                                         occ. 1231

                                1   2
[*c.* 1170]   Hugh de Hastings = Helen = Robert Vipont
               dead 1203   │ under age
                                 │ 1189
                      Thomas de Hastings

                            ∧

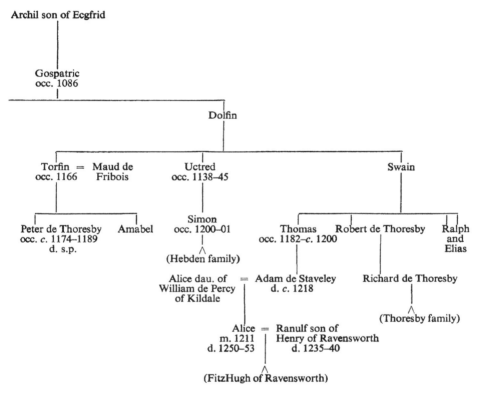

Archil son of Ecgfrid

Gospatric
occ. 1086

Dolfin

Torfin = Maud de
occ. 1166   Fribois

Uctred
occ. 1138–45

Swain

Peter de Thoresby   Amabel
occ. c. 1174–1189
d. s.p.

Simon
occ. 1200–01

∧
(Hebden family)

Thomas   Robert de Thoresby   Ralph
occ. 1182–c. 1200   and
                                                      Elias

Alice dau. of   = Adam de Staveley
William de Percy   d. c. 1218
of Kildale

Richard de Thoresby

∧
(Thoresby family)

Alice = Ranulf son of
m. 1211   Henry of Ravensworth
d. 1250–53   d. 1235–40

∧
(FitzHugh of Ravensworth)

son of Hervey, whose gift to the Templars of land in West Witton, a member of the honour of Richmond in Yorkshire, he confirmed with the description of Robert son of Hugh de Tadeshal'.[1] As Robert son of Hugh son of Eudo de Tateshal' he permitted Kirkstead abbey to move to a more convenient site, giving pasture in Tattershall and elsewhere, c. 1187.[2] He can be identified as the Robert son of Hugh de Westwittone who held half a knight's fee of the honour of Richmond in Yorkshire in the twelfth century.[3] His father Hugh son of Eudo can therefore almost certainly be the Hugh son of Eon[4] who held 2 knights' fees for castle-guard at Richmond in a return mainly of the time of Henry I, one of the fees being at Horningtoft, Norfolk.[5]

From Robert son of Hugh de Tattershall the family descended in the male line to Robert de Tattershall who was summoned to Parliament from 1295 to 1297, and so to the latter's grandson Robert who died without issue shortly before 30 January 1305-6, when his heirs were his three aunts, one of whom, Joan, married Robert de Driby. In 1316 West Witton and Swinithwaite in West Witton were held by Joan de Driby.[6]

THORESBY and STAVELEY
§1.

The traditional pedigree of the Thoresby family was due to a Cottonian roll, compiled in the time of Henry VI and now lost, which was printed by Roger Gale in 1722.[7] The descent given there was from Gospatric son of Archil through his son Dolfin. Both A. S. Ellis[8] and Farrer[9] were not satisfied of the existence of a son of Gospatric named Dolfin. A charter, however, is now available, cited in the Hebden section above, in which Gospatric is described as the grandfather of Uctred son of Dolfin.

Among his many holdings at the Survey Gospatric held of count Alan a carucate in Thoresby, in Carperby, par. Aysgarth, and a manor in Askrigg, par. Aysgarth, formerly held by Archil.[10]

---

[1] *E.Y.C.*, v, no. 389 and note.
[2] *Danelaw Charters*, no. 180.
[3] *E.Y.C.*, v, p. 14.
[4] A note on the identity of the names Eudo and Eon is in *Complete Peerage*, loc. cit., p. 645n.
[5] *E.Y.C.*, v, pp. 12, 337.
[6] *Feudal Aids*, vi, 186.
[7] *Reg. Honoris de Richmond*, App. between pp. 56–7. It was probably based on this source that Ralph Thoresby's own pedigree in *Ducatus Leodiensis*, 1st ed. 1715, p. 71, supplied to him by Peter Le Neve, shows the descent from Dolfin son of Gospatric.
[8] 'Notes on Ralph Thoresby's Pedigree' in *Miscellanea*, Thoresby Soc., ix, 112–25.
[9] In his Introduction to the Domesday survey of Yorkshire in *V.C.H. Yorks.*, ii, 184.
[10] *Ibid.*, p. 236. From Gospatric's son Uctred descended the family of Allerston (*q.v.*).

In the Cottonian roll Dolfin is given three sons Torfin, Uctred and Swain. Certainly Uctred son of Dolfin was the father of Simon the ancestor of the Hebden family (*q.v.*). Torfin is given as the father of Peter de Thoresby, and Swain as the father of Robert de Thoresby, to whom Thoresby passed from his cousin Peter who died without issue; and further Swain is given as having three other sons Ralph, Thomas from whom the Staveley family descended, and Elias, and also a daughter Gonelle wife of John Morville. Documentary evidence in proof of these statements is far from satisfactory; but some light is given by the following notes.

In 1166 Torfin son of Dolfin was amerced in the wapentake of Hang for a concealment.[1] In *c.* 1174–1189 Peter son of Torfin de Askrigg (presumably the same man as Peter de Thoresby) gave to Marrick priory a third of 6 bovates in Carperby, together with Amabel his sister, the second witness being Thomas son of Swain; and on the same occasion, the witnesses being the same, Alan son of Adam made a similar gift describing Amabel as his maternal aunt.[2] Swain son of Dolfin gave to Jervaulx abbey a carucate in Horton [in Ribblesdale]; and Ralph son of Swain, mentioned in the Cottonian roll, gave 2 bovates and the service of another bovate there.[3]

No documentary evidence has been found for Robert de Thoresby, said to be a son of Swain. If he was the cousin of Peter son of Torfin he would have been living late in the twelfth century. There is no reason to doubt the descent from him in the male line.[4] Richard de Thoresby, given in the Cottonian roll as Robert's son, can be identified as the Richard de Thoresby who witnessed a Marrick charter before 1204.[5]

In 1286–87 of the 9 carucates in Carperby Peter son of Hugh de Thoresby held 18 bovates of Avice Marmion, who held of the earl of Richmond; and of the 3 carucates in Thoresby he held all except 2 bovates of the heirs of William son of Nicholas of York,[6] who held of the steward's fee of the earldom, the remaining 2 bovates being held of Peter by Hugh de Thoresby.[7] In 1316 Thoresby was held by Hugh de Thoresby.[8]

---

[1] *Pipe Roll 12 Hen. II*, p. 48. Thoresby is in Hang West wap.
[2] *E.Y.C.*, v, nos. 216–7. Farrer, cited there in no. 216*n*, was of opinion that the descendants of Dolfin given in the roll and the descent of the Thoresby and Staveley families from Swain son of Dolfin are in the main correct.
[3] *Mon. Ang.*, v, 576; a confirmn of Henry III, 12 Feb. 1227–8; and see the gift in Horton by Adam de Staveley in §2 below.
[4] See A. S. Ellis, *ut sup.* Ralph Thoresby's pedigree in *Ducatus, ut sup.* has considerable variations from that in the Cottonian roll, and also from that in *Glover's Visitation*, Add. Pedigrees, p. 635; but they all give a descent from Robert de Thoresby and his son Richard.
[5] *E.Y.C.*, v, no. 126.
[6] Heir of the Hebden family (*q.v.*); he died in 1282.
[7] *Feudal Aids*, vi, pp. 85, 87.
[8] *Ibid.*, p. 186.

§2.

In the Cottonian roll the Staveley family is given as descending from Thomas son of Swain son of Dolfin, and then from Thomas to his son Adam de Staveley, whose daughter and heir Alice married Ranulf son of Henry of Ravensworth, the ancestor of the family of FitzHugh (q.v.). Evidence given below shows that these statements are correct; and as it has been shown above that Dolfin was a son of Gospatric son of Archil it can be deduced that the Staveley family, as that of Thoresby, descended from Gospatric.

Thomas son of Swain de Staveley gave land in Airton, retaining the lordship of the vill, late twelfth century.[1] Thomas son of Swain and Adam his son witnessed a Threshfield charter,[2] and with Elias son of Swain and Acaris his son an Arncliffe charter, 1182–c. 1200.[3] Adam de Staveley gave to Bolton priory land in Calton;[4] he confirmed to Fountains abbey all lands held of his fee in Ilton, Swinton and Warthermarske (in Swinton);[5] and was named with other free tenants, including Simon de Hebden, in Ilton and Swinton in 1200–01.[6] In Ilton an interest had been held of count Alan at the Domesday survey by Gospatric, a manor having been previously held there by Archil.[7] Adam de Staveley gave to St. Clement's priory, York, 2 bovates in Horton in Ribblesdale, which were attached to the church later given to the priory by his daughter Alice in her widowhood;[8] and it was there, as noted above, that Swain son of Dolfin gave a carucate to Jervaulx abbey.[9] In an Assize roll of 1203–4 it is recorded that William de Mowbray and Adam de Staveley made an agreement by which the latter acknowledged to the former all his forest of Lonsdale, receiving several facilities, Adam's men of Ingleton and High and Low Bentham being mentioned, but his claim to gallows in Sedbergh being disallowed.[10] His interest there is shown in his charter to Fountains abbey, addressed to his bailiffs of Lonsdale, by which he granted free transit for the monks' cattle through his land of Lonsdale.[11] He held land of the honour of Knaresborough in Farnham, where in 1211 he held a quarter of a knight's fee together with a knight's fee in Staveley,[12]

[1] E.Y.C., vii, no. 140.
[2] Ibid., xi, no. 262.
[3] Ibid., no. 231. Elias is given as another son of Swain son of Dolfin in the Cottonian roll (see above). It is probable, as Ellis suggested (ut sup., p. 115), that Thomas was the eldest of Swain's sons.
[4] E.Y.C., vii, no. 142; lands in Calton and Airton, par. Kirkby Malham, were held of the honour of Skipton, and descended to the family of FitzHugh (ibid., p. 216).
[5] Fountains Chartulary, ii, 857.
[6] Ibid., p. 702.
[7] V.C.H. Yorks., ii, 238. 3½ car. in Swinton were a berewick of the manor of Masham formerly held by Gospatric (ibid.).
[8] E.Y.C., i, no. 359n, citing Cal. Ch. Rolls, iv, 26.
[9] Adam de Staveley was also a benefactor of Jervaulx, giving land in Sedbergh (Mon. Ang., v, 576).
[10] Yorks. Assize Rolls, p. 7.
[11] Fountains Chartulary, i, 458.
[12] Pipe Roll 13 John, p. 90.

3 carucates in Farnham having been confirmed by king John in 1204 to Adam son of Thomas de Staveley for a quarter of a knight's fee.[1] Adam de Staveley witnessed several charters late in the twelfth and early in the thirteenth century, including two issued by William de Stuteville, who held Knaresborough in 1191–94 and c. 1201–1203.[2] He married Alice daughter of William de Percy of Kildale (q.v.), who brought Barwick-on-Tees in frank-marriage;[3] and in 1211 he owed 100 marks and 2 palfreys for a licence for the marriage of his daughter with the son and heir of Henry son of Hervey,[4] the heir being Ranulf son of Henry, mentioned above. In an assize held in 1218–19, after Adam's death, Hugh de Maunby complained that Ranulf and Alice his wife and others had disseised him of a tenement in Thoresby, but his case was unsuccessful as although Adam had given the tenement to him on his deathbed there had been no seisin.[5] In 1218–35 Alice and her husband were parties to several final concords, illustrating her inheritance including land in Thoresby, Carperby, Bentham, Barwick-on-Tees, Farnham, Horton in Ribblesdale, Ilton and Dent.[6] In 1235 they had a quitclaim of all the lands of Thomas son of Swain and Adam de Staveley in Yorkshire.[7] Alice died in 1250–53, when her inheritance passed to her descendants, the family of FitzHugh of Ravensworth (q.v.) which continued in the male line to early in the sixteenth century.[8]

THORNHILL

The family descended from Jordan, one of the many sons of Essulf.[9] The late W. Paley Baildon made a detailed examination of the available evidence for Essulf and his descendants.[10] He regarded Essulf as the probable grandson of Gamel and possibly a son of Ulf. He noted that Gamel, the holder of several lands in the West Riding before the Conquest, which included an interest in Thornhill,[11] held the manor of Birkin of Ilbert de Lascy at the Domesday survey,[12] a place which gave its name to the family of Birkin (q.v.) descending from Peter eldest son of Essulf;[13] and that in the Claims Gilbert de Gant had a carucate of the land of Ulf in Birkin.[14] Gamel, probably

---

[1] Rot. Chart., p. 136. At the Survey Gospatric held 3 car. in Farnham (V.C.H. Yorks., ii, 283).
[2] E.Y.C., ix, nos. 29, 33; and cf. nos. 23, 26, 113.
[3] Complete Peerage, v, 416n.
[4] Pipe Roll 13 John, p. 29.
[5] Rolls of the Justices, Selden Soc., vol. lvi, no. 342.
[6] Yorks. Fines, 1218–31, pp. 10, 15, 26, 64, 81, 97, 116, etc. A final concord of 23 Feb. 1239–40 shows that Alice was then a widow (ibid., 1232–46, p. 58).
[7] Ibid., p. 40.
[8] Complete Peerage, v, 416n; and pp. 416–33, with chart pedigree.
[9] An account of the family is in Y.A.J., xxix, 286–321, with chart pedigree.
[10] Baildon and the Baildons, ii, 15–34, with chart pedigree.
[11] V.C.H. Yorks., ii, 251.
[12] Ibid., p. 245.
[13] A chart pedigree of Peter's descendants, whose son Adam took the name of Birkin, is in E.Y.C., iii, p. 359.
[14] V.C.H. Yorks., ii, 294.

the same man, together with Ulf, held Hazlewood (par. Tadcaster) before the Conquest;[1] and the Claims relating thereto refer to the land of Gamel son of Osmund.[2] Moreover, Kilnsey was held by Gamel before the Conquest and by Ulf at the Survey.[3]

Baildon supposed that Jordan was a son of Essulf by a second or third wife, being born in 1120–30.[4] As Jordan son of Essulf he was constable of Wakefield in the period 1174–78;[5] and there are numerous references to him from 1155 onwards.[6] On 25 January 1194–5 he and his son Richard were granted by final concord the land of Thornhill, Hunsworth and East Bierley by Richard de Tong for the service of a quarter of a knight's fee and 10s yearly.[7] The principal interest of Jordan is his connexion with one of the many miracles said to have been performed by St. Thomas of Canterbury, and nine scenes from the legend are in the thirteenth-century glass in the Trinity Chapel in Canterbury cathedral.[8]

Richard, elder son and successor of Jordan, took the name of Thornhill; and from him the family descended in the male line to Simon de Thornhill, who died in 1369–70 leaving an only daughter Elizabeth. She married Sir Henry Savile, second son of Sir John Savile of Elland and Tankersley; and the Thornhill estates passed to their descendants.[9]

A younger branch of the family descended from Thomas de Thornhill and his wife Margaret a daughter of the family of Lacy of Cromwellbotham; and their son Richard acquired the manor of Fixby by marriage with Margaret de Totehill.[10] Fixby descended in the male line to the middle of the nineteenth century.[11]

Another branch held land in Wath upon Dearne, where one of the manors was known as Thornhill Hall, a member of the honour of Tickhill. William son of John de Thornhill who held it can be identified with William son of John son of Essulf.[12] John son of Essulf, a brother of Jordan, occurs in the Pipe Rolls from 1168 to

---

[1] *V.C.H. Yorks.*, ii, 259.

[2] *Ibid.*, p. 294.

[3] *Ibid.*, p. 289.

[4] *Op. cit.*, p. 22.

[5] *E.Y.C.*, viii, no. 71.

[6] *Y.A.J.*, xxix, 287–9.

[7] *E.Y.C.*, iii, no. 1767. Richard was another son of Essulf (*ibid.*, note). In 1322 John de Thornhill held the manors of Thornhill and Hunsworth of the heir of Richard de Tong, a minor in the kg's wardship, each by the service of ⅛ k.f. (*Y.A.J.*, xxix, 302–3).

[8] Baildon, *op. cit.*, pp. 28–31, gives a translation of the story narrated by two monks of Canterbury. An abstract is in *Y.A.J.*, pp. 289–90, and a photograph of the panel of the last scene showing Jordan with his wife and his son miraculously restored to life and his performance of his vow at the shrine of St. Thomas.

[9] For these see 'The Savile Family', by J. W. Clay in *Y.A.J.*, xxv, 1–47.

[10] *Ibid.*, xxix, 313–6, where it is suggested that Thomas, closely connected with the main line, was a younger brother of Sir John de Thornhill who died in 1322.

[11] *Dugdale's Visitation*, ed. J. W. Clay, i, 80–3.

[12] *Y.A.J.*, xxix, 308, giving an account of this branch.

1185; he gave land in Wentworth, par. Wath, to Monk Bretton priory and land in Holdsworth in Ovenden, par. Halifax, to the canons of Nostell.[1] William son of John de Thornhill was probably the father of Sir William de Thornhill, known also as Sir William de Wath, who died shortly after 1266; and his son William son of William de Wath granted the manor of Thornhill Hall to Sir Roger de Woodhall, in whose issue it descended.[2]

THORNTON (of Thornton Steward)

The family descended from Wimar, a tenant in Richmondshire of count Alan at the Domesday survey, subsequently acquiring other holdings of the honour, including lands in Cambridgeshire and Norfolk. He occurs as steward in 1096–98 and died before 1130, his Yorkshire lands being divided between his sons Roger and Warner, the former receiving Thornton Steward. Roger held the office of steward under count Stephen. His son Ralph, who succeeded by 1145, was the father of Roger, who in a final concord of 1195 was described as Roger son of Ralph de Thornton, and who through his son Wimar was the grandfather of Matthew de Thornton. By the death of the latter's sons without issue the heir was his daughter Mary wife of Humphrey de Bassingbourn, who in 1280 held besides 2 knights' fees in Thornton Steward land in Cambridgeshire which had been acquired by his wife's ancestor Wimar the Domesday tenant.[3] The manor of Thornton Steward passed to Mary's descendants, and it was sold to Richard le Scrope of Bolton in 1371.[4]

THWENG

The family took its name from Thwing, E.R., a member of the Brus fee,[5] and held a tenancy of the Percy fee at Legsby, co. Lincoln.[6]

Living in the reign of Henry I Robert was the father of Robert son of Robert de Thweng, who gave to Sixle priory the church of Legsby not later than 1166;[7] and as Robert son of Robert, with the assent of Emma his wife, the vill of Legsby subject to the forinsec service of half a knight.[8] The gift of the vill was confirmed by William de Percy II and later by Jocelin of Louvain and his wife

---

[1] *Y.A.J.*, xxix, 309; and for the charter to Nostell *E.Y.C.*, viii, no. 146, to which Jordan son of Essulf described as 'de Tang' [Tong] was a witness.
[2] *Y.A.J.*, xxix, 310–2.
[3] Authority for these details is in the account of the family and the steward's fee in *E.Y.C.*, v, pp. 17–26, where there is a chart pedigree; *cf.* also Farrer, *Feudal Cambridgeshire*, p. 147.
[4] *V.C.H.*, *N.R.*, i, 266, giving details of the descent.
[5] *E.Y.C.*, ii, p. 16.
[6] An account of the family is in *Complete Peerage*, xii(i), 735–44, which refers to the notes of William Brown in *Guisborough Chartulary*, ii, 100–2, and the MS. material collected by William Hebditch now *penes* Yorks. Arch. Soc. For the Percy holding see also *E.Y.C.*, xi, pp. 203–7.
[7] *Ibid.*, no. 173.
[8] *Ibid.*, no. 174.

Agnes de Percy.[1] In 1166 Robert son of Robert held a knight's fee of the old feoffment of William de Percy;[2] and the returns of 1212 show that the latter had given to Robert de Thweng land in Legsby and land in Holtham (in Legsby) and Ludford, each for the service of half a knight.[3] Although no 1166 *carta* for the Brus fee is available it can be assumed that Robert de Thweng's holding lay in Thwing, where his grandson Robert de Thweng held 1½ knights' fees and 3 carucates of the Brus fee in 1242–43,[4] and where his descendant Marmaduke de Thweng III held land by knight-service in 1284–85.[5]

Robert son of Robert de Thweng married Emma one of the three sisters and coheirs of Duncan Darel of Lund,[6] and was succeeded by his son Marmaduke de Thweng I, whose son Robert, living in 1242–43, acquired by marriage the castle of Kilton, with lands in Kilton Thorpe and Kirkleatham.[7] The family descended in the male line to Marmaduke de Thweng III, who was summoned to Parliament from 1307 to 1322;[8] and a coheirship passed to the representatives of his daughters on the death of his last surviving son in 1374.[9]

TISON

Gilbert Tison held lands in the East and West Ridings and in Lincolnshire and Nottinghamshire at the Domesday survey. With the exception of most of his holdings in the West Riding, which passed mainly to the Percy and Skipton fees or reverted to the Crown, the greater part of his service was given by Henry I to Nigel d'Aubigny before 1118;[10] and in 1166 15 knights' fee swere held by William Tison, Gilbert's grandson, of Roger de Mowbray.[11]

Gilbert Tison, a benefactor of the abbeys of Selby[12] and St. Mary's York, died before 1130, perhaps not later than 1124; and his son Adam succeeded him as a tenant of the honour of Mowbray.[13] Besides his son William, Adam Tison had a daughter Avice or Amice, the wife of Henry Hose of Harting, Sussex, who held in her

[1] *E.Y.C.*, xi, no. 70.
[2] *Ibid.*, no. 88.
[3] *Bk. of Fees*, p. 171.
[4] *Ibid.*, p. 1098. The entry gives Robert's tenure as *in eadem*, the previous entry being in Foxholes, a neighbouring parish to Thwing, but *eadem* can be taken as Thwing itself.
[5] *Feudal Aids*, vi, 30; Marmaduke then had no holding in Foxholes (*ibid.*, p. 28).
[6] *E.Y.C.*, xi, p. 205; and Darel chart pedigree p. 188.
[7] *Ibid.*, pp. 205, 227; and see the Kilton section above.
[8] *Ibid.*, pp. 205–6; *Complete Peerage*, xii(i), 738–40.
[9] *Ibid.*, p. 743.
[10] *E.Y.C.*, xii, pp. 4–6; *Mowbray Charters*, p. xxv. *Cf.* a similar grant of the Arches tenancy-in-chief (*q.v.*).
[11] *Mowbray Charters*, no. 401. Lists of Gilbert's holdings, the first table including those which passed to the honour of Mowbray and the second those which did not so pass, are in *E.Y.C.*, xii, pp. 20–1.
[12] A facsimile of his charter to Selby, not later than 1100, is in *ibid.*, facing no. 15.
[13] *Ibid.*, pp. 6, 7.

right an interest in Swinton, par. Wath upon Dearne, and in Averham
and other lands in Nottinghamshire, all of which had been held by
Gilbert Tison in 1086.[1]

William Tison, the Mowbray tenant in 1166, died before
Michaelmas 1180, leaving four daughters as his coheirs. Of these,
one, whose christian name is not known, married Robert Constable I
of Flamborough and her share of the Tison inheritance, including
Holme upon Spalding Moor, descended to the Constable family
(*q.v.*).[2]

There is an undetermined relationship with other branches of
the Tison family holding land in Gainsborough, co. Lincoln, and
Northumberland.[3]

TRUSSEBUT

The family descended from William Trussebut who, as Orderic
records,[4] was among those of ignoble parentage promoted by Henry I.
He occurs in Normandy in 1126 and as castellan of Bonneville-sur-
Touques in 1138.[5] The supposition of Dugdale and others that he
was son of Geoffrey son of Pain, the founder of Warter priory and
holder of the manor of Market Weighton, cannot be accepted;[6]
but the succession of the Trussebut family to Market Weighton by
right of succession from Geoffrey son of Pain, as recorded in a
case of 1204,[7] suggests that William Trussebut married Geoffrey's
sister.

William Trussebut was succeeded by his son William Trussebut
the younger, who in 1166 held 10 knights' fees in Yorkshire and
married Aubreye de Harcourt, a coheir of William Peverel of Bourn,
co. Cambridge.[8] Their eldest son Geoffrey succeeded in 1175–76,
and on the death of his brother Robert Trussebut in 1193 the heirs
were their three sisters Roese, Hilary and Agatha. Roese married
Everard son of Robert de Ros of Helmsley, and Agatha married as
his second wife William d'Aubigny of Belvoir. Hilary and Agatha
both died without issue, and on the latter's death in 1246–47 the sole
heir was William de Ros, Roese's grandson, and the inheritance
descended in the Ros family.

---

[1] *E.Y.C.*, xii, p. 7. Charters relating to Averham, issued by Adam and
William Tison and the Hose family are pd in *ibid.*, nos. 107–16, the Mowbray over-
lordship being shown in nos. 111 and 114; and for the Hose family in Swinton
nos. 77–9.

[2] *Ibid.*, pp. 145 *et seq.*, with chart pedigree facing p. 145.

[3] *Ibid.*, pp. 11–18.

[4] Ed. Le Prévost, iv, 164.

[5] *E.Y.C.*, x, pp. 5–22, giving an account of the family with chart pedigree
p. 6.

[6] *Ibid.*, pp. 3, 5.

[7] *Ibid.*, p. 14, citing *Curia Regis Rolls*, iii, 148.

[8] *Ibid.*, pp. 8–11. References for the ensuing statements are given in this
account of the family.

VAVASOUR

The family, of which there were several branches, descended from Malger, who at the Domesday survey held land at Hazlewood, par. Tadcaster, Edlington and elsewhere of William de Percy,[1] and who witnessed a charter of Alan de Percy to Whitby, 1100–c. 1115.[2]

William le Vavasour, king's justice, held 2 knights' fees of the old feoffment of William de Percy II in 1166, and half a knight's fee also of the old feoffment of the honour of Skipton, the Percy lands held by Malger having been considerably extended and the Skipton lands in Craven having been acquired.[3] In a charter to Bolton priory, 1175–90, with the consent of Robert and Malger his sons, he confirmed land in Yeadon of the gift of Robert son of Malger his uncle (*avunculus*).[4] It can be deduced that William was a grandson of Malger the Domesday tenant, but it is uncertain whether this was by paternal or maternal descent. The balance of evidence, including Dodsworth's statement that William's father was named Malger, suggests that Malger of the Survey had two sons Robert and Malger, William being the heir of Robert who presumably died without issue.[5] William le Vavasour died in 1189–91. Robert, his elder son and successor at Hazlewood, had by his first wife a daughter who married Theobald Walter, ancestor of the Butlers later earls of Ormond, and had the manor of Edlington as part of her endowment;[6] and by his second wife a son John le Vavasour. The latter was the father of William le Vavasour who was summoned to Parliament in 1299, and from whom the family descended in the male line to Sir Thomas Vavasour, who died in 1826, when Hazlewood passed by will to Edward Marmaduke Stourton.[7]

From Mauger le Vavasour, younger son of William le Vavasour the justice, descended the Vavasours of Denton and their younger branch the Vavasours of Weston, the latter descending in the male line to the nineteenth century.[8]

VEILLY

The family, tenants of the Lascy fee in Yorkshire, took its name from Villy-Bocage, dept. Calvados, arr. Caen, cant. Villers-Bocage.[9] At the Domesday survey Hunfrid was a tenant of Ilbert de Lascy in

---

[1] *E.Y.C.*, xi, p. 119, where his holdings are given in detail.
[2] *Ibid.*, no. 2.
[3] *Ibid.*, p. 119.
[4] *Ibid.*, iii, no. 1873. Robert son of Malger's charter, *ante* 1156 is in *ibid.*, xi, no. 120.
[5] *Ibid.*, p. 120.
[6] This daughter Maud married secondly Fulk FitzWarin; and by a charter (photograph kindly given by Sir Francis Hill) they granted and quitclaimed all Edlington to her father.
[7] *Ibid.*, vii, 166–72, with chart pedigree of the early generations; and xi, pp. 120–4; *Complete Peerage*, xii(ii), 230–8; *Dugdale's Visitation*, ed. J. W. Clay, ii, 224–9.
[8] *Baildon and the Baildons*, i, 506–49.
[9] *Anglo-Norman Families*, p. 109.

Newton [Wallis], par. Ledsham, Ackworth and Snydale, par. Normanton.[1] As Humfrey de Villeio he gave 2 thraves of his tithe in Snydale and Newton to the chapel of St. Clement in Pontefract castle *ante c.* 1093.[2] The tenancy in these places did not descend permanently to the Veilly family. This is shown by a charter of Robert de Lascy giving 3 carucates in Snydale to Kirkstall abbey, 1177–93;[3] by a claim, evidently unsuccessful, by a later Humphrey de Veilly against Robert de Lascy and Robert le Waleys in 1191 for 3 knights' fees in Ackworth, Snydale and Newton;[4] and by the fact that Newton became known as Newton Wallis from its tenancy by the family of Waleys.[5]

No member of the Veilly family occurs in the list of holders of knights' fees of Henry de Lascy in 1166;[6] but in 1242–43 Robert de Veilly held 3 knights' fees of the Lascy fee;[7] and in 1284–85 Humphrey de Veilly held 2 knights' fees less half a carucate in Thorner, [East] Rigton, Gipton, 'Wriglay' and Eltofts.[8] As Roger son of Alvred granted land in Thorner, 1160–75[9] it is possible that it formed part of the 3 knights' fees which he held of Henry de Lascy in 1166,[10] and that they were connected with the Veilly family, Roger holding them as custodian of the lands of Humphrey de Veilly.[11] It is probable that in addition to Thorner a further knight's fee, making up the total of 3 lay in Owston, where Humphrey de Veilly held a fee from which he gave rights to Hugh son of Walter in marriage with Rohaise his sister, 1180–95;[12] and as late as 1401 there is mention of the Veilly fee in Owston.[13]

Although there are no references to prove it there is little doubt that Humphrey de Veilly was the lineal descendant of the elder Humphrey living before 1100. He occurs in 1181, 1182, 1207 and 1212,[14] and witnessed charters *c.* 1170 to 1210.[15] He was evidently the predecessor of the Robert who, as noted above, held 3 knights' fees in 1242–43; and who made a presentation for the church of Thorner in 1246.[16] He made a final concord with the prioress of St. Clement, York, for common of pasture there in 1268,[17] and he occurs on a

---

[1] *V.C.H. Yorks.*, ii, pp. 245, 247, 250.
[2] *E.Y.C.*, iii, no. 1492.
[3] *Ibid.*, no. 1606.
[4] *Ibid.*, no. 1585*n*, where there are some notes on the family.
[5] *Complete Peerage*, xii(ii), 319.
[6] *E.Y.C.*, iii, no. 1508.
[7] *Bk. of Fees*, p. 1102.
[8] *Feudal Aids*, vi, 22. Wriglay from this reference is given as a medieval field-name in Thorner (*Place-Names of W.R.*, Eng. Place-Name Soc., iv, 106).
[9] *E.Y.C.*, iii, no. 1583. Roger's daughter Emma married Thomas Hay (*q.v.*).
[10] *Ibid.*, no. 1508.
[11] *Ibid.*, note.
[12] *Ibid.*, no. 1585.
[13] *Feudal Aids*, vi, 596.
[14] *E.Y.C.*, iii, nos. 1584, 1585*n*, 1620*n*.
[15] *Ibid.*, i, no. 497; iii, nos. 1549, 1632, 1638.
[16] *Reg. Gray*, p. 98.
[17] *Yorks. Fines*, 1246–72, p. 146.

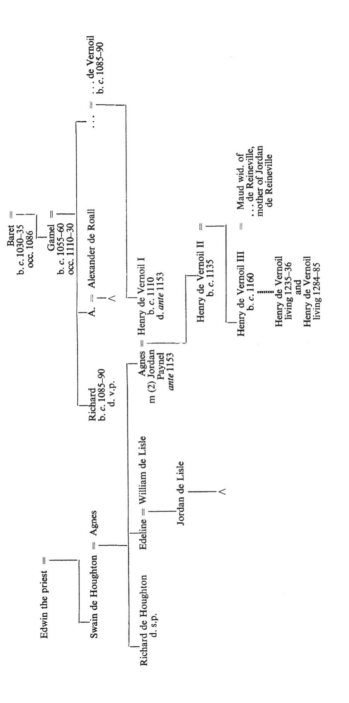

grand assize as a knight on several occasions from 1246 to 1268.[1] He was succeeded by his son Humphrey,[2] who, as noted above, was living in 1284–85, and who gave to William de Hamelton his interest in the manor of Thorner in 1285, and in 1286 land in Cowlam and Croom which he held in right of Lucy his wife.[3]

VERNOIL

The notes on the family of Roall (*q.v.*) show that the interest of Gamel son of Baret in Eggborough and elsewhere became shared by the families of Vernoil and Roall, and the notes on the family of Houghton (*q.v.*) that the tenure of Swain de Houghton descended in equal portions to the families of Vernoil and Lisle. It can therefore be deduced that the Vernoil family acquired interests by two separate marriages with coheirs in two different generations.

The notes on Roall suggest that a member of the Vernoil family – whose christian name is not known – married a daughter of Gamel son of Baret and sister and coheir of his son Richard and also sister of A. wife of Alexander de Roall, and that by these marriages he and Alexander acquired interests in Kellington, Roall, Eggborough, Brayton and Hensall, all held of the Lascy fee. Henry de Vernoil I, whose mother was thus Gamel's daughter, married Agnes daughter and coheir of Swain de Houghton, acquiring in her right an interest in Great Houghton which was shared by William de Lisle, the husband of her sister Edeline.[4] Before 1153, with his wife Agnes, described as daughter of Swain son of Edwin de Houghton, he confirmed to Nostell priory gifts of land in Great Houghton made by Swain son of Edwin;[5] and in 1155–70 Henry de Lascy, the tenant in chief, confirmed to St. Peter's hospital land in Eggborough given by Henry de Vernoil and his mother.[6] In 1180–90 Henry de Vernoil III confirmed to the hospital a bovate in Eggborough given by Agnes his grandmother of her dower.[7] This suggests that Henry de Vernoil I, husband of Agnes, was holding land in Eggborough in his own right and not in right of his wife, and that he had inherited it from his mother, the coheir of Gamel son of Baret.

Henry de Vernoil II, as heir of Agnes, then wife of Jordan Paynel,[8] gave his consent to a gift by Jordan his step-father to Nostell priory of land in Great Houghton, later than 1153;[9] and he confirmed his father's charter to the priory.[10] It was either he or his son Henry

---

[1] *Yorks. Fines*, 1232–46, pp. 132*n*, 144*n*; 1246–72, pp. 23*n*, 28*n*, 31*n*, 69*n*, 158*n*, 159*n*.
[2] *Knights of Edw. I*, Harleian Soc., v, 122, giving details about him.
[3] *Yorks. Fines*, 1272–1300, pp. 75, 78.
[4] See the Houghton section above.
[5] *E.Y.C.*, vi, no. 119.
[6] *Ibid.*, iii, no. 1502.
[7] *Ibid.*, no. 1630.
[8] For him see the Houghton section.
[9] *Ibid.*, vi, no. 117.
[10] *Ibid.*, no. 119*n*.

who gave to the Templars land and pasture in Eggborough, 1175–77;[1] and in 1177, naming him and members of the Roall family, also his tenants, Henry de Lascy confirmed gifts made there to the Templars.[2]

It was probably Henry de Vernoil III, living in 1180–90, as noted above, who was the Henry son of Henry de Vernoil who gave land and extensive pasture in Eggborough to Nun Appleton priory, *c.* 1175–1189,[3] and meadow in Kellington to Pontefract priory, 1185–1210.[4] In 1202 he was party to a final concord for a messuage in Kellington;[5] and in 1208 he and Maud his wife and the latter's son Jordan de Reineville (*q.v.*) were parties against Jordan Foliot for land in Ramesholme.[6]

It is difficult to distinguish members of the family named Henry in the thirteenth century. In 1242–43 Henry de Vernoil held half a knight's fee of the Lascy fee.[7] In 1246 Henry de Vernoil made a presentation for a moiety of the church of Brayton;[8] but in 1263 he recognised that the advowson was the right of the abbot of Selby.[9] In 1284–85 Henry de Vernoil held Great Houghton of Robert Luterel (the successor of the Paynels of Hooton Pagnell)[10] for half a knight's fee.[11] The family's inherited interest in Hensall, par. Snaith, held by Baret before the Conquest, where an interest was similarly held by the Roall family, is seen in an undated deed by which Henry son of Henry de Vernoil sold land and villeins there, mention being made of Henry the grantor's father.[12] In 1302–03 William de Hamelton held a moiety of a knight's fee in Great Houghton of Geoffrey Luterel,[13] which, as noted above, had been held by Henry de Vernoil in 1284–85. In 1305 the right of William de Hamelton in a messuage and a carucate there (*Halghton*) was recognised.[14] In the same year William de Hamelton granted the manor of Marr to John de Metham and Sibyl his wife at a yearly rent of a rose;[15] and in 1306 he and Adam his brother granted them land in Hambleton (*Hamelton*) and elsewhere, with remainder to Sibyl's right heirs.[16] Sybil was

[1] *E.Y.C.*, iii, no. 1626.
[2] *Ibid.*, no. 1629.
[3] *Ibid.*, no. 1631.
[4] *Ibid.*, no. 1632.
[5] *Yorks. Fines, John*, p. 15.
[6] *Ibid.*, p. 139. Ramsholme is given as a lost place in Pollington, par. Snaith (*Place-Names of W.R.*, Eng. Place-Name Soc., ii, 22).
[7] *Bk. of Fees*, p. 1103, where the name is Vernon in error. The mistake, from *Testa*, p. 365, was noticed by Farrer (*E.Y.C.*, iii, no. 1626n).
[8] *Reg. Gray*, p. 97.
[9] *Yorks. Fines*, 1246–72, p. 127; and *cf.* the charter of Henry described as a kt, remitting his claim, in *Selby Coucher*, i, no. 337. The family of Roall also had an interest in the church.
[10] *E.Y.C.*, vi, pp. 44–6.
[11] *Feudal Aids*, vi, 2. For the other half see the section on Houghton.
[12] *Yorks. Deeds*, x, no. 283; mid or late 13th cent.
[13] *Feudal Aids*, vi, 130.
[14] *Yorks. Fines*, 1300–14, no. 265.
[15] *Ibid.*, no. 274.
[16] *Ibid.*, no. 303.

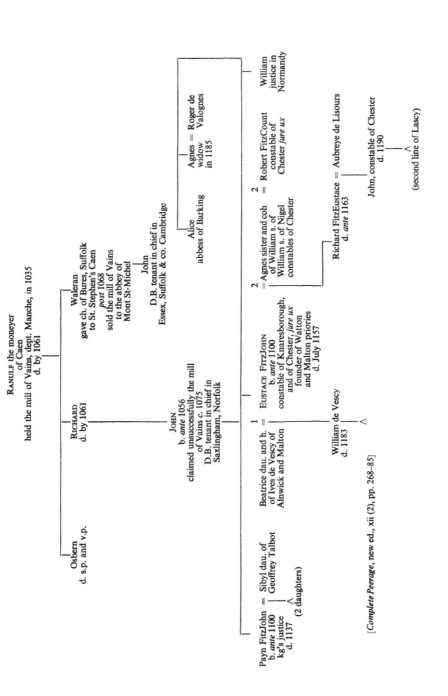

RANULF the moneyer
of Caen
held the mill of Vains, dept. Manche, in 1035
d. by 1061

Osbern
d. s.p. and v.p.

RICHARD
d. by 1061

Waleran
gave ch. of Bures, Suffolk
to St. Stephen's Caen
post 1068
sold the mill of Vains
to the abbey of
Mont St-Michel

John
D.B. tenant in chief in
Essex, Suffolk & co. Cambridge

Alice
abbess of Barking

Agnes = Roger de
widow   Valognes
in 1185

William
justice in
Normandy

JOHN
b. *ante* 1056
claimed unsuccessfully the mill
of Vains c. 1075
D.B. tenant in chief in
Saxlingham, Norfolk

1
Beatrice dau. and h.
of Ives de Vescy of
Alnwick and Malton   =

EUSTACE FITZJOHN
b. *ante* 1100
constable of Knaresborough,
and of Chester, *jure ux*
founder of Watton
and Malton priories
d. July 1157

2
= Agnes sister and coh
of William s. of
William s. of Nigel
constables of Chester

2
= Robert FitzCount
constable of
Chester *jure ux*

William de Vescy
d. 1183

∧

Richard FitzEustace = Aubreye de Lisours
d. *ante* 1163

John, constable of Chester
d. 1190

∧
(second line of Lascy)

Payn FitzJohn = Sibyl dau. of
b. *ante* 1100   Geoffrey Talbot
kg's justice
d. 1137
       ∧
   (2 daughters)

[*Complete Peerage*, new ed., xii (2), pp. 268–85]

doubtless the daughter and heir of Adam de Hamelton.[1] John son of Thomas de Metham died in 1312, leaving Sibyl his widow and Thomas his son and heir aged twelve.[2] In 1316 the king ordered the delivery to Sibyl widow of John de Metham of lands taken into the king's hand when Robert de Steeton, who had afterwards married her, had fled after an indictment; these included the manor of Pollington, lands in Hambleton, Great Houghton, Eggborough and 'the park of Vernoil'.[3]

These details show that between 1284–85 and 1302–03 the interests of Henry de Vernoil in Great Houghton and Eggborough, due to his descent from Swain de Houghton and Gamel son of Baret respectively, passed through William de Hamelton to his niece Sibyl wife of John de Metham. Her interests were inherited by the Metham family, which descended in the male line to the eighteenth century.[4] In 1401–02 Sir Thomas de Metham held half a knight's fee in Eggborough of the fee of 'Vernon',[5] lately of Sir William de Hamelton.[6]

VESCY

The second line of Vescy descended from Eustace FitzJohn and his first wife Beatrice only daughter and heir of Ives de Vescy, lord of Alnwick and Malton, their son William taking the name of Vescy.[7] Evidence is available to show that Eustace descended in the male line from Ranulf the moneyer who held the mill of Vains, dept. Manche, arr. and cant. Avranches, and whose son Waleran gave to the abbey of St. Stephen, Caen, the church of Bures, Suffolk, with land there, by a charter issued in the presence of king William and queen Maud.[8] John, Eustace's father, was son of Richard (an elder brother of Waleran), who so described gave the tithe of Saxlingham, Norfolk, to St. Peter's abbey, Gloucester, and who, described as John *nepos Walerami* or *nepos W.*, was a tenant in chief in Norfolk and Essex at the Domesday survey, his lands including the manor of Saxlingham, where Eustace FitzJohn gave a rent to the same house.[9] Payn FitzJohn was Eustace's elder brother.[10]

From William de Vescy, Eustace's son, the family descended in the male line to William de Vescy, summoned to Parliament in

---

[1] *Glover's Visitation*, p. 252; Adam being heir to his brother William. The latter was dean of York from 1298 and chancellor of England from 1305 to his death in 1307.

[2] *Cal. Inq. p.m.*, v, no. 316.

[3] *Cal. Close Rolls*, 1313–18, p. 362.

[4] *Dugdale's Visitation*, ed. J. W. Clay, ii, 82–7. The family quartered the arms of Hamelton.

[5] Evidently intended for Vernoil; *cf.* the error in *Bk. of Fees* noted above.

[6] *Feudal Aids*, vi, 598.

[7] *Complete Peerage*, xii(ii), 272–4.

[8] *Ibid.*, app. B, where other gifts of Waleran to St. Stephen's are noted. The charter, of which a facsimile forms the frontispiece to Prof. Galbraith's Raleigh Lecture, *The Literacy of the Medieval English Kings*, is now in the British Museum.

[9] *Complete Peerage, ut sup.*, pp. 269–72.

[10] *Ibid.*, pp. 270–1.

1295, who died in 1297 without surviving legitimate issue; his illegitimate son William de Vescy was summoned in 1313 and died without issue in 1314.[1] In 1316 and 1317 the claim to the Yorkshire and Lincolnshire estates was established by Gilbert de Aton, who was descended from Margery daughter and heir of Warin de Vescy, younger son of William de Vescy son of Eustace FitzJohn.[2]

WARENNE

William de Warenne, first earl of Surrey, from whom the family in England descended, was a younger son of Rodulf de Warenne, probably by a niece of duchess Gunnor, wife of duke Richard I; the family derived its name from the hamlet of Varenne, north of Bellencombre, on the river Varenne, dept. Seine–Maritime.[3]

William de Warenne was present at the battle of Hastings, and was given lands in England which at the Domesday survey extended over thirteen counties, including the extensive manor of Conisborough in Yorkshire, most of the rape of Lewes in Sussex, and Castle Acre in Norfolk.[4] His son William, the second earl, acquired the manor of Wakefield, which had been in the king's hand at the Survey.[5] Isabel, daughter and heir of William, the third earl, married first William of Blois son of king Stephen, by whom she had no issue, and secondly Hamelin, an illegitimate son of Geoffrey count of Anjou and half-brother of king Henry II, by whom she was the mother of William, the sixth earl, who took her name of Warenne. From him the family descended in the male line to his great-grandson John, the eighth earl, who died in 1347 without legitimate issue, his heir being his nephew Richard FitzAlan, earl of Arundel.[6]

WENNERVILLE

A William de Wennerville (*Wenrevilla*) is among the witnesses to three charters of Robert de Lascy to Pontefract priory;[7] although

---

[1] *Complete Peerage*, xii(ii), pp. 274–85.

[2] *Ibid.*, pp. 275n, 285n, by reason of a settlement of Feb. 1296–7 (*ibid.*, p. 282). For Gilbert de Aton, whose son was summ. to Parl. in 1371, see *ibid.*, i, 324–6.

[3] L. C. Loyd, 'The Origin of the Family of Warenne' in *Y.A.J.*, xxxi, 97–113. This has been used for the accounts of the family in *E.Y.C.*, viii, pp. 1 *et seq.;* and *Complete Peerage*, xii(i), 491 *et seq.*

[4] *Ibid.* The controversial question of the identity of his wife Gundreda is discussed in *E.Y.C.*, viii, pp. 40–6; the result given is that she was certainly a sister of Gerbod the Fleming, earl of Chester, and probably of a certain Frederic who had held lend in Norfolk (*cf.* Loyd, *op. cit.*).

[5] *E.Y.C.*, viii, p. 9.

[6] *Ibid.*, pp. 13–26; *Complete Peerage, loc. cit.*, where it is noted (p. 511n) that the Warrens of Poynton were an illegitimate line, being descended from Edward, a bastard son of the last earl by Maud de Nerford.

[7] *Pontefract Chartulary*, nos. 1, 2 and 7. They were examined by Farrer in *E.Y.C.*, iii, no. 1485n, where no. 7, mentioning kg Henry I, is pd and dated 1108–?1114; he regarded it as of doubtful authenticity, but perhaps based on a genuine charter.

these are either spurious or interpolated there is no reason to doubt that he was a genuine witness.[1]

It was presumably a later William de Wennerville who gave land near Collierstih (in Hemsworth) to Nostell priory, which was confirmed by his son Adam with Adeliz his wife, 1154–c. 1170.[2] Adam de Wennerville held a knight's fee of the old feoffment of Henry de Lascy in 1166,[3] which can be located in Hemsworth; and he witnessed a charter of Henry de Lascy to Pontefract priory, c. 1160–1177.[4] His son and successor was William de Wennerville III, who confirmed to Nostell the gift made by William de Wennerville his grandfather and confirmed by Adam his father, 1175–90.[5] With Ralph his brother he witnessed a charter, 1180–90.[6] No documentary evidence is available to prove that the next two holders of the fee, Adam II and William IV were the son and grandson of William III; but the fact is probable.[7]

Adam de Wennerville II as lord of Hemsworth gave to Nostell priory at the petition of Emma his wife a yearly rent of 2s, to be paid by the hand of Jordan de Wennerville and his heirs from a toft and meadow in Hemsworth, c. 1190–1220[8] (probably late in that period); and in 1204–09 he with Ralph de Wennerville, Adam his son and Jordan his brother witnessed an agreement in the wapentake court of Staincross.[9] He occurs as a juror on an assize in 1223.[10] In 1242–43 William de Wennerville IV held a knight's fee of the honour of the earl of Lincoln[11] (the Lascy fee); and on 4 August 1242 he made a presentation for the rectory of Hemsworth.[12] He died before 26 December 1244, when orders were issued for the assignment of dower to Hawise his widow;[13] and the inquisition after his death, the writ being dated 21 January 1244–5, states that he held Hemsworth

---

[1] This was Farrer's view in *E.Y.C.*, iii, no. 1590*n*.

[2] *Ibid.*, no. 1590, where in his note he regarded William de Wennerville I as presumably father of William II. There was, however, a Ralph de Wennerville who with tenants of the honour of Pontefract witnessed a charter to Spalding priory, c. 1135 (*ibid.*, no. 1490); and chronology makes it possible for an intervening generation between the two Williams.

[3] *Ibid.*, no. 1508.

[4] *Ibid.*, no. 1773.

[5] *Ibid.*, no. 1591.

[6] *Pontefract Chartulary*, no. 107; and for the date *E.Y.C.*, iii, no. 1590*n*.

[7] This seems to have been Dodsworth's view; but Hunter in his account of Hemsworth (*South Yorkshire*, ii, 423–4) could not confirm Dodsworth's series of the descent. Chronologically there is no difficulty if it is assumed that Adam I was born c. 1130, William III c. 1155, Adam II c. 1180, William IV c. 1205; and it is known (see above in the text) that the latter's son Adam III was born in 1231.

[8] *E.Y.C.*, iii, nos. 1592–3.

[9] *Ibid.*, no. 1784. Hemsworth is in Staincross wap. Ralph was perhaps the brother of William III, mentioned above; it is not clear whose brother Jordan was, but he was evidently the Jordan also mentioned above.

[10] *Curia Regis Rolls*, xi, no. 1319.

[11] *Bk. of Fees*, p. 1102.

[12] *Fasti Parochiales*, i, 135.

[13] *Exc. e Rot. Fin.*, i, 429.

and Kinsley in that parish for the service of a knight's fee, his heir male attaining the age of fourteen on 1 September next.[1]

The heir was evidently Adam de Wennerville III, as in 1258 his fee of one knight was assigned among others in dower to Alice widow of Edmund de Lascy.[2] A presentation for Hemsworth church was made in 1247 by William provost of Beverley, guardian of the land and heir of Sir William de Wennerville; and presentations were made by Adam de Wennerville in 1279 and 1282.[3] In 1284–85 a carucate in Easington, par. Slaidburn, evidently a new acquisition, was held of the earl of Lincoln by Adam.[4] He died before 20 November 1288, when a presentation for Hemsworth church was made by dame Alice de Lascy, guardian of the lands of Adam son of Sir Adam de Wennerville.[5] In 1302–03 a carucate in Easington was held by the heir of Adam de Wennerville, and Adam de Wennerville held Easington in 1316.[6] The latter, Adam IV, as a knight, witnessed charters in 1310, 1317 and 1321;[7] and he died shortly before 14 June 1324, holding, besides the manor of Hemsworth for a knight's fee and a messuage and 2 carucates in Easington, a messuage and 2 carucates in Gargrave of the honour of Skipton, his heir being Adam his son aged thirty and more.[8] In May 1326 Adam de Wennerville [V] made a settlement by final concord of the manor and advowson of Hemsworth, by which two-thirds of the manor and the reversion of the remaining third held by Agnes widow of Sir Adam [IV], together with the advowson, were to be held by Adam and Alice his wife, with remainders to John son of Sir Adam for life and to Adam's right heirs.[9] It was presumably he who presented for Hemsworth church in 1327, 1352 and 1357,[10] and who died in 1363–64, leaving two daughters Isabel and Elizabeth,[11] wives respectively of Simon de Marton and Nicholas de Wortley, between whom a partition was made, the advowson of Hemsworth becoming a joint possession.[12]

The question whether Ralph de Warneville, treasurer of Rouen and York and bishop of Lisieux from 1181, was a member of the same

---

[1] *Cal. Inq. p.m.*, i, no. 44.

[2] *E.Y.C.*, iii, no. 1782n.

[3] *Fasti Parochiales*, i, 135.

[4] *Feudal Aids*, vi, 10; there are no details for Hemsworth.

[5] *Fasti Pariochiales*, i, 135.

[6] *Feudal Aids*, vi, pp. 111, 195.

[7] *Yorks. Deeds*, i, no. 316; x, nos. 304–5.

[8] *Cal. Inq. p.m.*, vi, no. 530, cited in *E.Y.C.*, vii, p. 284. Hunter, *loc. cit.* gave the date of this inq. wrongly as 1 Edw. II.

[9] CP 25(1)/272/101, no. 31, kindly checked by Mr. Michael Roper; it is given incompletely by Hunter, *loc. cit.*

[10] *Fasti Parochiales*, i, 137.

[11] There was also a third dau. Agnes, a nun at Nun Monkton (*Yorks. Deeds*, vii, no. 220).

[12] Hunter, *loc. cit.*, giving an abstract of the partition made in 1364. Presentations were subsequently made alternately, in 1365 and 1369 (*Fasti Parochiales, ut sup.*). The Wennerville arms, 3 crescents, occur on a seal in 1362 (*Pudsay Deeds*, no. 226); they were impaled by John de Wortley in 1413 (*Yorks. Deeds*, vi, no. 345; possibly the seal of his father Nicholas).

family has been discussed in the notes on the treasurers of York.[1] Although both Farrer[2] and Delisle[3] from different points of view supported this, no corroborative proof has been found. It can be added that the land given by Roger de Mortemer to the abbey of Jumièges, his charter being witnessed by Walter de Warneville, knight, 1192–98, lay in Beaunay, arr. Dieppe, cant. Totes,[4] which is about six miles north of Varneville [-aux-Grès] near St-Victor-en-Caux, which Stapleton, without any documentary evidence, gave as the place from which the treasurer took his name.[5] It is possible, therefore, that the Wennerville family in England derived its name from there.

WYVILLE

In 1121 Robert de Wituila was at a meeting at Durham of the principal men of Northumberland;[6] and in 1130 Robert de Widuilla and Henry de Mont[fort] accounted for the farm of the land of Roger de Mowbray.[7] He is probably the Robert de Wituile to whom Nigel d'Aubigny had given Kirby Hill, Langthorpe and Milby in that parish, and the service of the land of Grafton; but these places did not remain members of the Wyville fee.[8] Robert de Witvilla or Wyvilla witnessed a charter of Thomas provost of Beverley to Bridlington priory, c. 1130–1132;[9] and one of Bertram de Bulmer to St. Peter's hospital, 1130–36.[10] He gave a carucate in Sherburn, E.R., to Bridlington, which was confirmed by Roger de Mowbray,[11] who also confirmed to St. Andrew's Northampton the mill of Welford, co. Northampton, 1138–c. 1150, for the soul of Robert de Witville of whose gift it had been.[12]

It is probable[13] that he was the father of Ralph de Wyville who witnessed charters of Roger de Mowbray in the period 1138–54;[14] and with William his brother one in 1142–43.[15] Ralph was given Thorpe le Willows, par. Coxwold, by Roger de Mowbray, c. 1147.[16] This was later held by his brother William, who gave it to Byland

[1] *Y.A.J.*, xxxv, 20–4.

[2] *E.Y.C.*, iii, no. 1590*n*,

[3] Delisle, *Rec. des Actes de Henri II*, Introd., p. 100*n*. There are many variations of spelling in the names of Ralph the treasurer and the Wenneville family, some being common to both.

[4] Vernier, *Chartes de l'Abbaye de Jumièges*, ii, no. 165, cited in *Y.A.J.*, xxxv, 24.

[5] Stapleton, *Rot. Scacc. Norm.*, i, pp. cxxvi–vii.

[6] *Symeon of Durham*, Rolls Ser., ii, 261.

[7] *Pipe Roll 31 Hen. I*, p. 137.

[8] *Mowbray Charters*, no. 3 and note.

[9] *E.Y.C.*, i, no. 102.

[10] *Ibid.*, ii, no. 783.

[11] *Mowbray Charters*, no. 22.

[12] *Ibid.*, no. 403 and note.

[13] Definitely so given in Farrer's MS notes on the Mowbray honour (*penes* Yorks. Arch. Soc.).

[14] *Mowbray Charters*, nos. 21, 298, 379.

[15] *Ibid.*, no. 195.

[16] *Ibid.*, no. 400.

abbey, his gift being confirmed by Roger de Mowbray,[1] and by William's son Richard.[2] William was presumably the William de Wyvill who held 4 hides and a virgate of the Mowbray fee in Welford,[3] and was the founder of an abbey there, later known as Sulby.[4] He witnessed a charter of Gundreda mother of Roger de Mowbray, *c.* 1138–43;[5] and several of Roger's, 1154–57,[6] being named as his dapifer in 1154.[7] He was succeeded by his son Richard, who named Ralph as his uncle and William as his father in his confirmation of Thorpe le Willows to Byland abbey, noted above.

In 1166 Richard de Wiville held 5 knights' fees of the old feoffment of Roger de Mowbray, which can be located in Burnby, Sherburn and Sledmere (E.R.); Coulton, Slingsby, Thornton Dale and Thorpe le Willows (N.R.); and Cold Ashby, Elkington, Sulby and Welford, co. Northampton.[8] He also held half a knight's fee of Warter, for which half a mark was paid for the aid in 1168.[9] He gave land in Sledmere to Kirkham priory,[10] and confirmed his father's gifts to Sulby abbey.[11] He witnessed charters of Roger de Mowbray and his son Nigel, 1163–69, 1166–86 and 1186–90,[12] and a Byland charter 1204–09.[13] Eustacia his daughter married Nicholas de Yeland,[14] with whom she made agreements with Sulby in 1225 and 1229.[15] In 1224–30 Nicholas held 2 knights' fees of the Mowbray fee in Slingsby (*Lengeby*) and elsewhere in Yorkshire, and had held 1½ fees in Welford;[16] and in 1235–36 dame Eustacia de Wivilla held the latter holding.[17] In 1223–27 Nicholas and Eustacia were parties to several final concords for land in Sledmere and Slingsby, and one quit-claiming the advowson of Thornton [Dale].[18] Before 1242–43 Eustacia married secondly William de la Launde or de Lande, when they were holding 1½ fees in Welford, William holding 2 fees in Yorkshire presumably in her right.[19] In 1251, when Roger de Mowbray had ejected William de Landa after Eustacia's death, the

---

[1] *Mowbray Charters*, nos. 50–1.
[2] The text of Richard's charter is pd at no. 16 below.
[3] 'Northamptonshire survey' in *V.C.H. Northants.*, i, 379.
[4] *Mon. Ang.*, vi, 902–3. Transcripts of his charter to the abbey, addressed to Robert bp of Lincoln, giving the ch. of Welford, *c.* 1155, and of his son Richard's confirmn are pd in H. M. Colvin, *White Canons*, p. 338.
[5] *Mowbray Charters*, no. 232.
[6] *Ibid., e.g.* nos. 202, 236, 242–3.
[7] *Ibid.*, no. 237.
[8] *Ibid.*, no. 401 and p. 264.
[9] *E.Y.C.*, x, p. 109.
[10] Charter no. 17 below.
[11] *Mon. Ang.*, vi, 903.
[12] *Mowbray Charters*, e.g. nos. 72–4, 206–7, 249.
[13] *E.Y.C.*, xi, no. 192.
[14] The custody of Richard de Wyville's land in Welford had been granted to Robert de Yeland, 28 Dec. 1215 (*Rot. Claus.*, i, 244).
[15] *R. R. Hastings MSS.* Hist. MSS. Comm., i, 134–5; they were described as patrons of the abbey, Eustacia being descended from the founder.
[16] *Bk. of Fees*, p. 1460.
[17] *Ibid.*, p. 498.
[18] *Yorks. Fines*, 1218–31, pp. 48, 63, 90, 93, 103.
[19] *Bk. of Fees*, pp. 932, 944, 1097.

king ordered restoration; but William de Wiville, her son and heir,[1] claimed greater right, denying that William de Landa had issue by her.[2] He was evidently successful and in 1253 was granted free warren in Slingsby, Sledmere and Coulton.[3]

In 1284–85 William de Wyville held of the Mowbray fee land in Sledmere, $7\frac{1}{2}$ carucates in Slingsby, a moiety of the vill, Coulton for a third of a fee, and 3 carucates in Thornton Dale for a quarter.[4] He was succeeded by John de Wyville, whose holdings at his death in 1301 included lands in Slingsby, North Holme and Coulton for a knight's fee, with rent in Sherburn, and the manor of Welford for a knight's fee, his heir being his son William aged twenty-six.[5] In 1316 William held Sledmere, Coulton and a portion of Slingsby;[6] and as lord of Welford granted facilities there.[7] In 1326 he enfeoffed his eldest son John of the chief messuage in Welford;[8] and in 1329 his son William of messuages and land in Sledmere.[9] The latter evidently succeeded, as in 1343 he sold to Sir Ralph de Hastings the manors of Slingsby, Sledmere and Coulton,[10] and also that of Welford,[11] both subject to the dower of Agnes his father's widow. In 1428 Sir Richard de Hastings held $7\frac{1}{2}$ carucates in Slingsby for half a knight's fee of the Mowbray honour.[12]

The Wyville family continued in a younger line. From William Wyville of Slingsby, who died in 1430 his family descended in the male line at Osgodby to early in the eighteenth century,[13] when the manor passed to Sir Marmaduke Wyville of Constable Burton.[14]

There is no conclusive proof of the place in Normandy from which the family derived its name. But in his general confirmation charter to the abbey of Conches king Henry I included a gift of Robert de Guidvilla of a moiety of the tithe of Guidvilla;[15] and in king Henry II's confirmation the place is given as Widvilla, being 'peutêtre Iville, dept. Eure, arr. Evreux, cant. le Neubourg'.[16] Iville is just north of Le Neubourg and no great distance from Conches.

[1] Evidently her son by Nicholas de Yelond, taking his mother's name.
[2] *Cal. Close Rolls*, 1247–51, pp. 548, 555, 559, 561. Unless William de Landa had such issue, he could not hold 'by the curtesy of England'.
[3] *Cal. Pat. Rolls*, 1247–58, p. 246.
[4] *Feudal Aids*, vi, pp. 39, 62–4, 82.
[5] *Yorks. Inq.*, iii, no. 105; *Cal. Inq. p.m.*, iv, no. 32. At an inq. of kts' fees held by Roger de Mowbray, who died in 1297, John de Wyville's holdings included 11 car. in Sledmere for a k.f. (*Yorks. Inq.*, iii, no. 107; *Cal. Inq. p.m.*, iii, no. 472, p. 362).
[6] *Feudal Aids*, vi, pp. 171, 174.
[7] *R. R. Hastings, ut sup.*, p. 137.
[8] *Ibid.*, p. 136.
[9] *Yorks. Fines*, 1327–47, p. 24.
[10] *Ibid.*, p. 165.
[11] *R. R. Hastings, ut sup.*, p. 136.
[12] *Feudal Aids*, vi, 314.
[13] *Dugdale's Visitation*, ed. J. W. Clay, iii, 90–2; *V.C.H. Yorks.*, N.R., ii, 433.
[14] *Dugdale's Visitation*, p. 92.
[15] *Gallia Christiana*, xi, Inst., p. 132.
[16] Delisle-et-Berger, *Rec. des Actes de Henri II*, i, no. 423 (p. 553); iii, 261.

It is recorded in a Mowbray genealogy that Henry I enfeoffed Nigel d'Aubigny of the *vavasaria* of the lord of Wyvil,[1] which may be the same place; and if Robert de Guidvilla was the same man as Robert de Wituile the tenant of Nigel in Yorkshire (see above), it is not improbable that the latter came from Iville.

No proof has been found for a connexion with Hugh de Widville who held land at the Domesday survey in Northampton and Leicester,[2] and his descendants.[3] If he was the same man as Hugh de Guitville, a benefactor of St-Georges-de-Boscherville[4] it is not unlikely that he took his name from Yville-sur-Seine, dept. Seine–Maritime, arr. Rouen, dept. Duclair,[5] a great distance from Iville.

---

[1] *Mon. Ang.*, vi, 320.

[2] *V.C.H. Northants.*, i, 302; *V.C.H. Leic.*, i, 306.

[3] In both references Round stated, though with no documentary evidence, that from this family Elizabeth (Woodville), queen of Edward IV, descended. The account of her family in *Complete Peerage*, xi, 15, only begins with Richard de Wydeville, born *c*. 1310.

[4] *Regesta*, ii, no. 1012, and text p. 325; being a confirmn by Henry I, 1112–13.

[5] It was near here, Wiville being the spelling, that the neighbouring abbey of Jumièges held land (Delisle-et-Berger, *ut sup.*, ii, no. 527, p. 92). The place occurs as Vuitvilla and Witivilla in a charter for Jumièges in 1025 (*Rec. des Actes des Ducs de Normandie*, 911–1066, no. 36).

ILLUSTRATIVE DOCUMENTS

1. Confirmation by Roger de Flamville and Juetta [de Arches] his wife to St. Peter's hospital, York, of land in Beningbrough (N.R.), given by William son of Warin and by Henry son of William.

[*c.* 1154 x 1169]

Bodl., MS. Dodsworth vii ff. 21^v–22^r, from an original charter formerly in St. Mary's Tower, York; also (abbreviated) MS. Dodsworth cxxB f. 50^v, from lost third vol. of St. Leonard's cartulary, f. 9.

Notum sit omnibus qui audierint vel viderint has litteras quod ego Rogerus de Flamavill' et Juetta sponsa mea concessimus et hac presenti karta nostra confirmavimus Deo et pauperibus hospitalis beati Petri Ebor' totam terram in Beningburg quam Willelmus filius Garini dedit eis in puram et perpetuam elemosinam, liberam et quietam ab omni seculari servicio, preter orationes in Christo, scilicet in bosco in plano et in omnibus aliis pertinenciis, et illam terram quam Henricus filius Willelmi et heres ejus dederunt eisdem pauperibus in eadem villa cum matre sua quam in sororem susceperunt, sicut continetur in karta Henrici de donatione patris sui Willelmi et sua donatione. Insuper hac eadem karta nostra concessimus atque confirmavimus predictis pauperibus illam terram quam in eadem villa de Henrico susceperunt, tenendam de eo et heredibus suis in perpetuum in feudo et hereditate et sicut de ea in karta Henrici continetur. Hii sunt testes, Nicholaus presbyter, Hugo filius Rogerii de Flamm', Willelmus de Ruhford senescaldus, Henricus de Beningburg.

Juetta was the heiress of William de Arches, who died after *c.* 1154; her husband Roger de Flamville was dead by 1169 (above p. 30).

Land in Beningbrough had first been given to the hospital before 1148.[1] Henry son of William's gift[2] was confirmed by pope Alexander III in 1173.[3]

2. Confirmation by Juetta de Arches to St. Peter's hospital, York, of the gift by William son of Henry of Beningbrough of two bovates in Beningbrough.

[?*c.* 1190]

Bodl., MS. Dodsworth cxxB f. 50^v, from lost third vol. of St. Leonard's cartulary, f. 8.

Omnibus Christi fidelibus ad quos presens scriptum pervenerit Juetta de Arches eternam in Domino salutem. Noverit universitas vestra me [concessisse]^a et confirmasse hospitali Sancti Petri Ebor' donationem illam quam Willelmus filius Henrici de Benyngburgh et Maria uxor ejus^b eis fecit de duabus bovatis terre in Beningburgh, cum

---

^{a} Omitted in MS. ^{b} Repeated in MS.

---

[1] *Mowbray Charters*, no. 295.
[2] *Cal. Ch. Rolls*, ii, 443–4.
[3] *E.Y.C.*, i, no. 197.

toftis et quodam assarto quod vocatur Brienriding etc. Test[ibus],
Willelmo de Perci, Alano filio Elie de Hamerton tunc seneschallo
Juette, Willelmo de Corneburgh, Simone clerico fratre ejus, Radulfo
Nuuel, Bertramo de Stiveton, Willelmo filio ejus, Thoma Lardenario,
Roberto de Wivelesthorp, Alano de Knapton.

Seven of the witnesses occur in a charter of Juetta confirming a gift by
William son of Henry of Beningbrough to Ralph Nuuel, dated by Farrer 1187
x c. 1190.[1] The first witness is William de Percy of Kildale, a son-in-law of
Juetta (above p. 30).

3. Gift by Robert de Daiville to G[eoffrey] de Rouen and Alice his
wife of a *mansura* on the River Ouse in York, in free burgage for
12*d* p.a.   [1135 x *c.* 1150]

B.M., Add. MS. 40009 (cartulary of Fountains) ff. 112ᵛ–113ʳ (old
pp. 224–5). Pd (abstract): *Fountains Chartulary*, i, 277.

Robertus Daivilla omnibus videntibus vel audientibus has litteras
salutem. Sciatis me dedisse et concessisse et hac carta confirmasse
G. de Rotom' et Ael' uxori sue et heredibus suis unam mansuram terre
in Ebor' super Usiam, juxta mansuram quam ipsi tenent de domino
meo Rog[ero] de Molbr', tenendam de me et heredibus meis in franco
burgagio liberam et quietam ab omnibus consuetudinibus, preter .xii.
d[enarios] quos michi et heredibus meis annuatim debent persolvere.
T[estes], Rogerus de Molb', Nicolaus capellanus, Bertrammus Haget,
Walterus de Riveria, Hugo de Mannilhermer, Robertus Maltalent, et
G. de Condeio, Ricardus de Morevilla, Oliverus de Buci, G. de Ramp',
Walterus Buhere, Aldelin et Landri et Rogerus de Condi.

Several of the witnesses occur in Mowbray charters of the period between
1138 and *c.* 1150.[2]

Geoffrey de Rouen went on a pilgrimage to Compostella before 1157.
After his death Alice (Careu) granted this and the next *mansura* to Fountains,
the gift being confirmed by Henry II in August 1175.[3]

4. Agreement between the monks of Byland and Robert de Daiville
over a fishpool near Kilburn and other matters, including pasture
rights.   [*c.* 1147 x 1186]

Bodl., MS. Dodsworth xciv f. 31ʳ (no witnesses), from an original
charter formerly in St. Mary's Tower, York; B.M., Egerton MS.
2823 (cartulary of Byland) f. 52ᵛ.

Sciant omnes has [litteras]ᵃ visuriᵇ vel audituriᶜ quod hec est
compositio, pactio et concordia inter monachos Sancte Marie de
Bellalandaᵈ et Robertum de Dayvill' et heredes ejus, scilicet quod

---

ᵃ Omitted in MSS.   ᵇ *lecturi*, Egert.
ᶜ *audituris*, Dodsw.   ᵈ *Beghl'*, Egert.

---

[1] *E.Y.C.*, i, no. 552.
[2] *Mowbray Charters*, nos. 156, 363, 403.
[3] *Ibid.*, no. 351 and note.

monachi dimiserunt quietum Roberto predicto vivarium cum stagno inter Kileburn[e] et Midelbergh[f] et semitam circa vivarium hominibus ejus ad piscandum. Concesserunt etiam eis sartare a fundo vallis ubi terra lucrabilis ferit super viam recta linea usque Rauthekeldsic versus Kileburnam.[e] Robertus vero dimisit monachis terram de ductu juxta gardinum de Wildona per divisas quas fecerunt et perambulaverunt usque ad Wlsiker[g] et totum Wlsiker et exinde recta linea per viam ad caput del north de Wlsiker[g] usque ad capud sarti de Ketelberne et exinde recta linea per transversum usque ad terram lucrabilem de Wildona, in proprium ad faciendum quicquid [h]inde facere[h] voluerint imperpetuum. Totum vero nemus de Rosebergha a capite sarti de Ketelberne del west usque ad magnam viam que vadit a Karletuna[i] usque ad Killeburnam non omnino[j] sartabitur, sed remanebit in communem pasturam per divisas quas fecerunt et perambulaverunt, a magna autem via usque ad angulum de Dritraneker[k] versus le west per divisas quas perambulaverunt et deinde[l] usque ad angulum de Dritraneker del nord[m] et exinde usque ad terram lucrabilem Roberto remanebit ad pratum et bladum, ita quod postquam pratum et bladum messuerit erit eis in communem pasturam, et extra Traneker sartabit ad libitum suum usque ad viam que vadit de Kileburna[n] versus Angotebi del nord[o] de Traneker. Hec sarta et has terras seminabit annuatim ad libitum Robertus et faciet si voluerit vivaria inter Killeburna et Hod.[p] Monachi vero si voluerint claudent xv acras ad faciendum quod inde facere voluerint in Caldecothedala. Habebunt etiam plenarie communam pasturam per totam terruram de Killeburna averiis suis de Wildona et de Stocking[q] et liberos et congruos introitus et exitus averiis suis et sibi et hominibus suis ad pasturam suam per totam terram Roberti. Robertus vero annuatim habebit unam defensionem pasture bobus et equis suis consideratione sua et utriusque grangiarii de Wildon' et de Stocking' quandam tempus defensionis debet durare.[r] Hiis testibus, Rogero de Molbray, Hugone Malabisse, Hugone junior Malebisse et ceteris.

This charter undoubtedly records a genuine agreement and some grants made by Robert de Daiville before 1186. The Byland chronicle refers to a dispute over land near Kilburn between Daiville and Byland in 1147, and also mentions Daiville's gift of 15 acres in 'Calcotedale' and pasture in Kilburn. [1] But the detailed boundaries given in this document are unusual for a charter of the mid-twelfth century, and later interpolation (fairly common in Byland charters) must be suspected. This may have occurred in 1224, when Robert abbot of Byland brought a case against John de Daiville over pasture in Kilburn; the fine not only has some expressions reminiscent of the present

---

[e] *Killeburnam*, Egert.	[f] *Midelbergam*, Egert.
[g-g] Omitted in Dodsw.	[h-h] Omitted in Dodsw.
[i] *Carletuna*, Egert.	[j] Omitted in Egert.
[k] *Drytraneker*, Egert.	[l] *exinde*, Egert.
[m] *north*, Egert.	[n] *Kilburna*, Egert.
[o] *north*, Egert.	[p] *Hode*, Egert.
[q] *Sthockyng'*, Egert.	[r] Dodsw. version ends.

[1] *Mon. Ang.*, v, 351*b*–352*b*.

charter (including *per visum grangiarorum de Wildon' et de Stockyng'*), but also actually refers to this charter. [1]

5. Gift by Robert de Daiville to St. Peter's hospital, York, of 13*d* from the farm of his mill of Baxby (par. Husthwaite, N.R.).

[*ante* 1190]

Bodl., MS. Dodsworth cxxB f. 52[v], from lost third vol. of St. Leonard's cartulary, f. 22.

Notum sit omnibus tam presentibus quam futuris quod ego Robertus de Daivilla et uxor mea et heres meus concessimus et dedimus Deo et Sancto Leonardo et pauperibus hospitalis Sancti Petri xiij denarios de firma molendini nostri de Baxeby, in puram et perpetuam elemosinam, ut simus participes omnium beneficiorum que fiunt in illa sancta domo in vita et in morte. Quare precipimus ut semper fratres hospitalis illos xiij d. ad festum Sancti Martini omni occasione remota habeant. Hujus rei testes sunt Radulfus de Herovilla, Gilbertus de Cressi, Ancht[illus] de Huc, Galterus de Davidd[villa], Robertus de Surdevilla, Willelmus de Croccesl[aio].

Robert de Daiville died by 1190 at the latest. [2] The charter may be later than 1173 as the gift is not mentioned in the detailed confirmation of pope Alexander III of that year.[3]

6. Gift by Roger de Flamville, with the assent of Juetta de Arches his wife, to Malton priory, of the church of Norton.

[*c.* 1150 x July 1169]

B.M., Cotton MS. Claud. D. xi (cartulary of Malton) f. 57[r] (old f. 55[r]).

Cunctis Christi fidelibus Rogerus de Flamevilla salutem. Vobis omnibus innotescat quod ego Rogerus de Flamevilla divino ductus instinctu concessi et dedi quantum fas est laico[a] persone et hac carta mea confirmavi ecclesiam de Nortona cum omnibus pertinenciis suis in perpetuam elemosinam canonicis beate Virginis Marie de Maltona ad sustentationem duorum canonicorum, quos ipsi concesserunt michi et heredibus meis habere in perpetuum in domo sua ad profectum animarum nostrarum et patrum et matrum et specialium amicorum nostrorum. Cui rei quia domine Juete de Archis uxoris mee specialiter desideratur assensus quoniam hoc beneficium de dote sua est, sciatis omnes ipsam ultro suum accomodasse assensum similiter ad profectum anime sue et omnium amicorum suorum etc.

Malton priory was founded *c.* 1150. The gift was confirmed by pope Alexander III on 30 July 1169, and also by Roger de Mowbray, to whose honour Flamville's fee belonged.[4] In her widowhood, Juetta confirmed the church of All Saints, Norton, to Malton.[5]

---

[a] *laice*, MS.

---

[1] *Yorks. Fines*, 1218–31, pp. 55–6; *cf.* Egerton MS. 2823 ff. 52[v]–54[r].
[2] *Mowbray Charters*, no. 361.   [3] *E.Y.C.*, i, no. 197.
[4] See *Mowbray Charters*, no. 183 and note.
[5] *Mon. Ang.*, vi(2), 971, probably 1194 x *c.* 1206.

7. Confirmation by Hugh de Flamville to the hospital of Norton of the church of Marton, which his father had given; an earlier confirmation having been made before he had given his sister Maud in marriage to Robert de Hastings. [1169 x 1212]

> B.M., Cotton MS. Claud. D. xi (cartulary of Malton) f. 60ʳ (old f. 58ʳ). Pd, *Mon. Ang.*, vi(2), 972.

Cunctis Christi fidelibus Hugo de Flamvill' salutem. Notum vobis facio omnibus me concessisse et confirmasse Deo et beate Virgini Marie et beato Nicholao et elemosinarie domui de platea apud Nortonam et canonicis ordinis de Semplingham procuratoribus pauperum Christi ibidem, ecclesiam de Marton' in Burgersire*ᵃ* in perpetuam et liberam elemosinam cum omnibus pertinenciis et libertatibus antiquis et novis, quam ecclesiam pater meus eidem loco antea dedit et carta sua confirmavit in puram et perpetuam elemosinam, et quam etiam ecclesiam ego ipse concessi et confirmavi predicte elemosinarie antequam sororem meam Matildem Flamvill' Roberto de Hastings in matrimonium dederam, ut habeantque perpetuoᵇ possideant in liberam et perpetuam elemosinam, pro salute anime mee et omnium antecessorum meorum. Et ego et heredes mei warantizabimus ipsis hanc predictam ecclesiam erga dominos et omnes homines et de omnibus rebus quantum pertinetᶜ ad laicumᵈ personam. Hiis testibus, etc.

The site of the hospital had been given to the canons of Sempringham (at Malton) by mag. William de Flamville,[1] whose identity has not been ascertained. He may be the mag. William who made an agreement in 1173 for tithes between the chapel of Welham and the mother-church of Norton,[2] and witnessed charters of the dean and chapter of York, 1189 x 94,[3] and of Hugh de Flamville (below no. 8). The church of St. Mary, Marton, had been given to Malton by Roger de Flamville before 1169.[4]

8. Gift by Hugh de Flamville to Byland abbey of one acre of meadow in Fryton. [*c.* 1175 x *c.* 1190]

> Bodl., MS. Dodsworth vii f. 176ᵛ, from an original charter formerly in St. Mary's Tower, York; also (short extract) MS. Dodsworth xciv f. 39ʳ, from same source.

Eboracensi archiepiscopo totique capitulo Sancti Petri et omnibus sancte ecclesie filiis Hugo de Flammavilla salutem. Sciatis me dedisse et concessisse et hac [carta]ᵉ mea confirmasse Deo et monachis Sancte Marie de Bellalanda unam acram prati mei in terrura de Fritona, juxta quatuordecim acras prati quas dedi eis et carta mea confirmavi in puram et perpetuam elemosinam antequam iter arripui versus Jerusalem. Hoc autem pratum dedi predictis monachis in puram et perpetuam elemosinam, liberam, propriam, solutam et quietam ab omni terreno

---

ᵃ *Sic*; *Burgesire, Mon. Ang.*
ᶜ *pertinent, Mon. Ang.*
ᵉ Omitted in MSS.

ᵇ *habeant perpetuoque, Mon. Ang.*
ᵈ So *Mon. Ang.; laicam*, MS.

---

[1] *Mon. Ang.*, vi(2), 972.
[3] *Ibid.*, vi, no. 135.

[2] *E.Y.C.*, iii, no. 1888.
[4] *Mon. Ang.*, vi(2), 972.

servicio et exactione seculari, ad faciendum quicquid inde facere voluerint imperpetuum, pro salute anime mee et patris et matris mee et omnium antecessorum et heredum meorum. Dedi etiam liberos et congruos introitus et exitus sibi et caretis et hominibus suis per terram meam ad predictum pratum suum, quod monachi circumfossare facient si voluerint. Et ego et heredes mei hanc donationem manutenebimus et warantizabimus predictis monachis et defendemus contra omnes homines imperpetuum. Hiis testibus, magistro Willelmo de Flammavilla, Johanne persona ecclesie de Hovingham, Ricardo de Widevilla, Hamone Beler, Radulfo de Surdevall', Hugone de Holthorp, Omundo Croer, Roberto de Vado et Radulfo fratre ejus, Willelmo de Daivill', Drogone de Harum.

MS. Dodsworth xciv fo. 39^r notes: 'Seale faire on horsebak'.

Five of the witnesses occur in a charter of the period *c.* 1175 x *c.* 1190.[1]

9. Gift by Hugh de Flamville to Robert son of Patrick de Hotunia of a toft [? in High Hutton, N.R.], for an annual rent of one pound of pepper. [1169 x 1201]

> Bodl., MS. Dodsworth vii f. 176^{r-v}, from an original charter formerly in St. Mary's Tower, York.

Hugo de Flamavill' omnibus hominibus et amicis suis, clericis et laicis, Francis et Anglis, presentibus et futuris salutem. Sciatis me dedisse et hac mea carta confirmasse Roberto filio Patricii de Hotunia totam tuftam quam Arkil tenuit, tenendam de me et de heredibus meis illi et heredibus suis in feodo et hereditate, libere et quiete et integre, pro una libra piperis annuatim reddenda michi pro omnibus serviciis que ad me pertinent. Et pro donatione predicte tufte et carte mee confirmatione prefatus Robertus dedit michi in cambiam totam toftam quam Patricius pater prefati Roberti tenuit in feodo et hereditate de Rogero de Flamavill' patre meo imperpetuum, absque venditione ejusdem Roberti et heredum suorum. Et ideo ego et heredes mei garantizabimus predictis Roberto et heredibus suis contra omnes homines predictam toftam. Hujus rei isti sunt testes Rogerus de Coniers, Galfridus de Conyers, Hugo de Houlthorp, Gilebertus de Rugemont, Robertus Haget, Reginaldus[a] filius Walteri, Rogerus filius Ricardi, Henricus de Flamavila, Ricardus[a] de Houltorp, Hugo Brito, Rogerus[a] de Suffolchia, Rogerus Pensif, Wadinus de Bartun', Paulinus de Bothalia, Willelmus filius Ulfi, Ricardus de Dunestapel, Ricardus prepositus de Hotun', Galfridus Fergus, Rogerus Fossardus, Rogerus Gerrun, Simon de Hemelesheie, Rogerus de Kenebi, Willelmus Haget et multi alii.[a]

Gilbert de Rougemont was probably dead by 1201.[2]

---

[a] Given in ablative case in MS.

---

[1] *E.Y.C.*, ix, no. 77.
[2] *York Minster Fasti*, ii, no. 78.

10. Gift by Agnes de Flamville to St Peter's hospital, York, of nine bovates and a third part of a bovate, two tofts and a croft, and three tenants in Marton. [1203 x 1217]

> Bodl., MS. Dodsworth cxxB f. 73ᵛ, from lost third vol. of St. Leonard's cartulary, f. 174.

Omnibus Christi fidelibus Agnes de Flamagvill' salutem. Noverit universitas vestra me concessisse et pro salute anime mee et animarum patris et matris mee et domini Petri de Brus et virorum meorum Willelmi de Perci et Johannis de Birkyn et liberorum meorum dedisse in puram elemosinam hospitali Sancti Petri Ebor' tres bovatas cum duobus toftis et terciam partem unius bovate terre in Marton in Burghshire quas Hugo de Merston tenet et tres bovatas terre cum crofto quod Thomas Briddesmudh tenet et tres bovatas terre quas Willelmus filius Petri tenet, cum predictis hominibus et tota eorum sequela etc. Test[ibus], Hamone thesaurario Ebor' ecclesie, Hugone de Touleston, Roberto Everingham, Ricardo de Hudleston, Roberto de Barkeston, Roberto de Rivill', Waltero de [   ]ᵃ, Simone de Corneburg', Thoma de Langwath, Roberto de Stow.

Agnes did not marry John de Birkin until after 1203; Hamo was treasurer of York until 1217.

This gift was confirmed with the same witnesses by John de Birkin, the grantor's second husband, and some time between October 1218 and October 1219 by Walter de Percy of Kildale, the grantor's son by her first marriage. These documents are copied on the same folio in the Dodsworth MS., together with a deed recording that the master and brethren of the hospital were to find a chaplain to celebrate masses for the souls of Agnes and the others at the altar of St. Michael in the infirmary of the hospital.

11. Confirmation by William Gramary to the hospital of Jerusalem of half an acre and a toft in Aberford. [c. 1188 x c. 1229]

> Bodl., MS. Dodsworth viii f. 215ᵛ, from an original charter formerly in St. Mary's Tower, York.

Sciant presentes et futuri quod ego Willelmus Gramaticus concessi et hac presenti mea carta confirmavi donationem quam pater meus dedit Deo et fratribus hospitali Ierusalem in territorio de Edburford in puram et perpetuam elemosinam pro salute animarum omnium parentum meorum, scilicet dimidiam acram terre et toftum inter toftum qui fuit Angoti et toftum qui fuit boniᵇ Roberti et decem acras in Asegerecroft inter crucesᶜ cum omni communione predicte ville pertinente. Hiis testibus, capitulo de Ansti, Hugone de Altarive, Roberto Walais, Waltero de Lechertun, Jordano de Poterinton, Thoma Gramatico, Roberto de Wiflestorp, Ada clerico de Ascheham, Helia clerico de Ruforde, Willelmo filio Roberti de Oustorp, Willelmo filio

---

ᵃ Name omitted in MS.
ᵇ *Sic.*
ᶜ Dodsworth gives a marginal note: 'vulgo Osgodcross wapentak'.

Rann[ulfi], Thoma clerico de Poteringtun et Laurentio fratre ejus et multis aliis.

Drawing of outline of circular seal on tag: a lyon passant to the sinister in a roundell'.

12. Gift by Emma de Hay, with the assent of Thomas her son and heir, to St. Peter's hospital, York, of half a carucate in Oglethorpe (W.R.), for the light of St. Leonard.   [c. 1197 x 1198]

Bodl., MS. Dodsworth cxxB f. 75ᵛ, from lost third vol. of St. Leonard's cartulary, f. 182.

Omnibus sancte matris ecclesie filiis Emma de Hay salutem. Noveritis me assensu Thome Hay filii et heredis mei, pro salute animarum nostrarum et Rogerii sponsi mei, dedisse hospitali beati Petri Ebor' ad luminariam Sancti Leonardi dimidiam carucatam terre in Oclestorp de illis duabus carucatis terre quas Hugo filius Willelmi de Oclestorp de nobis tenet. Tenendum sicut elemosina etc. Ita quod assignavimus predictum Hugonem filium Willelmi de Oclestorp ad solvendos sex solidos annuatim predicto hospitali pro predicta dimidia carucata terre. Test[ibus], Simone decano, Reginaldo Arundel cantore, Hamone thesaurario et capitulo beati Petri Ebor', Rogero de Batvent tunc vic[ecomite] et comitatu Ebor'.

Reginald Arundel did not become precentor, and Hamo did not become treasurer, until c. 1197. Roger de Bavent ceased to be [deputy] sheriff after Michaelmas 1198. As Emma's husband was Thomas I (pp. 40–1 above) Roger must be a mistake, possibly for Thomas son of Roger.

13. Gift by Simon son of Uctred to Walter his brother of all his land in Ilton and half the mill and a toft, and half a carucate in Conistone.   [1179 x c. 1200]

Bodl., MS. Rolls Yorks. 21 (cartulary of Hebden family) m. 3.

Omnibus visuris vel audituris has literas Simon filius Huthred' salutem. Noverit universitas [vestra]ᵃ me dedisse concessisse et hac presenti carta mea confirmasse Waltero fratri meo et heredibus suis totam terram meam de Ilketon' et medietatem molendini et illud toftum quod in predicta villa de Ilketon' habeo et meam dimidiam carrucatam terre in Coningston' pro homagio et servicio suo, tenendam de me et heredibus meis libere et quiete in bosco et in plano, in pratis et pasturis et in omnibus ayseamentis ad prenominatas terras adjacentibus, adeo libere et quiete ex omni consuetudine et exactione ut ego et heredes mei liberius tenemus de dominicis meis. Et sciendum quod ego Simon et heredes mei habebimus de dominio meo in bosco de Ilketon' lx porcos quietos annuatim de pannagio. Et hac donatione prenominatus Walterus et heredes sui fidei interpositione et sacramento confirmante quietamclamavit ante dictum Simonem et heredes suosᵇ totam terram que

ᵃ Omitted in MS.
ᵇ MS. reads: *an' dicto Simon' et her' suos;* text might therefore be: *autem dicto Simoni et heredibus suis.*

fuit Uthred' filii Dolfini patris mei et Herberti des Arches filii prenominati Huthredi. Hiis testibus etc.

This charter was presumably given after the death of the grantor's father, Uctred son of Dolfin, that is after 1179.[1] The grantor was still alive in 1200, but Herbert de Arches does not otherwise occur later than c. 1195.[2]

The beneficiary of this charter, who is sometimes called Walter son of Uctred de Ilton,[3] gave to Fountains four bovates and half the mill of Ilton.[4] Walter de Ilton, his son, returned to William of Hebden, son of Simon son of Uctred, two bovates in Conistone.[5]

Herbert de Arches, described here as son of Uctred son of Dolfin, also appears as brother of Simon son of Uctred.[6] In view of the details given by Farrer[7] it is almost, if not quite, impossible that this description of Herbert's parentage can be correct. It is known that Alice dau. of Uctred married Elias de Rilston;[8] and Farrer[9] was of the opinion that Herbert de Arches married Ingonilda, Alice's sister.[9] If so Herbert would be the brother-in-law and not brother of Simon son of Uctred; and the only possible solution of the problem is that *filii* in the present charter must be taken as meaning son-in-law and not son.

14. Confirmation by Richard de Huddleston to St. Clement's nunnery, York, of meadow given by his uncle Gilbert son of Nigel.
[1166 x 1208]

Bodl., MS. Dodsworth xciv f. 111[r], from an exemplification, presumably in St. Mary's Tower, York.

Ego Ricardus de Hudleston confirmavi monialibus Sancti[a] Clementis Eboraci[b] donationem quam Gillebertus filius Nigelli patruus meus eis dedit, videlicet totum pratum tam hospitatum quam non hospitatum. Test[ibus], Petro de Toulestcn, Hugone filio ejus, Willelmo de Ria, Johanne filio ejus, Gilberto de Hudleston, Roberto filio ejus.

15. Confirmation by Lisiard de Musters to St. Peter's hospital, York, of a toft and a carucate in Theakston (N.R.), and a toft and a carucate in Kirklington.
[1184 x 99]

Bodl., MS. Dodsworth cxxB f. 78[v], from lost third vol. of St. Leonard's cartulary, f. 197.

Archiepiscopo Eboracensi et capitulo Sancti Petri et omnibus filiis sancte matris ecclesie Lisiardus Musters salutem. Noverit

---

[a] *Sancto*, MS. [b] *Eboraco*, MS.

---

[1] E.Y.C., vii, no. 92. [2] Ibid., iii, no. 1586.
[3] *Fountains Chartulary*, ii, 729.
[4] *Yorks. Deeds*, iii, nos. 159, 160; and see E.Y.C., vii, p. 249.
[5] Bodl., MS. Rolls Yorks. 21 m. 2.
[6] Yorke Deeds at Halton Place, no. 42; cf. E.Y.C., vii, p. 252 and n. 1.
[7] E.Y.C., iii, no. 1586n.
[8] Ibid., vii, no. 93.
[9] Loc. cit., where it is shown that Herbert had a dau. named Ingoliena; cf. E.Y.C., vii, no. 113n.

universitas vestra me concessisse et per cartam meam confirmasse Deo et pauperibus hospitalis Sancti Petri Ebor' unum toftum et unam carucatam terre in Textan' cum omnibus eidem terre pertin[entibus]. Et preterea confirm[avi] eidem hospitali dimidiam carucatam terre in Kirclington cum omnibus ad eam pertin[entibus] et unum toftum in eadem villa. Test[ibus] Hamone precentore ecclesie beati Petri Ebor', P. de Musters, Rogero de Bavent, etc.

Robert de Musters died after 1184. Hamo had become treasurer of York by 1199.

The property in Kirklington had been given to the hospital by Lisiard's great-grandmother, Muriel, who was the wife of Robert de Musters the Domesday tenant.[1] The land in Theakston had been given before 1157 by Lisiard's father Robert,[2] whose charter follows this in the Dodsworth MS, with a confirmation charter of Basilia, named as wife of Robert de Musters.

16. Confirmation by Richard de Wyville to Byland abbey of Thorpe le Willows (par. Coxwold, N.R.).   [c. 1160 x 1186, perhaps c. 1176]

> Original charter, deposited at Northallerton, N.R. Record Office (Newburgh Priory document). Cal., Hist. MSS. Comm., *Var. Coll.*, ii, 6.

Eboracensi archiepiscopo totique capitulo Sancti Petri et omnibus sancte ecclesie filiis Ricardus de Widevilla salutem. Notum sit vobis me concessisse et hac presenti carta confirmasse Deo et monachis Sancte Marie de Bellalande Torp cum omnibus pertinentiis et aisiamentis ad illam pertinentibus villam in bosco et plano in terris et aquis in pratis et pasturis in viis et semitis simul cum incremento foreste quod Rogerus de Molbrai dedit prius Radulfo avunculo meo et postea concessit Willelmo patri meo per metas et divisas que continentur in cartis ipsius Rogeri de Molbrai et Willelmi patris mei. Hec omnia concessi et confirmavi predictis monachis in perpetuam elemosinam liberam solutam et quietam ab omni terreno servicio et exactione seculari pro salute anime mee et omnium antecessorum et heredum meorum. Et ego et heredes mei manutenebimus et warentizabimus hec omnia predictis monachis contra omnes homines in perpetuum. His testibus Rogero de Molbrai, Radulfo de la Hai, Simone de Staingriva, Roberto de Surdevals, Willelmo de Hairum, Willelmo Dod, Ricardo Silvain, Herberto fratre ejus, Ricardo de Dalt[ona], Gerardo stabulario, Walkelin Trussevilain.

Five of the witnesses to the present charter occur together at Nottingham in March 1176.[3]

Roger de Mowbray gave Thorpe le Willows to Ralph de Wyville in c. 1147,[4] and it was given to Byland by Ralph's brother William before c. 1154.[5]

---

[1] *E.Y.C.*, v, no. 333 and note.
[2] *Mowbray Charters*, no. 301 and note.
[3] *E.Y.C.*, ix, no. 160.
[4] *Mowbray Charters*, no. 400.
[5] *Ibid.*, no. 50 and note.

17. Gift by Richard de Wyville to Kirkham priory of one rood and a half of land in the field of Sledmere (Yorks., E.R.).

[late 12th or early 13th cent.]

Bodl., MS. Dodsworth vii f. 196^v, from an original charter formerly in St. Mary's Tower, York; and cartulary of Kirkham, MS. Fairfax vii f. xxxiv^v (abstract).

Omnibus visuris vel audientibus literas istas Ricardus de Wivilla salutem. Noverit universitas vestra me dedisse et concessisse et hac carta mea confirmasse pro salute anime mee et antecessorum et heredum meorum canonicis de Kirkeham unam rodam terre et dimidiam in campo de Sledemere juxta mansuram ipsorum canonicorum, que jacent juxta terram Ricardi Bellehus versus orientem, quas Ricardus filius Lecelini et Thomas filius Gileberti de me tenuerunt, in liberam puram et perpetuam elemosinam, tenendas et habendas libere et quiete et pacifice perpetuis temporibus ab omnibus serviciis et exactionibus. Et ego et heredes mei warantizabimus prefatis canonicis predictam rodam terre et dimidiam in puram et perpetuam elemosinam in perpetuum. Hiis testibus, Willelmo Salvain, Gileberto de Thoreni, Willelmo de Gulevilla, Radulfo de Fribi, Waltero Wildeker, Johanne . . . . ,^{a} Roberto . . . . ham,^{a} Johanne de Vado, Galfrido . . . . . ^{a}

^{a} *Sic.*

INDEX

www.ingramcontent.com/pod-product-compliance
Ingram Content Group UK Ltd.
Pitfield, Milton Keynes, MK11 3LW, UK
UKHW042152280225
455719UK00001B/300